FULL EMPLOYMENT WITHOUT INFLATION

FULL EMPLOYMENT
WITHOUT INFLATION

Manifesto for a
Governed Economy

Tim Hazledine

MACMILLAN

First published 1984 by
THE MACMILLAN PRESS LTD
London and Basingstoke
Companies and representatives
throughout the world

Typeset in Great Britain by
STYLESET LIMITED · Salisbury
and
Printed in Hong Kong

British Library Cataloguing in Publication Data
Hazledine, Tim
Full employment without inflation.
1. Manpower policy — Great Britain
I. Title
331.12′5′0941   HD8391
ISBN 0–333–36983–1
ISBN 0–333–36984–X pbk

To my parents

Contents

Contents

Foreword

The public appearance of the ideas developed in this book dates back a decade, to a seminar on price controls that I gave to the Economics Department at Warwick University in the spring term of 1973. My original interest in controls as a permanent anti-inflation policy probably stemmed from a remark made in 1971 or 1972 by Professor John Williams, of the University of Otago in Dunedin, New Zealand. Williams conjectured that markets adjust to long-term changes in supply and demand more by shifts in output than by changes in relative prices. This could imply that a permanent price controls policy, which would have to match any trends in relative prices, might not be as difficult to operate as was (and is) commonly supposed.

Whatever the empirical validity of Williams's conjecture (and neither my own nor others' research has yet established this), it inspired me to look more closely at the possibility of a direct anti-inflation policy. I found that such had been employed with great success in many economies as recently as the Second World War, but with little subsequent attempt to look openmindedly at their possible peacetime application. For ideological as well as intellectual reasons most well-trained economists are uncomfortable with the very idea of 'controls', and though with no great expertise in the area tend automatically to invoke insuperable 'administrative difficulties' against them when other arguments fail.

My investigations lead me to believe that a successful direct anti-inflation policy is indeed administratively and economically feasible, and is thus highly desirable, given the benefits of a stable price level, and the even larger benefits from a return to full employment which would become possible if the inflation threat were dealt with directly.

But developing the logic of the policy has taken me far from the form of either the wartime system, or the various 'incomes policies' that have been tried since. It has led, too, to the recognition of certain principles of policy-making which I suggest can be applied, under the rubric of 'the governed economy', to achieving important goals in addition to stable prices – a satisfactory trade balance, sensible use of energy, and very low unemployment rates.

And, perhaps equally important, the governed economy approach leads to a list of things that government should not be doing – industrial policy and trying to eradicate poverty, for example.

All this may seem rather radical. But I try to stress in the book that my proposals are fundamentally consistent with the basic commitment to efficiency and equity that is shared by most economists, and with the respect for decentralised competitive markets to which their commitment leads them. The problem is that competitive markets do not spring up spontaneously, as orthodox economics assumes. Market forces must be stimulated and protected. In many situations ideal markets are impracticable, and then the challenge is to somehow simulate their beneficial effects on economic behaviour.

All this mandates a role for government. But the policies of the governed economy look rather different from our present assortment of attempts to 'manage' the economy. And assessing my proposals requires a firm commitment to openmindedness on the part of the reader, perhaps especially the reader with some formal training in economics.

Of course, openmindedness doesn't necessarily lead to agreement. Nor should it. It is most unlikely that everything in this book is correct, but I do not know which bits are wrong. I am fairly sure, though, that the extent of error has been significantly limited by the comments and suggestions received at seminars given at various institutions around the world. Apart from Warwick, I am grateful to economists at Oxford, Otago, Canterbury, McGill and Queen's. The New Zealand Institute of Economic Research and Victoria University, both in Wellington, and University College, London, provided sabbatical hospitality while I was working on the book. Individuals whose comments and criticisms have been particularly useful include Keith Cowling, Geoff Bertram, Brian Philpott, Martin Prachowny, Chris Green and Richard Lipsey. Vicky Chick and Anne O'Malley were kind enough to read the entire manuscript, and are responsible for many improvements in style and substance.

T.H.

1 Introduction and Summary

'May you live in interesting times.'

OLD CHINESE CURSE

Economists have lost their nerve. Faced with the collapse, under the on-slaught of simultaneous inflation, unemployment, and chronic deficits, of the structure of policy activism built on foundations laid by John Maynard Keynes, the economics profession is, almost *en bloc*, scurrying back to the caves of its traditional *laissez-faire* fatalism.

Instead of accepting the challenge of learning from our mistakes to rebuild a more durable framework for economic policy-making, the cleverest economists have devoted themselves to devising a string of rationalising theories − 'monetarism', the 'natural rate', 'rational ex-pectations' − that purport to demonstrate that successful policy activism is, in fact, actually impossible. The gist of these is that best-attainable economic performance can be achieved only by the operation of 'free' market forces, so that any intervention by government in the working out of these forces will just make things worse.

It is the thesis of this book that these new fatalists are wrong. Substantial improvements in economic performance *can* be achieved, but we will have to work for them. Leaving it to *laissez-faire* will not do the job. An active role for government in our economic affairs *is* necessary. This fact may be unpalatable, but it must be faced.

It is true that our traditional hypocrisy of paying lip-service to the official ideology of the free-market-private-enterprise system while more or less apologetically sanctioning, as even conservative politicians have in office continued to do, thousands of interventions to 'correct' per-ceived inadequacies in the performance of this system, is not working very well. It is even true that the accretion of five decades of 'papering over' the cracks of capitalism has manifestly reached the point where the layers of government involvement are in themselves now a significant drag on the economy.

But it does *not* follow that the answer to our problems is simply to rip away all the government paper, and give free enterprise its head, as the

1

revivalist enthusiasts of the 'new right', egged on by significant proportion of my economist colleagues, are now proclaiming. There *is* a basic
flaw in our economic system, and this must be recognised and understood,
if we are to have a chance both of rectifying the muddle-headed inadequacies
of 'band-aid' interventionism, and of avoiding the excess dose of 'free'
market forces to which the new right would subject us.

The basic problem is that we are running dangerously low on the one
resource that is crucial to the operation of any modern economy. This
resource is not energy, or raw materials, or land – in fact, our difficulties
with these factors are themselves due to the more fundamental shortage.
What we have critically depleted is our stock of the intangible resource
that economists call 'elasticity'. Elasticity is the measure of the economy's
flexibility; of its capacity to accommodate and adapt to the ceaseless
bombardment of 'shocks' – of changes in environment and circumstance
– to which it is routinely subjected.

It is elasticity that is behind the workings of Adam Smith's famous
'invisible hand', the apparent miracle whereby millions of firms and
households, each acting independently but all crucially affected by the
actions of others, are somehow co-ordinated, so that supplies on one side
of the market, and demands on the other, add up to numbers that are
mutually consistent.

The symptom of what can now be reasonably called an *elasticity
crisis* is that the numbers are chronically failing to add up. We are ex-
periencing persistent and increasing gaps between the total supply of
people willing to work, and the demand for their services; between the
supply and demand of goods at non-inflated prices; between the government's revenues and its expenditures; between exports and imports;
and perhaps between the sustainable supply of energy and our demands
on it. This persistent decline in the 'big number' performance of our
economies by now dominates the business cycle – the year-to-year fluctuations in unemployment and inflation which hitherto have been the
focus of economists' attention.

Why has this happened? In the present book, it is first pointed out
that elasticity basically depends on the *variety of choices* open to decision-
makers; on the number of options that they have available to deal with
each economic situation that they must face. I then argue that there is
an inherent tendency in our sort of economy for each decision-maker –
each 'agent', in economists' jargon – to act in such a way that the number
of options open to other agents is reduced. This is because subjecting
ourselves to the discipline of market forces is like giving up a bad habit –
it is something that we find easier to prescribe for others than to suffer

through ourselves. No one enjoys being pushed around by the invisible hand, however much they may applaud its operation on others, and a good deal of purposive economic activity is in fact devoted to finding ways of insulating ourselves from the vagaries of the market.

The most important manifestations of this activity are the inexorable trend to concentration of business in ever fewer and larger units, and the increasing role of government as a supporter of the apparent interests of particular economic interest groups, as well as its larger direct role in economic affairs through its own spending and taxation.

Each merger, or acquisition, or new regulatory program, or grant, represents a perfectly rational attempt by the private — or public — sector decision-maker to increase control over the economic environment in the direct interest of some organisation or pressure group. These *direct* effects may or may not be judged to be truly in the public interest, and it is on such issues that the attention both of economists and politicians concerned with economic policies has traditionally been focused.

What have largely been missed, however, are the less obvious *indirect* consequences of control-increasing activities. An index of their success, from the point of view of the decision-makers concerned, is the extent to which they allow resources to be safely 'tied up' in uses which are insulated from the unpredictable fluctuations of the market. But such tying-up means that, when the economic environment *does* change, more of the burden of making the appropriate adjustments must be carried by the rest of the system. As the process of escaping from market forces proceeds, the economy has ever fewer uncommitted or adaptable resources available, so its capacity for change — its elasticity — declines. Since it is elasticity that determines how quickly market shocks are absorbed and neutralised, the end result is that fluctuations in market conditions are actually *more* violent than before.

Thus we have what can be called a *planning paradox*. Each successful attempt by a firm or interest group to control or 'plan' its own immediate environment reduces 'plannability' for everyone else. The net effect of each agent acting in their own best interest is a system in which they are all worse off. Such is the process whereby the stock of elasticity in the economy has been depleted to crisis levels.

What to do? If this diagnosis of the problem is correct, then it should be clear that the remedies currently being debated are not likely to be effective. On the one hand, the proposals for less government involvement — for a 'return' to *laissez-faire* — err fundamentally in neglecting the inherent tendency of the system to gobble up the very elasticity on which the effectiveness of any decentralised and interdependent economy depends.

On the other hand, the alternative of 'more of the same' — of intensifying policy efforts along the old grooves — is equally flawed. The macro level 'Keynesian' approach of demand management, 'fine tuning', and the like, misses out because it too depends on the economy having plenty of elasticity. And the efforts at direct intervention at the micro level to which government and its bureaucracy increasingly are turning in their frustration (grants, subsidies, tax write-offs, bail-outs, import quotas, planning agreements) seem almost perfectly designed to eliminate as fast as possible such elasticity as remains, so that, even if their short-run impact is in the desired direction (usually towards 'saving' some jobs), they are policies virtually guaranteed eventually to worsen the crisis.

In this book I propose an approach to economic policy-making tailored explicitly to the reality of the elasticity crisis. This approach builds from two guiding principles:

(1)   government must accept *direct* responsibility, at the macro level, for ensuring that the big numbers in the economy *do* add up; and
(2)   it should do what it can to increase elasticity throughout the economic system — that is, to increase flexibility and efficiency at the micro level of individual decision-makers — to make adding-up as painless and productive as possible.

The specific policies that are consistent with these principles are discussed in detail. The elasticity-augmenting measures basically aim at increasing the range of options open to decision-makers, and adding to the information they have available to assess these options. These involve hacking away at the tangled web of impediments to the free exchange of goods and services erected over the years by private and public sector elasticity-reducing efforts, stepping up the flow of useful publicly-provided information, and implementing a more sceptical monitoring of that information produced through advertising, labelling, and so on, by the private sector on its own behalf.

Few of the particular elasticity-augmenting policies proposed are novel. Most already have the support of one group or another; though existing platforms tend to be more selective than they should be. Thus, there is a good deal of support from the 'new right' for the current modest movement in the US towards 'deregulation' — the removal of publicly-erected restrictions on competition — largely unaccompanied by any matching enthusiasm for the activist 'liberal' concern with the private sector's own efforts in restraint of trade, which has resulted in the now almost defunct apparatus of anti-trust and anti-collusion legislation.

Less familiar will be the proposals for implementing the other principle of policy; namely that government can and should ensure that the big numbers of macroeconomic performance do add up. In fact, in the first flush of post-war enthusiasm for Keynesian activism, a number of countries – the US, Canada, and Britain among them – did actually *legislate* a public responsibility for full employment and for maintaining a high and stable level of economic activity. Unfortunately, the strength of governments' commitment to these goals has waned as the perceived ineffectiveness of the orthodox tools of fiscal and monetary policy has grown. Our expectations have simply been revised downwards.

This is a great mistake. Highly satisfactory levels of macroeconomic performance *are* achievable, but only if we adopt a radically different approach to policy-making.

The basic idea is very simple. Instead of the present panoply of taxes, subsidies, grants, and administrative *fiats*, with which government attempts to blackmail, bribe, or bully the private sector into acting in ways which, it hopes, will indirectly lead to the macro numbers adding up, it should simply use its ultimate legislative authority to mandate directly that the macroeconomic goals be met, and let the producing sector get on with achieving this as best they can. That is, government should *govern* in the economy as it does in other spheres of social activity, and it should abandon its unsuccessful and inappropriate efforts to *manage* our economic affairs.

In theory, the governed economy approach has a lot to recommend it. All 'policies', in public and private sectors, basically involve someone influencing someone else's actions in the expectation thereby of achieving some desired goal. Such activity must be assessed against three criteria: the standards of *knowledge*, *power*, and *propriety*. That is, we must ask whether the policy-makers *know* enough about the workings of the system to be able to set appropriate goals, and to predict what behaviour would achieve them; whether they have the *power* to accordingly influence behaviour; and whether it is *proper* that they should try and do so.

It can be shown that the orthodox 'managed' economy fails to measure up to any of these standards. Even when they know what the goals are, macroeconomic policy-makers simply lack sufficiently precise and fine-grained information on how the private sector works to predict what changes at the micro level, with all their feedbacks and side-effects, would achieve the desired goals. Furthermore, their power to effect any changes in micro-level behaviour has been eroded with the general drying-up of elasticity in the economy, the effect of this being to reduce the sensitivity of the private sector to the penalty/incentive mechanism relied on by fiscal and monetary policy. Finally, legitimate doubts can be raised about the propriety of constitutional government meddling in an often *ad hoc* and almost personal way in the detailed economic affairs of its citizens.

A governed economy could avoid these difficulties. By restricting public sector policy activism to 'performance policies' — that is, ensuring that high-level macroeconomic targets are met, but without attempting to specify the details of micro-level behaviour that will achieve this — it both takes advantage of the fact that high-level performance targets are rather simple and uncontroversial (we all can agree on the desirability of a stable price level, full employment, and suitable balances on the various public sector and foreign payments accounts), and does not make the, almost certainly unreasonable, demands on economists and bureaucrats to supply detailed and accurate models of how firms and households will respond to the assortment of stimuli and penalties that are the tools of the managed economy.

As for the criterion of *power* — the ability to effectively implement a policy — the governed economy can play from a position of strength, namely government's unquestioned monopoly of the legislative or law-making process, rather than 'mixing it' down in the market-place with private sector agents against whom the bureaucracy is inherently at a disadvantage. Reliance on its legislative powers is also no doubt a more proper posture for government to take than is its current flirtation with interventionism, given the latter's susceptibility to corruption, special pleading, and whimsical reversals of favour.

If all these theoretical advantages of the governed economy approach be granted, the next question must be: 'Yes, but how do we actually *do* it? What *are* the concrete programs that will ensure that the big numbers add up?' I argue that appropriate policies are available to us, though to recognise them may take an open-minded effort on the part of the public, of policy-makers, and especially, of economists, to escape from habits of thought, endemic in liberal democracies, that mistakenly equate the means of *laissez-faire* capitalism with the legitimate ends of personal freedom and economic efficiency.

For inflation, the book proposes a system of 'retail-level commodity price controls'. The controllers would be required, by legislation, to periodically adjust maximum prices of a 'basket' of consumer goods and services such that the consumer price index remained stable, while the prices of individual items moved up or down to reflect long-run changes in the relative costs of producing them. The rather long-winded title of this policy is needed to differentiate it from the so-called 'price' (actually profit-margin) controls to which frustrated governments resort from time to time in generally unsuccessful — indeed, counter-productive — attempts to somehow force down the inflation rate by intervening directly with

the decision-making of individual firms. In fact, the two policies are fundamentally different. Whereas firm-level profit-margin controls attempt to
suppress 'market forces' (and in so doing violate all three of the principles
of knowledge, power and propriety), the commodity price system aims
to *accommodate* genuine pressures for adjustments of relative prices,
while chopping off the useless and unpleasant general upward trend in
the average price level that is inflation.

Indeed, commodity price controls would, in effect, simulate that
discipline of competitive market forces which, economists do agree, leads
to the most efficient allocation of resources, but which is unobtainable
under a pure *laissez-faire* regimen due to the unfortunate but inherent
tendency of the latter to gobble up the very elasticity on which its proper
functioning depends. Thus, in addition to stopping inflation, a properly
designed price control system could make significant contributions to
meeting other goals; notably improving productivity and increasing the
power of orthodox monetary and fiscal policies (which, as noted above,
depend on competitive market conditions for their effectiveness) to move
towards and maintain full employment.

For 'quantity' problems at the macro level, such as imports exceeding
exports (or the threat of them doing so being a constraint on policies to
stimulate the economy), or the demand for energy exceeding sustainable
long-run supplies, the appropriate governed economy solution is to deploy
systems of 'negotiable permits'. Government decides, each year, say, on
the desired *total* consumption of imports or of energy that will achieve
the macro adding-up goals. It then issues permits or licences to import
goods or purchase energy up to the desired total level, and legislates that
their use be mandatory. Since the licences are deemed fully negotiable
(ie can be freely traded) there is no need for government to specify,
at the micro level, just who should consume and how much – the free
exchange of licences will result in their being allocated to the uses in
which they are most valued. Methods for the initial allocation of each
year's stock of permits can vary – import licences could be auctioned
off directly by government (with the proceeds used to effect a general
reduction in sales taxes), whereas the rights to purchase energy, given
the common-property nature of this resource, might most equitably
be distributed evenly on a per capita basis.

Some encouragingly eminent economists have recently come out
in favour of negotiable permit schemes of one sort or another, and we
can perhaps hope that there will be increasing recognition of the virtues
of the approach – that it allows individual firms and households maximum
freedom to allocate the resources available to them, while ensuring that

the aggregate implications of their behaviour are consistent with the achievement of the essential high-level adding-up goals.

As for imbalances on the public sector account, experience suggests that government cannot be trusted to issue the correct number of spending licences to itself! Perhaps some more fundamental limitation on public spending, such as constitutional requirements for budgets to be balanced over some reasonably long time period, is needed. Any attempt to reduce public sector deficits would be greatly aided by a reduction in that substantial proportion of public sector outlays that is 'locked in' by statutory commitments of various sorts, with the effect of throwing the burden of adjusting to budget cuts on a rather small sector of recipients of portions of the publicly-disbursed pie. That is, the elasticity of public sector spending should be increased.

In any case, we can reasonably expect that most, perhaps all, of the government deficit would disappear should the economy do better at achieving the other macro performance goals. Indeed, it is generally true that the governed economy approach escapes from the 'trade-offs' that are implicit in traditional policies, such as the famous 'Phillips curve' trade-off between inflation and unemployment. The trade-offs surface as the undesired – and often unpredicted – side-effects of managed-economy policies, due to the latters' 'bluntness' relative to the complexity of behaviour at the micro level on which they operate. At the level of the ultimate economic goals which are the concern of the governed economy, things are much simpler, so that there is a good chance of coming up with a list of policy targets which is short enough to be tractable, yet comprehensive enough to leave no significant 'gaps' through which unpleasant side-effects may emerge.

The final, though probably most important, item on the list of targets to be considered here is full employment. Our currently viciously high unemployment rates are a sign of another 'quantity' imbalance between supply and demand; in this case the shortfall is on the side of the demand for labour.

There are good reasons to expect that a governed economy could enjoy an unemployment rate of approximately zero, without resorting to the micro-meddling of grants, subsidies and so on, that are the best that the practitioners of the present managed economy approach can come up with.

First, the array of elasticity-augmenting programs, some of which would be aimed directly at the labour market (such as reducing the minimum wage for youths) would work to reduce the rigidities whereby we now get excess demand for some worker categories, and excess supply of others.

Secondly, federal and provincial governments can subsidise lower levels of government, and other providers of public goods, to provide 'employment of last resort', in a deliberately counter-cyclical way. As well, tax incentives can be used to vary the length of a backlog of private sector investment projects.

Thirdly, as noted above, with the adding-up constraints in place, and with an injection of elasticity, the economy would be much more responsive than it is now to the Keynesian demand management tools of monetary and fiscal policy. These could then be used to maintain the economy in a permanent state of full employment, by keeping a small but permanent margin of excess demand (in aggregate) over supply. The excess is necessary because:

(1) the econometric evidence shows that it is excess demand that, more than anything else, gives entrepreneurs the confidence to invest in the new plant and machinery that generates new and more productive jobs;

(2) the economy will always be subject to cyclical swings due to exogenous 'shocks' such as fluctuations in world prices. Maintaining a state of permanent excess demand means that the brunt of these shocks will be borne by variations in the length of the 'queue' of inventories and unfilled orders, rather than, as at present, partially by inventories and orders, and partially by the queue of unemployed people looking for work.

Of course, permanent excess demand is not at present feasible (in the managed economy) because it leads to inflation and deficits; in the governed economy these are kept in check by price controls and auctioned-licences schemes, so that the pressure of demand is channelled usefully to encourage the expansion of supply — of the output of real goods and services.

The advantages of running a 'queueing economy' are, (1) that it can escape from the callous exploitation of real people as the 'buffer' to bear the brunt of cyclical fluctuations; and (2) that the 'distance' from policy to economic activity would be rather shorter when changes in inventories and orders are the trigger of stabilisation policy, thus enabling us to avoid the lags that have often resulted in government's interventions *intensifying*, rather than stabilising, economic fluctuations.

The governed economy approach, of using performance policies to *ensure* that the end targets of economic performance are met while allowing the private sector maximum room to achieve these as efficiently as possible, can be applied to other areas of policy, such as income redistribution and maintaining environmental standards. Some of these are discussed in the book. In all cases, the thrust of the argument is the same: By giving new answers to the questions 'What is wrong with the economy?', and 'What is wrong with economic policy?' we can develop a reformulation of government's role in our economy that promises, not a nirvana, but at least a secure and stable economic environment within which people can get much closer than at present to achieving their full creative potential.

Part I
The Problem

2 Charting Economic Decline

'Nothing is so bad that it cannot get worse tomorrow.'

VARIATION ON GRESHAM'S LAW

The good thing about economic slumps used to be that they were followed by a boom. But this seems no longer to be the case. We are now coming out of the great recession of the early 1980s. Economic growth is picking up, and unemployment falling a few percentage points. But the improvements that are being forecast will still leave us with unemployment at levels – perhaps 8 per cent of the labour force, if we are very lucky – which only a decade ago would have marked the most vicious of slumps. Indeed, the really disturbing thing about the recent recession is not that it has been worse than any other of the post-war period, unpleasant though this fact may be. What is really worrying is that almost every recession since 1950 was the worst to date; that every recovery or boom was weaker than the last.

Thus, those who look for special factors – OPEC, or the unfortunate synchronisation of the recessions of the major Western economies – to 'explain' our current difficulties, are missing the point. The real concern is not that the recent recession is different from the others, but that it is *not* – that it merely continues an ominous pattern of declining economic performance.

It is only in the last few years that our hindsight has become long enough to enable this process of decline to emerge from the confusing ups and downs of the year-to-year fluctuations in economic activity that have traditionally preoccupied economists and governments. Indeed, the perception of long-term deterioration is still not widespread. Much less is there evidence of efforts to understand and deal with the problem.

Yet the old tools of 'stabilisation policy' – of our efforts to smooth the bumps in the business cycle – seem clearly powerless to halt the slide into mass unemployment. Indeed, many of the economists' most cherished policy prescriptions are actually predicated on the firm assumption that large-scale unemployment is impossible!

13

Evidently, something rather different is called for. First, though, we should see for ourselves just how our economies have deteriorated. An apparently inexorable pattern emerges from the 1950s and 1960s through the OPEC period, looking at the three biggest 'big numbers' of economic performance: unemployment, of course, inflation and productivity growth. The data are plotted for Britain for each of the thirty years from 1953 to 1982, on Figure 2.1. During the first half of the period (the fifteen years up to 1967) all three variables fluctuate up and down a lot, with no sign of any permanent tendency towards increases or declines. The economy seems dominated by 'cycles' — year-to-year ups and downs —

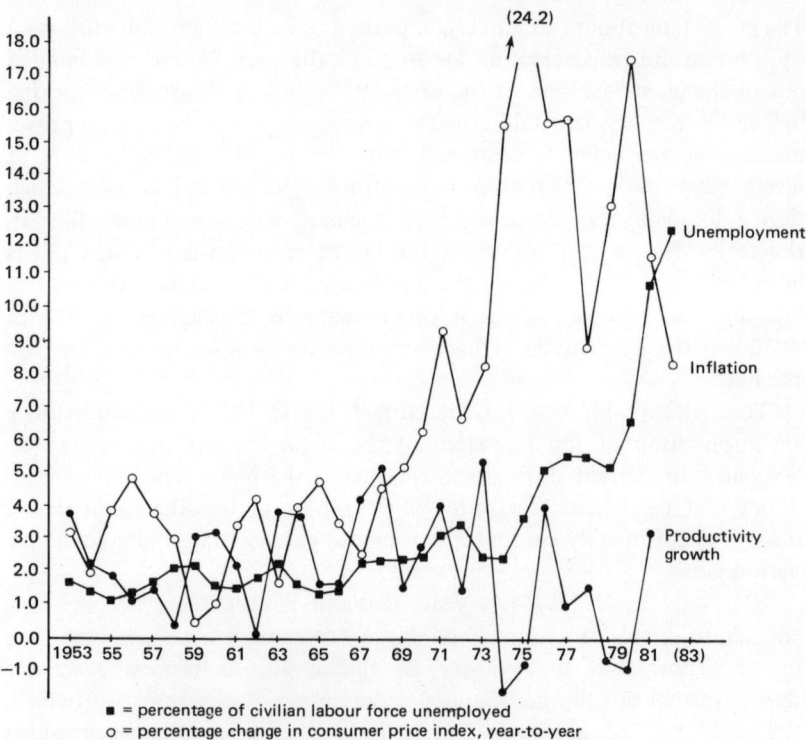

■ = percentage of civilian labour force unemployed
o = percentage change in consumer price index, year-to-year
● = percentage change in real GDP per employee, year-to-year

SOURCES   Calculated from OECD *Labour Force Statistics, General Statistics, Main Economic Indicators, Historical Statistics;* various issues.

FIGURE   2.1   *Unemployment, inflation and growth in Great Britain, 1953–82*

rather than by 'trends' – cumulative movements in one direction. Quite understandably, then, macroeconomics (the part of the subject concerned with understanding and predicting the behaviour of variables such as unemployment and inflation) concentrated attention on the cycle.

In particular, much was made of a relationship between inflation and unemployment discovered by A. W. Phillips, a New Zealander working at the London School of Economics. Using British data stretching back into the nineteenth century, Phillips uncovered a clear negative correlation between the two variables: when unemployment was relatively low, inflation tended to be high, and vice versa.[1]

To discern the relationships from the jumble of lines on Figure 2.1 we do what Phillips did, and plot inflation and unemployment against each

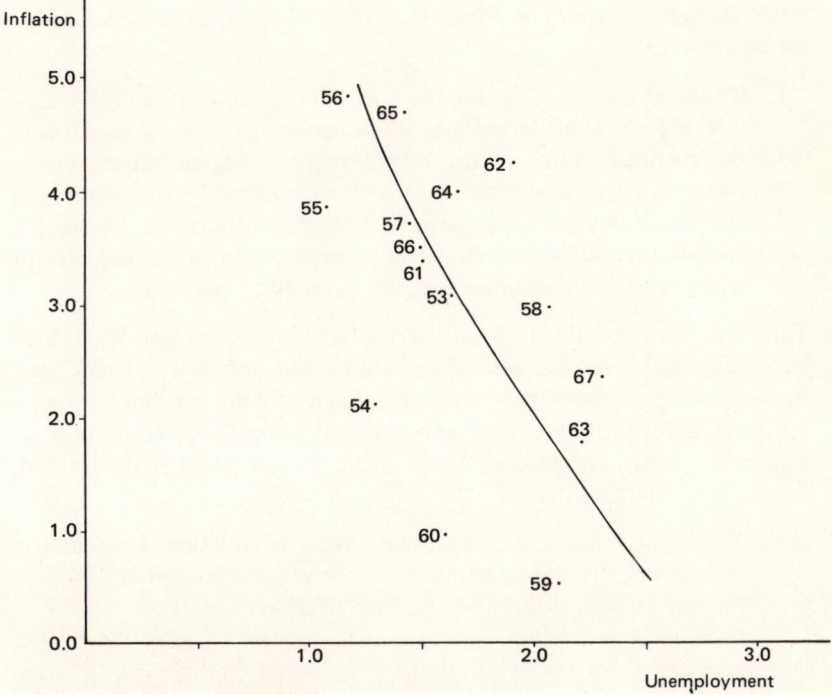

Annual percentage change in consumer price index plotted against annual average percentage of labour force unemployed.

SOURCES   As for Figure 1.1.

FIGURE 2.2   *Inflation and unemployment in the United Kingdom, 1953–67*

other.[2] The result for the period 1953–67 is shown on Figure 2.2. Although this is, statistically speaking, a rather crude procedure, it does reveal an inverse relationship between inflation and unemployment. Without too much imagination, this might be summarised by a downward-sloping line through the points, sketchéd in figure 2.2.

Using rather more formal techniques, Phillips fitted a line to his scatter of observations on inflation and unemployment. The result was quickly dubbed 'The Phillips curve', and was replicated by others for dozens of economies and time periods. Indeed, the discovery and propagation of Phillips curves was the biggest event in post-war macroeconomics, at least until the 'rational expectations' fad of the 1970s.

The economic rationale for the Phillips curve is important and controversial, and will be discussed later. At this point, the concern is with its historical significance. The Phillips curve was welcomed by economists for two reasons:

(1)   it imposed some order on the jumble of cyclical ups and downs – it 'explained' short-term fluctuations in unemployment and inflation;

(2)   the particular form of the relationship – a negative-sloped line – was exciting because it seemed to offer a 'trade-off' between inflation and unemployment. In particular, the line drawn on Figure 2.2 implies that inflation can be brought right down to insignificant levels by letting unemployment rise to around 2 per cent.

Thus the terms of the trade-off seemed entirely tolerable. What then happened as the second half of our thirty-year period unfolded? Alas! Economists' confidence that they had finally found the key to understanding and controlling the economy was short-lived. Look back at Figure 2.1. When the second fifteen years are compared with the first, two vivid differences emerge.

(1)   The cyclical ups and downs, particularly of inflation, are wilder in the second period, suggesting that efforts to smooth-out or 'stabilise' the economic cycle have become less effective over time.

(2)   Even more worrying, there are definite signs of long-term *trends* emerging from the confusion of year-to-year fluctuations. Inflation and unemployment seem inexorably to be edging up, and productivity growth, measured as the change in real Gross Domestic Product per employed person, to be slipping down.

These trends have now progressed far enough to dominate the short-term fluctuations of the cycle as determinants of how well, in any given year, our economy is performing. To see this, examine the 'peaks' and 'troughs' of the data series plotted on Figure 2.1. In the post-1967 period, the cyclical troughs in inflation – ie the 'good' years for inflation – which occur in 1972 and 1978, are both higher than the 'bad' peak years of the previous period (1956, 1962, 1965). The post-1967 good years for unemployment (1974, 1979) were both worse than the peak years of the earlier period, which came in 1959 and 1963. With growth in GDP per employee the comparison is not so simple, but we can see that, in the last ten years, this variable was negative four times, which did not happen at all in the previous twenty years.

Furthermore the perspective granted us by a full three decades of data lead to the suspicion that the worsening trends have been there all along. That is, although the speed of deterioration definitely picked up in the 1970s, inflation and unemployment, at least, may have been edging upwards from the beginning of the thirty-year period.

To examine this idea, it would help to cancel out the cyclical ups and downs in our data. The simplest way to do this is to take averages over periods of years. Table 2.1 shows the results of calculating the average values of unemployment, inflation and per capita growth for each of the six five-year periods from 1953 to 1982. For comparative purposes, the same calculations on equivalent data for the United States and Canada are also shown.[3]

These five-year averages reveal some very interesting patterns. In all three economies average unemployment rises over the thirty years in a sequence of successive increases broken only by the unusually recession-prone 1958–62 period. Inflation moves up from the beginning at a steadily increasing rate in Canada and the US. In the UK, the pattern is briefly interrupted by the 1958–62 period. Productivity growth seems to peak in the 1960s, and thereafter declines dramatically, becoming non-existent in North American economies in the 1978–82 period.

The engine of economic growth has always been rather mysterious, so it is not surprising that economists have been as puzzled as anyone by the collapse in productivity improvement which seems to date from 1973. But the deterioration in inflation and unemployment hit hard, because it became evident just when economists were beginning to feel confident about how the macroeconomy works, and how to translate this knowledge into useful policy advice. Figure 2.3 shows inflation plotted against unemployment for the whole thirty-year period. The axes have to be relabelled to accommodate the extremes of the last decade, with the result that the 1953–67 Phillips curve of Figure 2.2 gets crammed into the bottom left corner of the diagram. In 1968, the curve begins its long ascent, with both inflation and unemployment trending up to levels that were not experienced at any time of the 1953–67 period.

TABLE 2.1 *Economic performance: five-yearly averages*

	1953–7	1958–62	1963–7	1968–72	1973–7	1978–82
UK unemployment rate	1.3	1.9	1.8	2.9	4.0	8.4
UK inflation rate	3.6	2.4	3.3	6.5	16.0	12.1
UK per capita growth	2.1	1.8	3.1	3.1	1.7	1.1*
US unemployment rate	4.3	6.0	4.0	4.7	6.8	7.2
US inflation rate	1.2	1.4	2.0	4.6	7.7	9.8
US per capita growth	1.9	2.4	2.5	1.0	0.5	0.0*
Canada unemployment rate	4.0	6.6	4.4	5.5	6.7	8.4
Canada inflation rate	0.9	1.3	2.5	3.6	8.9	10.4
Canada per capita growth	2.3	1.5	2.3	2.8	1.0	−0.3*

* 1978–81.

Unemployment = % civilian labour force unemployed, annual average.
Inflation = % change in consumer price index, annual average.
Growth = % change in per employee GNP (Britain—GDP), annual average.

SOURCES   as for Figure 2.1.

Indeed, the upward trends have been so dominant, that it was for some time unclear whether the inverse Phillips relationship between the variables had survived. However, the extraordinarily high unemployment rates of the early 1980s do seem to have had a measurable impact on inflation (though with considerable assistance from lower import prices due to recession in the rest of the world).[4] In the US and Canada as well as in Britain, inflation seems finally to have cracked under the weight of unemployment levels of more than 10 per cent, and of the accompanying high rates of bankruptcy and excess capacity.

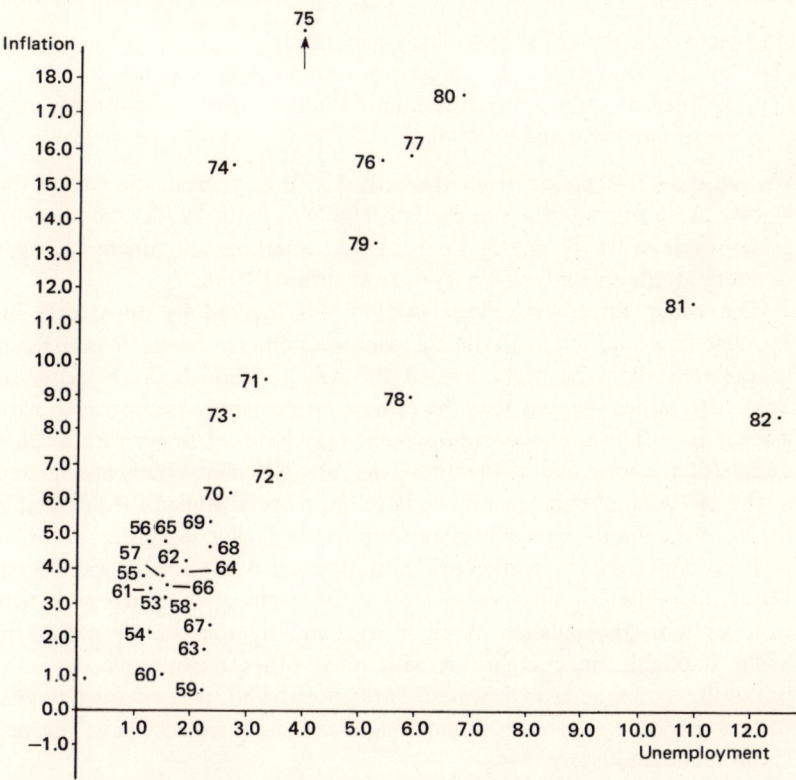

Annual percentage change in consumer price index plotted against annual average percentage of labour force unemployed.

SOURCES　As for Figure 2.1.

FIGURE 2.3　*Inflation and unemployment in the United Kingdom, 1953–82*

But if a line drawn between the 1980, 1981 and 1982 points on Figure 2.3 represents the Phillips curve that we now have to put up with, this offers an inflation-unemployment trade-off that is drastically – perhaps disastrously – poorer than the trade-off of the 1950s and 1960s.

All these facts and figures can be summarised in terms of two opposing forces, which seem to have dominated economic performance since the war in Britain and in other Western economies.

First, we enjoyed the long post-war boom (to be distinguished from the shorter, 'cyclical' booms that alternate with recessions every few years). This boom was characterised by:

(1)   economic growth at historically high rates;
(2)   cyclical fluctuations that were relatively moderate; and
(3)   a tolerable and apparently stable Phillips curve trade-off between unemployment and inflation.

We can date this period from the early 1950s (say, from the end of the Korean war) to some time in the late 1960s or early 1970s. Productivity growth stayed fairly strong up to 1973, inflation and unemployment began to attain uncomfortable levels from around 1968.

The other force – the 'long decline' – is marked by apparently in-exorable deterioration in all the big macroeconomic numbers. It is difficult to precisely date the beginnings of the decline, though the evidence of Table 2.1 rather suggests that the erosion of economic performance with respect to inflation and unemployment may have set in even in the first decade of the long boom. Certainly, the rate of decline visibly accelerated in the 1970s, and seems by now to have quite overwhelmed the favourable forces of the boom years. Nor is any end to the decline in sight.

It is important to realise just how unusual was the post-war boom. British memories of this period tend to be dominated by the persistent troubles with the balance of payments, and by the *relative* decline in living standards, in comparison with most other European economies. But, still, economic growth was smooth enough and strong enough to give Britain the 'quarter century of most rapid and sustained economic advance in our recorded history'.[5]

This matters because it gives a clue where to aim efforts to deal with the present predicament. If the boom was the result of a fortunate and fortuitous combination of 'one-off' events, we should perhaps not worry that economic growth seems now to have settled down closer to historically normal levels.[6] But we can, indeed must, concern ourselves with the deterioration in inflation and unemployment, since the evidence shown here seems to suggest that this cannot be passed off as a short, reversible run of bad luck, but, rather, is the culmination of persistent trends.

The consequences of these trends are uncomfortable enough today, and look positively dangerous if extrapolated into the future. How high could unemployment go before it threatened the very existence of our liberal democracies?

The main purpose of this book is to contribute to an understanding of the long decline, and to suggest remedies that could halt or reverse it. The starting point, which will occupy the next two chapters, is an analysis of why orthodox economics has not been able to do the job.

3 Keynesianism: The Incomplete Revolution

'I myself am not a Keynesian.'

JOHN MAYNARD KEYNES

Theories follow facts, and both eventually find their way into the text-books. It is interesting to plot how the economics taught to students has changed in response to the dramatic shift in economic performance that was documented in chapter 2.

When I first taught macroeconomics, at Oxford in 1974, the text I used was William H. Branson's *Macroeconomic Theory and Policy* (Harper & Row, 1972). This is a well-argued and quite demanding book, chosen because it seemed the best available. It has nearly 450 pages, of which 318 – more than 70 per cent – deal with the 'Keynesian model' – the theory of how the spending of the various sectors in the economy determines the level of Gross National Product. Following the Keynesian section, there is just one chapter, of 21 pages, on inflation. Only 6 pages of this are concerned with the Phillips curve. The remainder of the book – nearly 100 pages – deals with the theory of economic growth; with how GNP increases over the long term.

Five years later, in the 1979–80 academic year, I taught macro-economics again, at Queen's University in Ontario. The change over this quite short period was dramatic (and traumatic for the teacher!). The state-of-the-art text was now Rudiger Dornbusch and Stanley Fischer's *Macroeconomics* (McGraw-Hill, 1st edition, 1978). It is longer than Branson, at nearly 650 pages. The share taken up by the Keynesian model falls somewhat, to nearly 63 per cent. Within this there is a shift in emphasis, with about 70 pages devoted to the economics of 'open' (trading) econo-mies, which had only occupied Branson for 20 pages.

But the really striking change occurred with the other two topics – inflation and growth. The relative attention given them is reversed! Econ-omic growth now gets only one chapter, which reads like a diversion from the main flow of the book, and which many teachers (including me) never get around to covering in lectures. The rest of Dornbusch and Fischer, six hefty chapters, is about inflation and the Phillips curve, and introduces several important concepts, such as the 'natural' rate of unemployment, and inflation expectations, which do not appear at all in Branson's analysis.

On the face of it, these changes make sense. As the table and figures of the previous chapter showed, inflation did not become a really big problem until the 1970s. The post-war boom — the long period of high economic growth — vanished, apparently for good, a year after Branson's book was published. And the explosion in oil prices, as well as the general movement to 'floating' exchange rates in the 1970s, certainly justify increased attention being paid to trade and the balance of payments.

But, apart from the improved treatment of trade, the new macroeconomics has, on closer scrutiny, some disturbing features.

First, the collapse in productivity growth after 1973 is a puzzle, in the sense that it does not seem to be explicable in terms of the growth theory to which Branson devoted nearly 100 pages. The leading expert in the use of this theory to 'account' for economic growth, Edward Denison, confesses that what happened after 1973 is, to him, 'a mystery'.[1] It does not seem satisfactory to deal with this important puzzle by virtually ignoring it — that is, by compressing the topic down to one rather perfunctory chapter. This complaint is particularly pertinent given that the microeconomic underpinning of the discredited growth theory is the same as that of the new material on inflation and unemployment which has forced it out of the textbooks.

Second, this new macroeconomics of inflation and unemployment does represent a response to the changing circumstances of the real economy, but it takes a form which may, with justice, seem surprising or even reprehensible to the concerned non-economist. Of the two big trends marking the economic decline that was documented in the last chapter, only rising inflation is faced up to as a real problem. Unemployment is, in effect, waved off as a logical impossibility given the assumptions on which the new theory is built.

To find out how a theoretical movement that denies the very existence of an unemployment problem could virtually take over the frontiers of macroeconomics during a period when measured unemployment was rising to one member in eight of the workforce, we need to go back fifty years, to the founding of macroeconomics as a distinct discipline. I will argue that irresolution on the part of those responsible for implementing the 'Keynesian revolution' left the theory of unemployment vulnerable to

attack by the 'monetarists' who wish for a return to a less interventionist
era.

John Maynard Keynes' great book, *The General Theory of Employment
Interest and Money*, was written during the depression of the 1930s. It
explained how unemployment could result from an insufficiency of what
is called 'aggregate demand' – that is, a shortfall in total spending by
consumers, firms, and government, such that all available capital and
labour was not in productive use.

Before Keynes, economists had focused on what we now call 'microeconomics' – the study of how supply and demand interact in individual
markets. It was believed that if we could understand how *each* market
works we would then understand how *all* of them operate. That is, we
would understand the economic system as a whole.

It was the achievement of Keynes and his followers at Cambridge
to show that this need not be so. In particular, events in one market or
sector of markets might impinge on others in ways which could not be
predicted by standard microeconomic theory. For example, a confidence
crisis amongst entrepreneurs would cause a cutback in their investment
spending which would lead directly to unemployment in capital goods
industries. But this would not be the end of it. The unemployed workers
would have less disposable income, and would be forced to cut back their
spending on consumer goods, which would lead to unemployment in
those industries, further spending cuts, and so on. Thus, the original shock
to the system would be *multiplied* in its eventual impact on output and
employment. The process would work in either direction, so that an
increase in spending in one sector would result in a larger increase in the
aggregate economy.

The concept of multipliers is by now widely disseminated. It is used,
for example, by special-interest lobby groups in support of pleas for
government grants to a particular industry, on the grounds that the direct
effect of financial support will be multiplied in its ultimate beneficial
impact on employment in the economy.

But, to economists brought up in the microeconomic tradition, this
seemed a revolutionary, even subversive notion. Microeconomics relies
on the price mechanism as a self-correcting system. A sudden excess of
supply in a market will result in a fall in the market price. This should
both encourage demand, and discourage some supply, thus tending to
bring the market back into balance without disrupting other markets. But
Keynes seemed to be saying that the economy is not like that. An initial
imbalance would be self-magnifying, not self-correcting. In the language
of systems engineering, multipliers generate 'positive feedback', whereas

the price mechanism has negative, self-regulating feedback.

The revolution could not be quickly or easily digested. Thus, despite the mounting evidence, as the depression ground on, that the price mechanism really was not doing a very good job of restoring balance in labour markets, no determined test of the policy implications of Keynes' theory was tried until the advent of the Second World War offered a massive, if unwanted, experiment. There was suddenly an enormous expansion of aggregate demand, through armament spending, and, sure enough, unemployment was virtually eliminated.

This demonstration of theory in action sufficiently impressed the governments of Britain, the US, and Canada, that at the end of the war each took the unprecedented step of legislating upon themselves a commitment 'to maintain a high and stable level of employment and income'.[2]

The means of achieving this became known as 'stabilisation policy'. The idea was that government should make use of its control over a large portion of aggregate demand, through its own spending, taxation, and monetary policy, to lean against swings in private sector demand. If private investment fell, threatening output and employment, then public sector spending could be increased, or taxes reduced, or interest rates lowered, to compensate. When, at the other end of the business cycle, a boom in private sector spending built up inflationary pressure, governments would move in the other direction, pulling back the 'levers' of fiscal and monetary policy to restrict aggregate demand.

Disseminated in a vastly successful textbook by Paul Samuelson, the new doctrine of 'Keynesianism' rapidly became the dominant orthodoxy in economics.[3] Its political influence peaked in the 1960s, with the most famous policy example being the Kennedy-Johnson tax cut enacted in the US in 1964. This was a bold and deliberate attempt to increase consumer and corporate spending, and so, through the multiplier, increase GNP and employment.

The tax cut probably worked,[4] and the 1960s was a period of high economic growth and low unemployment. The Keynesian activists had every reason to feel pleased with themselves, and they did not resist the temptation. One of the leading architects of what was then the 'New Economics', Walter Heller, wrote

The significance of the great expansion in the '60s lies not only in its striking statistics of employment, income, and growth, but in its glowing promise of things to come.[5]

Yet, by the end of the next decade, Keynesians were out of intellectual and political favour. Though the Keynesian model still had its place in the textbooks, its activist aspirations had been almost obliterated by an even 'newer' macroeconomics which flatly denied that stabilisation policy could have any permanent effect on real GNP and employment.

What happened? There is a flaw in Keynesian doctrine that eventually proved fatal. It stems not from a weakness in Keynes' own arguments, but from a certain ideological timidity on the part of his disciples, who failed to carry through the full logic of the theory.

The crucial question concerns the failure of the price mechanism to eradicate unemployment. The old microeconomic view was (as noted above) of an economy made up of thousands of sets of criss-crossing supply and demand curves — one pair for each distinct economic activity or market. In each market there is a price at which supply equals demand (that is, a price where the two curves cross), and where all is well. If supply exceeds demand, the market price must be too high. These propositions apply as much to labour as to any other commodity which is bought, sold, or rented. Thus, unemployment, which means an excess supply of labour relative to the demand, could be eliminated if workers lowered their 'price' — the wage rate.

Now, Keynes emphatically rejected wage cuts as a cure for unemployment.[6] Why? Despite what Galbraith has called the 'almost unique unreadability' of the *The General Theory*,[7] I think that the answer shines forth clearly from that book, as well as from Keynes' other writings.

In effect, Keynes' crucial point was that for a large proportion of economic activity no markets exist. This is due to the gap in time between the decision to hire more labour and/or invest in new capital stock, and the realisation of the proceeds from the sale of the output produced by the labour and capital. That is, production decisions by entrepreneurs must be made in the *expectation* that they will be profitable.

Now some expectations are close to certainties. When goods and services are pre-sold — production on contract or 'to order' — the risk will, in general, be low. But a good deal, perhaps most, of economic activity is production 'to stock' — production undertaken in the hope that someone will want to buy it at a profitable price.

For a few commodities — copper and pork bellies, for example — the risk of production to stock can be hedged in 'futures markets', in which the guarantee of sale in the future is sold at a price determined now. But there are no futures markets for the vast majority of goods and services. General Motors cannot pre-sell the new models it tools-up for each year. Kelloggs cannot pre-sell a new, or even its existing brand of breakfast cereal. An expanding restaurant franchise cannot be sure that its tables will be full. In principle, there is no reason why futures markets should not exist for these commodities, but the risks are so great that such markets have not emerged.

Keynes pointed out that the economy cannot be assumed to be self-regulating if expectations are important. On the contrary, expectations may be self-reinforcing rather than self-correcting. If, for example, all firms expect a recession to occur, and adjust their own output and employment accordingly, there *will* be a recession. Keynes then argued that wage cuts would, if anything, tend to strengthen recessionary expectations. The cuts would result in some redistribution of income from workers to capitalists, which would be expected to reduce demand, since workers spend a larger proportion of their incomes than do richer owners of capital. And to the extent that wage cuts lead to general price cuts, individual firms would not expect much or any improvement in their own competitive position, and so would not bank on the cuts leading to a significant boost in demand.

As well as the difficulties due to the widespread lack of proper futures markets, there are problems with the markets that do exist. A lot depends on what economists call 'elasticity'. This is the measure of the response of one variable to a change in another. If, for example, a 1 per cent fall in the price of something results in a 3 per cent increase in the demand for it, economists would say that the price elasticity of demand is three. The elasticity concept can be used to summarise the strength of the relationship between any two variables, but it is most often mentioned in connection with the effect of price changes on demand and supply.

Why does elasticity matter? Suppose that a firm facing difficult times asks its workers to take a 10 per cent wage cut. This would lower the firm's costs, to an extent determined by the share wages are of total costs (which include, also, materials bought from other firms). Suppose that the cost effect would be 5 per cent. Then the firm could afford to lower its price by 5 per cent without reducing its percentage profit margin. The effect of this price change on demand determines whether the wage cut would be worthwhile. If demand elasticity was rather high, then the effect on sales and thus output and employment will be large. An elasticity of 5 would mean that the 5 per cent price cut would result in sales and employment being 25 per cent (5 x 5) higher than they would have been otherwise. Such an increase in jobs might be judged worth taking a 10 per cent wage cut for.[8]

But suppose demand were 'inelastic', by which is meant an elasticity number smaller than 1. Then the increase in jobs would be less than 5 per cent, and much less than the original 10 per cent wage cut. The arithmetic of this situation is not attractive, since it implies that, despite the slightly larger amount of work being done, the total wage bill would actually fall. It would therefore be foolish of the workers to offer a wage cut.

The effectiveness of the market price mechanism depends to a very considerable extent on elasticity. It will be a central theme in this book that demand in most markets is already inelastic, and is steadily getting more inelastic over time.

The combination of the expectations, or shortage-of-markets, problem stressed by Keynes and low elasticities in the markets that do exist reinforces the argument that wage and price flexibility cannot cure unemployment. Some more direct way of influencing demand is needed.

But, by and large, the 'Keynesians' – the economists who propagated Keynes' ideas as they saw fit in textbooks and policy advice – did not rest their case about the need for government efforts to stabilise demand on the evidence of missing or inadequate markets. On the contrary, they took a position on the other extreme. Implicitly at first, later explicitly, they assumed not only that the economy is well-supplied with a complete set of markets, but also that demand in these markets is potentially highly elastic. In technical terms, they assumed that the economy is 'perfectly competitive'.

A perfectly competitive economy is characterised by markets in each of which there are very many (and therefore small) firms. The significance of smallness is that it means that no individual firm can exert an influence on the market price. Perfectly competitive firms are 'price-takers', not 'price-makers'. It can be shown, with the aid of some mathematics, that for such an economy there must exist a set of wages and prices which, if adopted, would result in supply and demand being equal everywhere.[9]

How, then, did Keynesians explain unemployment – an excess supply of labour relative to demand? They claimed that wages (and, as a result, prices) were rigid, or, at least, 'sticky', so we would not normally find them at the full employment levels: it would take time to adjust.

This view, suitably elaborated, became known as the 'neoclassical synthesis'. In economics neoclassicists are people who believe that the world is made up of perfectly competitive markets. By grafting sticky wages onto the model, Keynesians were able to achieve a sort of synthesis between perfect competition at the microeconomic level, and unemployment at the aggregate or macro level of the economy. For example, if aggregate demand fell, instead of wages and prices falling to compensate, the burden of adjustment would have to fall on 'real' variables – output and employment. In the other direction, however, with wages rigid upwards as well as downwards, government could boost aggregate demand, and get a one-for-one increase in output and employment, with no leakage into higher prices.

And just *why* were wages rigid? At first, this question was left unanswered, or the rigidities were blamed on trade unions. This was not entirely satisfactory, especially in the US, where unions are not as important as in other economies. So, in the 1960s, a more sophisticated rationalisation began to emerge. Following a brilliant article by Robert Clower (which is said to have been developed from his rejected Oxford D.Phil thesis), and a provocative book by the Swede Axel Leijonhufvud, the idea began to circulate that the reason prices and wages did not change rapidly was that there was no-one around to change them.[10] An essential element in the full neoclassical model was missing; namely, the 'Walrasian auctioneer' whose job it is to call out a price, receive bids for both supply and demand, adjust the (provisional) price according to whether the supply bid was greater or less than the demand bid, receive new bids, and so on, until an equilibrium price was reached balancing supply and demand. It was observed that many markets had no-one answering the description of the Walrasian auctioneer. Instead, firms and workers had to change prices themselves, which would take time and involve mistakes, reflected in the under-employment of resources and labour.

Thus the emphasis shifted away from Keynes' notion of unemployment as a *permanent*, equilibrium phenomenon, with which most Keynesians, especially North Americans, had never been really comfortable, presumably because it implied that something was rather fundamentally lacking in the market system.[11] Much easier to digest was the idea that unemployment is just a by-product of an adjustment process; that firms and unions are continually groping their way towards the 'market-clearing price'.

The new doctrine was called 'disequilibrium economics', or the 'economics of temporary equilibrium'. It was bolstered in the 1970s by some interesting efforts, in particular by the late Arthur Okun of the Brookings Institution, to rationalise wage and price stickiness in terms of 'implicit contract theory'.[12] These invoked various adjustment costs, and the efficiency of long-term relationships between worker and employer, and between firm and customer, to justify wages and prices not fluctuating sharply enough to equate supply and demand in every short period of market activity.

There is little doubt that the notion of implicit contracts has some descriptive validity (though it is not clear why workers would prefer to stabilise wages rather than employment in such contracts).[13] However, it has not sufficed to save Keynesian economics. Both under the pressure of recent events, and as a result of a fierce attack from within the economics profession, Keynesian activism has had most of the stuffing knocked out of it. In its place, the critics have introduced, or, more accurately, resurrected, the doctrine known as 'monetarism', which is the subject of Chapter 4.

4 The Wacky World of Mark II Monetarism

'Flag? I see no flag.'

HORATIO, LORD NELSON

In the 'neoclassical synthesis', unemployment is not a permanent problem. The economy is always *tending* towards full employment, but the wage and price stickiness that slows it down does justify some stabilising intervention by government. Thus, Keynes' popularisers emasculated his revolution into a reform.[1] This view seemed to fit the facts of the 1950s and 1960s well enough. As shown in Chapter 2, these years were dominated by 'cycles' — ups and downs in economic activity of a few years' duration — which never strayed far from full employment.

But in the 1970s, insidious trends began to dominate the short-term cycles. The economy slipped away from full employment to the extent that the lowest levels achieved in the last ten years exceed the worst years of the previous two decades. Rather than tending towards full employment, we seem to be headed in the opposite direction.

But it was not, unfortunately, persistent high unemployment that was seized upon by the critics of Keynesianism. If it had been, we could be now in a much better position to understand and counter the current crisis. Instead, attention was focused on inflation. The monetarist critique took advantage of the incompleteness of the Keynesian revolution. This, as was pointed out in the previous chapter, never queried the basic neoclassical assumption of perfectly competitive markets. But, then, all the stories about wage rigidity due to absence of auctioneers or to implicit contracts were implausible. For why should firms and workers put up, even temporarily, with prices and wages that left them selling or working less than they wished? With the essence of perfect competition being that every 'agent' (buyer or seller) in the economy is small relative to its market, everyone would perceive that a quite small cut in their price or wage would suffice to generate enough extra demand to balance supply. That is,

31

with high elasticities everywhere, the incentive for the necessary price and wage adjustments to restore full employment would be so strong that no missing auctioneer or adjustment costs would impede the process for long.

The logic of this argument, *given the neoclassical preconditions that both sides accepted as common ground*, is so strong that two of the leading theorists of Keynesian disequilibrium models — Robert Barro and Herschel Grossman — have become strong advocates of anti-Keynesian positions.[2]

The argument justified a swing back to the pre-Keynesian faith in the efficacy of 'free' market forces. The economy, unaided, really would tend strongly to deliver a balance between supply and demand in all markets. Apparent unemployment, then, must in fact be appropriate, or 'natural'. Keynesian policy-makers attempting to hold unemployment below its natural rate would, in effect, be trying to generate *too little* unemployment. In microeconomic terms, they would be creating excess demand in labour markets. And the consequences of excess demand have always been predictable — inflation.

While the novelty of Keynesian activism may have fooled people in its first decade or so into producing more and working harder than they really wanted, this effect would surely (claimed the critics) wear off as everyone became accustomed to the new policy regimen. Then, stimulus of aggregate demand would just lead to higher wages and prices, not higher real GNP. That is, the Keynesian tools of demand management or stabilisation policy could not *permanently* hold output above, and unemployment below, their natural, market-determined levels. In the long-run, there would be no trade-off between inflation and unemployment.

The new doctrine was introduced by Milton Friedman and Edmund Phelps, notably in papers by each of them published in 1968.[3] Its major policy implication is that, with real output and employment at or tending strongly towards their natural equilibrium levels, the only available target for policy-makers is the rate of inflation, which, as a corollary of the theory, has a simple one-to-one relationship with the rate of growth of the money supply. If, say, the amount of money in the economy is increased by 10 per cent, and given that none of the increase can be permanently absorbed by increased real output, it must all eventually feed into a price level 10 per cent higher than before. That is, money is all that matters, and it matters only for inflation.

Thus, the new theory has been called 'monetarism', or 'monetarism mark II'. The 'mark II' is useful to mark the distinction of these ideas from an earlier debate, also largely stirred up by Milton Friedman, about the relative effectiveness of fiscal and monetary policy instruments in the

Keynesian tool-kit of stabilisation policies. In the 1950s and 1960s Friedman argued with Keynesians, notably James Tobin, about *which* instrument was more important in effecting changes in output and employment. By the 1970s, Friedman and others were claiming that *no* policy could permanently move real variables.

The monetarist movement was given a further injection of exciting ideas by the brilliant Chicago economist Robert Lucas, who is credited with introducing the notion of 'rational expectations' into economics. The idea here is that people form expectations of the results of their own and others' actions on the basis of their understanding of how the economy works. That is, they 'rationally' use all their information about the system.

This notion certainly was a step forward, since economists – both Keynesian and monetarist – had previously assumed expectations to be 'backward-looking'. For example, most models had inflationary expectations determined as a function of the actual past levels of inflation, heedless of any observable change in the fundamental determinants of price changes.

A striking implication of rational expectations was drawn out in the celebrated 'policy-ineffectiveness' proposition of Thomas Sargent and Neil Wallace.[4] This states that if everyone in the economy believes it to be neoclassical (perfectly competitive), and if they are correct [!], then should they all act rationally on this belief, no systematic government fiscal or monetary policy will have even a *temporary* effect on real output and employment. The market will be 'smart' enough to compensate fully for the intrusions of government. Government gets the blame for inflation; the private sector takes the credit for everything else.

Filtered through academia by some enthusiastic popularisers, mark II monetarism has achieved a quick and striking influence on the policy process. By now (1983) it has just about supplanted Keynesianism as the orthodoxy accepted by the political leaders of Britain and the United States. How well does it fit the facts?

Note first that the predictions of the monetarists (dropping the 'mark II', for brevity) seemed well on target as the post-war boom faded in the late 1960s. We saw in Chapter 2, Figure 2.3 how inflation in the UK began a rather steady ascent in 1968; apparently abandoning the relatively clear-cut Phillips curve of earlier years. This is consistent with both monetarist predictions: (1) that the inflation-unemployment trade-off would only last until people became familiar with the policies that were exploiting it; and (2) that these policies had been attempting to hold unemployment below its 'natural' rate, and were thus inherently inflationary. As Lucas recently put it:

A high-inflation decade should not have less unemployment on average
than a low-inflation decade. We got the high-inflation decade, and with
it as clear-cut an experimental discrimination as macroeconomics is
ever likely to see, and Friedman and Phelps were right.[5]

'It really is as simple as that', claims Lucas. But is it so straightforward?
The rise in inflation is consistent with monetarism. But it may be consistent with other theories, too.

There are at least two major economic 'facts', which are very difficult
to deal with from within a monetarist perspective, and which strongly
suggest that something quite different is demanded.

First, there are the actual results of application of monetarist policies
in Britain, the United States and, to an extent, in Canada. Since Lucas
wrote, governments and their central banks in these economies have
determinedly dragged down the rate of growth of the money supply in
order to reduce inflation. The result? Inflation has finally cracked, but
only after unemployment was deliberately screwed up to levels which
all but the most rabid new monetarist would admit to be well above
any conceivable 'natural' rate. But if everyone is 'rational', they should
have *known* that the lower money growth would result in lower inflation,
and have adjusted quickly their own wage and price changes to be consistent with this – that is, to validate the expectations – without going
through the great and wasteful fuss of heavy unemployment and bankruptcy rates.

The second problem is with the natural rate of unemployment itself.
Even adjusting for the recent recession, the underlying trend of unemployment is upwards, and seems to have been so at least from the 1960s, and
possibly from the very beginning of the post-war boom (as documented
in Chapter 2).

How do the monetarists deal with this? How indeed, do they rationalise
as 'natural' any significant positive level of measured unemployment? It is
appropriate now to look more closely at the underpinnings of monetarist
theory. We will find a disturbing example of the power of prior beliefs –
in this case, beliefs about the efficiency of the market system – to shield
even very clever economists from the painful intrusion of what Galbraith
might call 'an inconvenient reality'.

Monetarist reasoning can, without excessive caricature, be summarised
as follows: The world is, *unquestionably*, neoclassical. That is, the economy
is made up of many small, and thus individually powerless, buyers and
sellers competing 'perfectly' with one another. In such an economy there
can be no persistent involuntary unemployment of labour because market

forces always act to restore equality between supply and demand. There-fore, what *looks* like involuntary unemployment in the real world must, somehow, be voluntary.

How was such an about-turn in our perception of reality to be rationalised? The breakthrough was made by a group under the leadership of Edmund Phelps, who, in a well-known 1970 book, proudly announced the dis-covery of a 'new microeconomics' of unemployment and inflation.[6]

The gist of their idea is that what appears to the untutored eye to be enforced idleness − unemployment − is, in fact, voluntary, rational, and efficient 'search' activity, leading to better jobs for those undertaking it. Workers *choose* to become unemployed − they quit, rather than being laid-off − in order to devote all their time to searching for a better job. Thus unemployment is an essential and useful element of the market system − it is 'natural'. As Phelps put it (with a conciliatory bow towards the Keynesians)

> It would be as senselessly puritanical to wipe out unemployment as it would be to raise taxes in a deep depression. Today's unemployment is an investment in a better allocation of any given quantity of employed persons tomorrow.[7]

Any theory of unemployment must explain, not only its existence, but also why it fluctuates up and down. The search theorists did this by proposing that workers could be *fooled* by changes in the rate of inflation into extending or curtailing their search activity, and consequently into increasing or decreasing around the natural rate the proportion of the labour force out of work at any time.

Suppose that government caused aggregate demand − the total amount of spending in the economy − to increase. This, according to search theorists, would lead at once to a general increase in prices and wages − to an inflation. Each happily searching worker would receive higher wage offers. If they knew of the general increase in other wages and prices they would not be impressed. However, (it is assumed), it takes them time to find out what is going on elsewhere in the economy: in the meantime, they jump at the higher money wage, stop searching sooner, and so reduce the unemployment rate.

In the other direction, an attempt to reduce inflation by squeezing aggregate demand will reduce the size of wage offers. Searchers will, mistakenly, be disappointed (mistaken because, with all other wages and prices also cut, offers are, in real terms, as good as before) and will choose to search longer to attempt to satisfy their obsolete wage expectations. Thus, unemployment in the economy will increase, until searchers realize what is going on and return to their 'natural' habits.

Thus we derive the monetarist morals; first, that any attempt to use Keynesian policies to reduce unemployment below average will (a) increase inflation, (b) only temporarily reduce unemployment, and (c) be misguided, since workers *want* the unemployment, so that they can search efficiently; and second, that above-average unemployment will be necessary to pull down the inflation rate, with its extent and duration depending on how quick-witted workers are in realising what is going on. If workers are 'rational' as assumed in the rational expectations version of the model, then they should soon perceive the change in aggregate demand, and thus not deviate for long from their natural search behaviour.

The reader may find this tale improbable. Many economists have found it so, and have produced arguments and evidence against the search model. So far as I am aware, monetarists have made no serious effort to refute these arguments.

One assumption vital to the theory was quickly queried by Keynesians; for example, by James Tobin, in 1972.[8] It is that search from unemployment is more popular than search 'on-the-job' − than looking for your next job without leaving your current employment.

On the face of it, there seem to be useful advantages to searching on-the-job. You get paid a full wage while searching. If search is unsuccessful, then one's present employment can quietly be continued. Being currently employed may make the worker more attractive to a prospective employer − it at least proves employability. Certainly, most economists, including monetarists, search on-the-job − when they change jobs, it is without a voluntary intervening spell on the unemployment register.

Indeed, the evidence for the labour force as a whole seems overwhelmingly against the search unemployment model. Most unemployed people accept the first job they are offered, rather than 'sampling' from the limitless pool of offers assumed by search theorists.[9] Search itself typically takes only a few hours a week − hardly a full-time activity.[10] Most unemployment is relatively long-term and much ends in discouraged departure from the labour force, rather than a new and better job.[11] And, most damning, search on-the-job actually results, on average, in *higher* wage increases than search from unemployment.[12]

Thus, the empirical evidence strongly suggests that the 'natural' rate of unemployment, defined by monetarists as the rate willingly chosen by workers in full possession of the relevant information about government's aggregate demand policy, must be very small, even near zero. Workers do not seem to *choose* to become unemployed in order to search for a new job. If so, then the natural rate doctrine underlying monetarism is not able to explain why our average or trend unemployment rates are so high and increasing.

Monetarists have shown some interest in examining various 'structural' characteristics of labour markets in search of changes that might have raised the natural rate. Events such as more generous unemployment benefits and higher participation rates of women are often called on. But while such changes may have increased the time people spend searching, *once unemployed*, they do not make much more plausible the proposition that the unemployed chose that condition in the first place. In any case, the quantitative magnitude of the structural changes is not large enough to account for more than a quite small fraction of additional unemployment, even accepting the search theory's premises.[13]

A second key assumption allows the monetarists to rationalise fluctuations in unemployment around its average, and the relationship of these fluctuations to inflation. As noted, these are supposed to depend on workers being slow to pick up across-the-board changes in prices and wages due to changes in aggregate demand. This too seems to be empirically implausible. The rate at which workers quit jobs declines in recessions.[14] According to the search model, it should increase, as workers respond to what, mistakenly, they perceive as a too-low wage offer by quitting to search for something better. And there is evidence that workers tend to be adequately informed on the employment situation in their labour market.[15]

A simpler, and, to me, much more persuasive explanation of fluctuations in unemployment is that they come from changes on the *demand*, not the supply side of the labour market. It is the availability of jobs — the demand for labour — that determines how many will actually be employed. There is plenty of econometric evidence to support this proposition,[16] and we will come back to it later in the book.

Thus, the Keynesians' criticisms of monetarism seem well taken. The voluntary search unemployment model does not seem plausibly capable of explaining the sizeable and continuing trend to higher unemployment in our economies. And it is probably not very good at rationalising the cycle — the year-to-year fluctuations around the trend.[17]

But, on the other hand, monetarists have fired some effective salvos at Keynesian economics, which does not seem to have coped well with the other big macroeconomic trend — to higher inflation. And its underlying assumptions of rigid or 'sticky' wages and prices is hard to defend within the basically neoclassical paradigm shared by both theories. Something different is needed.

5 The Importance of Being Elastic

Robert Lucas concludes his critical review of some lectures by James Tobin with a story:

> The archaeologist Heinrich Schliemann, the discoverer of Troy, became convinced, we are told, that a particular skull unearthed in a later excavation was the head of Agamemnon. To the frustration of this creative and productive scientist, his associates confronted him with one devastating argument after another to the effect that this could not possibly be the case. Exhausted, Schliemann took up the skull and thrust it in the faces of his unconstructive critics: 'Alright then, if he is not Agamemnon, who is he?'[1]

Lucas, the monetarist, uses this story to illustrate a point against the Keynesian Tobin, but it might with at least equal appropriateness be turned on monetarism itself. Monetarists have 'named the skull'; that is, they have produced a logically cohesive theory of how the economy works. Keynesians and other critics can offer a long list of real-world reasons why the monetarist theory does not fit the facts – the length of business cycles, the evidence on expectation formation, the persistence of involuntary unemployment. But to all this monetarists can respond: 'OK, let us see *your* theory'. And this retort is embarrassing, because the Keynesian model has, as was argued in previous chapters, fallen through the rather thin ice of the 'sticky wage' assumption on which it rests.

Nevertheless, the awkward facts remain. Indeed, they become ever more intrusive as the trends in the unemployment/inflation trade-off continue to deteriorate. We do urgently need a theory to explain these important matters.

The story told in the previous two chapters provides the essential clue. Both the post-war orthodoxies (Keynesianism and monetarism) rely on what is code-named 'the neoclassical model'. This, in essence, is the proposition that everyone in the economy – firms, households, workers

38

— operates in markets that are extremely 'competitive', in the economist's special sense of the word. That is, economic activity is organised in markets in which both buyers and sellers are numerous, and all are small relative to the size of the total market. Then, 'market forces' — adjustments in the market price and responses to these — work effectively to balance supply and demand, and persistent unemployment is impossible.

In contrast, Keynes himself, who certainly did believe persistent unemployment to be possible, argued that, for rather fundamental reasons, many important markets are not perfectly or highly competitive in this sense. In particular, the gap between present actions and their future realisations makes it impossible for firms to rely on being able to sell all they wish at a known market price, as is guaranteed under perfect competition. The difference was summarised in chapter 3, in terms of differences in the *elasticity* of markets. This powerful concept requires further analysis.

The basic neoclassical assumption of perfect competition, that every firm and worker is small and unimportant, is equivalent to saying that price elasticities — the responsiveness of quantities to prices — are extremely large. The neoclassical economy is a high-elasticity economy. This is because the very essence of 'smallness' is that you get a lot of action from a price change. If one prairie wheat farm cut its price below the market level by one cent, it would be deluged with customers deserting the other thousands of farmers offering the same grade of wheat for one cent more. (It doesn't actually do this because it doesn't need to; being small, it can already sell all that can be profitably produced at the going market price.) In the other direction, an attempt to raise the price one cent above the market rate would quickly result in all the farm's customers melting away to the abundant alternative suppliers.

It is these powerful price effects that make both persistent unemployment and persistent inflation (assuming the appropriate monetary policies) impossible in a neoclassical world. Anyone can sell all they wish merely by shading by a fraction the market price or wage. And no-one can get away with charging more than the market will bear.

What about when market conditions *change*? How does the price mechanism cope? Suppose, for example, that an unforeseen change in consumer tastes reduces the demand for one of a firm's products, leaving it with unsold stocks. The firm could cut the price, to encourage a few extra consumers to buy up the excess supply. Over the longer run, the lower profits resulting from the lower price encourage the firm and its potential competitors to divert resources into other products for which demand is stronger. The price change is the means both of balancing supply and demand in the short term, and of signalling the appropriate long-term reallocation of investment.

The painfulness of these adjustments depends on elasticity. If demand is very elastic, then a small price cut suffices. Profits and wages will not be much affected, nor will substantial changes in long-run investment plans be needed. An elastic economy is quickly able to fill-in the gaps made by 'shocks' such as changes in tastes (or technological breakthroughs; or shortages of natural resources). This, of course, is the neoclassical economy assumed by monetarists.

Suppose, on the other hand, that demand is 'inelastic', as defined in Chapter 3. That is, the quantity response is less than the change in price, with each measured in percentage terms. Say, for example, that the shortfall in demand is 10 per cent and elasticity is 0.5. Then, a 20 per cent price cut would be necessary to balance supply and demand. This is more than the profit margin of many firms. Bankruptcy could result. Further, the loss in income of the firm's owners and workers would mean less spending by them – lower demand for the output of other firms. Thus, the original shock can become multiplied in its eventual impact on the economy.

An analogous story can be told of the effects of a sudden *increase* in demand. Consumers want to buy more of the firm's product at the going price. The firm, however, would do better if it could take advantage of the stronger market by raising its price, rather than going to the trouble and expense of increasing its production. What will actually result depends on elasticity. If this is high, then a price rise would result in a substantial loss of customers, so a firm will tend to choose increased production instead. On the other hand, low elasticity means that profit margins can be inflated at only a small penalty in lost sales.

All this has direct implications for the economy at large; for the 'big numbers' of macroeconomic performance. Take the problem of unemployment. This means a general shortfall of demand, firms in general being unable to sell enough goods at current prices to employ all the labour willing to work. The modern economy has two ways of dealing with this. First, market forces can operate – firms and workers cut prices and wages to increase sales and employment, as outlined above. Secondly, government can supplement the market by implementing policies to expand demand – tax cuts, public sector investments, easier credit, and so on.

If there is plenty of elasticity around, the price cuts will be quickly effective at increasing demand. Further, there will be a second-round effect – with employment and incomes increasing across the economy, demand will expand, increasing employment again, and tending to restore prices to their previous levels. Thus, the end result would be unemployment eliminated with no permanent erosion of profitability. In an elastic economy, government's expansionary policies would also be particularly effective, as firms feel constrained to respond to demand increases with higher output rather than price increases. However, if the economy is really very elastic, market forces alone may be sufficient to rapidly restore full employment, and government policies redundant, or even (if badly timed, for instance) a nuisance, as monetarists claim..

Contrast this with the circumstances of an economy which is low in elasticity. The size of the price and wage cuts needed to clear goods and labour markets are such that each firm believes it would thereby be bank-rupted, and/or its workers that they would be impoverished. So the price cuts do not get made. There may even be a pathological (from the point of view of market economics) tendency towards *increasing* prices when demand falls, in an attempt to maintain total profits by raising margins on a smaller volume of sales, and further reduce output and employment. In any case, the second round multiplier process, of each firm's boost-ing of its own demand leading to increases in the demand for the products of other firms, never gets underway. Nor can government intervention be expected to help much. With low elasticities, the flow of increased spending resulting from, say, a tax cut, will be largely diverted to higher prices — inflation — rather than towards increasing output and employ-ment.

All this is rather disturbing. It is not enough to have a comprehensive network of 'free' markets — the markets must also be well-supplied with elasticity if they are to function successfully. But this is not a proposition which one finds stressed in the technical journals or in the textbooks. This is because most macroeconomists are incorrigible 'elasticity optimists'. As we saw in the last chapter, both of the dominant macroeconomic ortho-doxies continue to be based on the neoclassical assumptions of perfect competition.

Chapter 6 documents the unrealism of the perfect competition assump-tion. The failure of macroeconomics to come to terms with this is par-ticularly difficult to understand given that *micro*economists — those charged with understanding how individual markets and the agents in them function — are well aware of the presence of low elasticities in markets, and are quite well-informed on the subject.

A typical microeconomics textbook, after developing at length the obligatory set-piece on how five different curves all meet at the same place in a perfectly competitive market,[2] will then admit that such markets are rare, if not extinct, and will take the student through chapters on imperfect and monopolistic competition, oligopoly, and monopoly. The oligopoly ('a few firms in a market') chapter will be disappointingly inconclusive, given the importance of this market type, but at least it is there.

But this plurality of market types is not carried through to the macro-economics texts, where the big numbers of unemployment and inflation are debated. There, battle is waged between Keynesians and monetarists on terrain restricted, by mutual agreement, to the smooth irrelevancies of perfect competition.

Fortunately, not all economists have been satisfied with this state of affairs. The most famous maverick is without doubt John Kenneth Galbraith. In many articles and books, Galbraith has put forward an iconoclastic and determinedly relevant analysis of how the economy works.[3] Certainly, his insistence that the world does not fit the neo-classical ideal type, and his success in propagating this view, has made things a lot easier for those who also wish to question the economic orthodoxies.

A few of the technical virtuosi in the profession have also begun to take an interest in the unfamiliar world of low elasticity. One of the most brilliant of the younger theorists, Oliver Hart, of the London School of Economics, has recently published a paper in which he demonstrates rigorously how an imperfectly competitive economy can settle down at an equilibrium at which there is involuntary unemployment.[4] He does so without recourse to the implausible assumptions of wage and price 'stickiness' that weaken 'Keynesian' analyses of unemployment.

The non-economist might well exclaim that this is just a case of theory catching up with the facts, and about time too! However, the walls of the ivory tower are dense – it seems to take a long time for the cries of the unemployed to be heard within – so that Hart's contribution is most encouraging, given the deserved respect in which his technical skills are held amongst his colleagues.

Less widely respected is the group of economists who call themselves 'post-Keynesians'.[5] These people attempt to follow the true spirit of what Keynes *really* meant, as well as developing the ideas of Keynes' distinguished contemporary, the Polish economist Michal Kalecki. Kalecki did build models in which it is explicitly assumed that markets are not perfectly competitive. Unfortunately, though, his primary interest was in the *distribution* of wealth, not its creation, which led him to make a number of simplifying assumptions, including one that there is full employment in the economy.

The ideas of the post-Keynesians deserve a better hearing than the economics profession at large has so far been prepared to give them. A recent book by Keith Cowling, of the University of Warwick (though Cowling probably would not describe himself as a post-Keynesian) has demonstrated how Kalecki's ideas can be extended to cover unemployment and inflation.[6]

Finally, we have the ideas of John Maynard Keynes himself, which certainly cannot be equated with the doctrine of Keynesianism propagated after his death in 1946. The latter, as pointed out in Chapter 3, is a rather timid attempt to graft Keynes' idea of aggregate demand being sometimes insufficient for full employment onto an orthodox neoclassical base of perfectly competitive markets, missing only the elusive 'Walrasian auctioneer'.

It should be noted that 'Keynesianism' as I have defined and criticised it is largely a North American hybrid. British economists tend to be less neoclassical, closer in spirit to Keynes himself (and, it must be admitted, less technically skilled than the Americans). This is probably due to the presence in British economics of some of the people who collaborated with Keynes in formulating the ideas that became his *General Theory* — the late Joan Robinson, Nicholas Kaldor, and Richard Kahn, in particular.

To summarise: events have demonstrated the inadequacy of received economic orthodoxies. A growing minority of economists recognise this, and are attempting to do something about it. However, there is no doubt that the neoclassical system is still intellectually far more refined and cohesive than the available alternatives. Much more work remains to be done. But we cannot sit back and fiddle theoretical tunes while the economy burns. The problem of stagflation must somehow be confronted.

I suggest that the confrontation be organised around the concept of elasticity. It is the assumption of high elasticities that makes a fairytale out of the neoclassical model. And, I conjecture, it will be low elasticity that emerges as the culprit when the theoretical dust has settled, and a successful model of stagflation has been constructed.

As a foundation for the new theory, it is important to establish just how much elasticity there is in our economies. A useful model of how all markets fit together must be grounded in a realistic appreciation of how individual markets work. The next chapter will survey the evidence on elasticity in markets.

6 An Elasticity Crisis in the Lumpy Economy

'It is not that the system of free private enterprise has failed, but that it has not yet been tried.'

F. D. ROOSEVELT

Elasticity is the oil that lubricates the market mechanism. This mechanism shows signs of seizing up. Is there direct evidence that this is due to depletion of the elasticity level in the economy?

It is not simply a matter of going out and inserting a statistical dipstick into the economy. Elasticity estimates are not 'hard' data, like acres of farm land. But there is compelling evidence that the economy (1) does not have the elasticity needed for automatic full employment; and (2) is inherently prone to gobble-up such elasticity as remains. That is, we have a shortage of elasticity, and the situation is deteriorating.

The crisis appears when a picture of a 'perfectly competitive' economy is overlaid by all the real-world qualifications. The actual economy is a long way from the high-elasticity neoclassical ideal.

The essence of perfect competition is that all economic activity is mediated by markets in which no individual participant is big enough to have a significant influence: the price mechanism controls everything, and no-one controls the price. Each individual goes out into the market every day, buys materials, adds some value to them (ie, produces something), and sells the result. Then the individual puts on the 'consumer' hat, and returns to the market to spend the income earned by producing. So long as everyone acts 'rationally' – that is, buys and sells to maximise profits from producing and utility from consuming – and so long as there is an 'auctioneer' to adjust prices as supply and demand change, and so long as a few other more technical conditions are met, then all markets should tend towards an equilibrium in which supply and demand for each commodity and service, including labour, are in balance.[1] This is the wonderful world of perfect competition. But:

44

(1) *Most people do not do business on their own account*. A majority (indeed, a large majority) of producers do what they do because they are told to, not because they choose it in response to market prices. There are about 25 million 'producers' (members of the labour force) in Britain. But there are only 2 million or so business units. This means, roughly speaking, that nine out of ten workers are not self-employed or top managers, but work for a wage or salary. That is, most of us work for someone else. When we have produced something, we don't go out and sell it, but hand it on to the next person in the organisation. We are not responding to prices: our day-to-day economic activities are carried out in an administered, or *planned* environment, not in a market.

The preponderance of planned environments is obvious enough. But it has escaped neoclassical economists, who persist with the misleading fiction of ubiquitous markets. They do this not only in theoretical models but also in evaluating the merits of different economic systems. Thus, the US and the USSR are set up as extreme cases of 'market' and 'planned' economies, and their relative economic success used as a yardstick of the efficiency of the two types of economic organisation. It is no doubt true that a larger proportion of economic activity in the US is co-ordinated by market forces than in the USSR, but, *in both countries*, most of the job is done by planning, without reference, at least from a short-term perspective, to the price mechanism.

The reasons for this have interested a few economists. Why do institutions within which activity is co-ordinated by management not markets — firms — arise in a market system? The classic answer, developed by R. H. Coase in the 1930s, stressed the costs of using markets when there are uncertainties and difficulties in tightly specifying contracts.[2] Imagine an assembly line where workers had to haggle over price at each stage of production! These kinds of costs make it worthwhile to forego some of the theoretical advantages of the price mechanism in order to give managers discretion to co-ordinate activity.

Thus, it is efficient at the micro-level to organise people into bureaucracies. *But the macro-level implications must be recognised*. Monetarists assume that all economic activity is co-ordinated by the price mechanism, which is why they expect price changes to be a powerful tool for eliminating imbalances, such as unemployment. Since much activity is, in fact, ruled by administrative *fiat* rather than market forces, we cannot be sure that the leverage prices can exert will be sufficient to restore macroeconomic balance.

Over the long term, of course, market forces matter in determining just what people inside organisations produce, and what they get paid for doing this. We cannot conclude that price plays a minor role. But market forces cannot be *all*-important, unless the 'power' wielded by the millions of managers and supervisors is entirely illusory, and the great superstructure of bureaucratic authority relationships just a veil over the mechanism of supply and demand.

(2)   *The imperfection of markets* is a second difficulty damaging the credibility of neoclassical theory. The preconditions for 'perfect' competition are rarely even approximated in the real world. Too much depends on suppliers and demanders in markets being 'small', in the sense of being individually unable to influence the market price.

There are plenty of industries, especially in the service sector, in which firms are physically small (for example, corner stores) but when important factors such as location are allowed for, each seller turns out to be operating in a small sub-market with just a few competitors. That is, relative to the *relevant* market, these firms are not small in the economic sense of being price-takers. If they want to sell more, they must reduce prices, and if their prices are slightly higher than their competitors', all their customers will not melt away. That is, even in the small business sector, demand is not necessarily highly elastic. And a very large proportion of GNP is produced by firms obviously of significant size relative to their markets. By now, the largest 100 firms produce around one half of the output of the UK manufacturing sector. On average, the five largest sellers in each industry account for more than 75 per cent of sales.[3]

Now, one cannot infer, just from the fact of a high degree of concentration of sales in the hands of the biggest firms, that these necessarily are able to escape from the price-taking constraint assumed in neoclassical theory: although markets may not *look* competitive, they may still behave so. But analysis of sixty separate case studies of British industries carried out by the late Price Commission provides strong evidence of non-perfectly competitive, 'price-making' behaviour being the norm, even in industries in which concentration levels are relatively low. Without necessarily resorting to illegal price-fixing collusion, the firms in an industry seem able to evolve mechanisms whereby they avoid mutually-destructive outbursts of price competition, and can co-ordinate their price increases. In most cases, some sort of a 'pecking order' emerges, such that one firm is accepted as a leader by the others, and initiates price changes which its 'competitors' dutifully follow.[4]

The economic implication of co-ordination on price is that firms get closer to the price that would be charged were a single firm — a monopolist — running the industry. And the implication of this for elasticity is that it will be lower, since by presenting a united front to buyers, selling firms limit the choice open to them. If a single firm raises its price, its customers have the opportunity to switch to the substitutes offered by other sellers in the market, at an unchanged price, as well as to leave the market altogether, and spend their money on something else. But if all the firms put up prices at once, only the leave-market option is open, so that the customer is more likely to shoulder the higher price. That is, elasticity – the response of demand to a price change – is lower when sellers act together as an industry, than when they operate as independent competitors. How much lower? Studies of demand elasticities at the market or industry level have almost always come up with estimated numbers smaller than one. That is, demand appears to be typically inelastic at this level.[5] These statistical estimates are very much subject to error, and there is no particular significance about elasticity being below rather than above one. However, it seems rash to assume that actual elasticities are high enough to generate the sort of perfectly competitive price-taking behaviour that is needed to validate the monetarist model.

More sensible, on the basis of this evidence, is the approach taken by Oliver Hart, who examined (as noted in chapter 5) the macroeconomic implications of an economy of generally imperfectly competitive markets, and found these to include the likelihood of sustained unemployment. To emphasise again the nature of the problem: low elasticity means that, on the down side, firms and unions have less incentive to respond to a recession by cutting wages and prices (because the rewards in larger sales and employment are smaller), and are more likely to feel free to raise prices rather than increase output when demand recovers (because the penalty in lost sales is less).

(3) *Most market transactions are not at arms-length.* Economics can be described as the study of how people who do not know each other get along. It is as though the marketplace is bisected by a high wall, with buyers on one side and sellers on the other. On the top of the wall sits the auctioneer, calling out tentative prices, fielding the resulting supply offers from one side and demand bids from the other, and revising prices until one is found that clears the market. There is no direct contact between buyer and seller; no bargaining; no one-on-one deals. All transactions are made at 'arms-length'.

This may seem like a very awkward way of doing business, and so it is. The real value of the marketplace metaphor is that it allows the economic problem of co-ordinating supply and demand to be formulated mathematically. Then, after a satisfyingly difficult series of formal manipulations, it can be rigorously proven that a set of prices exists such that supply everywhere equals demand. This gives economics the intellectual distinction of being the only social science with real theorems.

Apart from its function as a prop for economists' self esteem, the arms-length model is not of great practical relevance. It depends on a degree of simplicity and homogeneity in goods and services that is difficult to match in the real world beyond the fields of the often-cited prairie wheat farmer. If all the details of product characteristics, delivery dates, payment terms, and so on were added on, the auctioneer would be out of breath before getting through the first of the many iterations of bids and offers needed to find the equilibrium price. And there would remain the problem stressed by Keynes, that the importance of time in economic affairs means that it is not even in principle possible to specify with certainty how each deal will eventually work out.

On the production side, the response to all this complexity and uncertainty is to form firms, as noted above, in which administrative rules and procedures replace the market as the means of co-ordinating workers and capital. As for the finished product, firms may eliminate the need to go through markets by 'vertically integrating' – that is, by merging with suppliers and/or customers into a larger firm. The extent of vertical integration is hard to measure,[6] but it is unlikely to be insignificant.

But even when not formally integrated by a take-over or merger – that is, even when left ostensibly to the market – many, perhaps most, economic transactions occur in the context of some longer-term relationship between buyer and seller. Because we cannot tie down every detail in advance, we choose to deal with people that we trust not to take advantage of the holes in the contract, and trust can only be developed by the experience of repeated transactions turning out satisfactorily for both sides. That is, it is common to forego the short-term advantages of using the anonymous market – getting the best price on a particular deal – in order to secure reliability over the longer term.

These informal but powerful linkages between buyers and sellers have been termed 'networks' by the economist G. B. Richardson.[7] They are particularly noticeable in the dealings between firms, when the size of individual transactions frequently results in quite close professional and even social relationships developing between employees of organisations doing business with each other. They are also powerful in the small business retail sector – the corner grocer establishes some sort of durable relationship with its neighbourhood clientele. And even large retail businesses, though obviously unable to establish bilateral relationships with each of their thousands of customers, find it worthwhile to instil in them some permanent attachment, or loyalty, by foregoing the temptation to vary prices freely so as to maximise short-term profit margins. These habits establish the 'implicit contracts' analysed by Arthur Okun.[8]

This shunting-aside of short-term market forces can be rationalised as economically efficient given the complexity of the real world. But it serves a wider purpose too. Most people do not *want* to deal with each other at arms-length. Most of us enjoy having non-fleeting relationships with other humans, both within and without the work place. 'Economic man' in the market model of neoclassical economics is an odd creature indeed — utterly selfish, and with no feelings of benevolence (or malevolence) to its fellows.

Thus, an accurate theory of economic behaviour would have to be imbedded in a wider model of social activity. This was better recognised when economics was called 'political economy'. More than 140 years ago, one of the last great political economists, John Stuart Mill, complained about the concentration on 'competition' to the exclusion of 'custom', by which he meant the non-economic forces leading to networks and implicit contracts. And what was the reason for this?

Only through the principle of competition has political economy any pretension to the character of a science.[9]

Mill's observation is even more apt today, after a century of development of neoclassical economics with all the mathematical trimmings. Yet it seems a silly sort of 'science' that must shed a sizeable proportion of what is interesting and important in economic life in order to get down to a problem within its analytical grasp. How useful would physics be to the designers of transportation systems if all its theorems began: 'assume there is no friction'? The economist Albert Hirschman, who is unusual in the range of his interests, notes the 'integrative' benefits of participation in real-world markets, and contrasts this with the depersonalised 'ideal' of perfect competition, concluding that economists have sacrificed 'sociological legitimacy' for economic.[10]

Clearly, it is important to at least try to note the implications of custom, networks, and the like for macroeconomic problems. The pervasiveness of informal linkages between buyers and sellers blurs the old dichotomy between the market and the administered, or planned, segments of the economy. The market-clearing leverage of the price mechanism is reduced when longer-term commitments impede its uninhibited use, as is the plausibility of the monetarist system that relies on prices to restore equilibrium.

(4) *In the real-world, contrary to the neoclassical ideal-type, governments mess with markets.* Markets do not flourish amidst anarchy. Even
in the most *laissez-faire* of market systems, a strong government is needed
to define and defend property rights and contracts. But few governments
have stopped there. As much as one quarter of US Gross National Product,
and an even larger proportion in Canada, is subject to some sort of direct
official control over price, or output, or entry into markets.

This topic is worth separate treatment (Chapter 20). We can note now
that the effect — indeed, the *aim* — of economic regulation is to further
impede the working of the price mechanism.

(5) *The private sector itself regulates markets.* Changes in market conditions affect profitability. In the neoclassical model underlying monetarism, firms are interested in nothing other than maximising a rather
short-term measure of profitability, which means that short-term changes
in the market (that is, events like a recession which are supposed to
engineer a reduction in inflation) are at their most effective.

The real world is more complex. Be it due to the benificence of the
people who run them, or to their fear of goading government into explicit
controls and regulation, businesses appear to aim at a wider set of goals
than pure profit maximisation. According to the chairman of a 'taskforce
on corporate responsibility' set up by the Business Roundtable, the lobby
group of the biggest US corporations

> Chief executive officers who have been out there facing reality know
> that corporations are surrounded by a complicated pattern of economic,
> social, ethical, and political ideas and expectations. They know that
> they have to be concerned not only about shareholders but about such
> constituent groups as customers, employees, communities, suppliers
> and society at large. And they believe a corporation best serves its
> shareholders by carefully balancing the legitimate interests of all
> constituents.[11]

This sort of stuff enrages conservative academics. Milton Friedman once
called 'fundamentally subversive' the notion that business has a social
responsibility any wider than maximising the profits of its nominal owners,
the shareholders. The Yale economist Paul MacAvoy, commenting on the
Roundtable's position, expands on this objection

> The Roundtable fails to understand that the corporation is the agent
> for the shareholder, who is the source of all corporate resources the

various constituencies are laying claim to. To use the shareholder's
risk capital to do all the things that are called 'socially responsible' is
actually responsible only if the shareholder agrees.[12]

There is a revealing internal contradiction in the conservative economists' position. They argue that business *should* only maximise its shareholders' profits, as in the neoclassical model. But their policy position on
macroeconomic issues such as inflation (as well as on some micro issues,
such as anti-trust) is that the economy does, *in fact*, conform to the
assumptions of perfect competition. But then anything other than pure
profit maximisation would be impossible, since competition prevents
anyone from earning more than the bare minimum 'competitive' return.
Thus MacAvoy continues

> In present-day competitive markets, profitable enough [to satisfy the
> shareholders] is all the profits that are available from production of
> goods and services. There is nothing left over with which to make the
> payments to these other hypothetical constituencies that the Round-
> table elevates in its statement.

But if this were so, why all the fuss? Why should MacAvoy even bother
to raise his pen to comment? Why, indeed, would a lobby group like the
Business Roundtable exist?

The resolution of the contradiction is not too difficult. Whatever
the normative merits of perfect competition as a *goal*, it does not describe
what actually goes on. The chief executives 'out there facing reality'
know well, and perhaps guiltily, that their shareholders are not the sole
source of corporate resources. Governments provide favours of various
kinds, consumers pay higher-than-competitive prices, workers toil. All
these groups must be 'paid-off' if the corporation is to remain politically
viable.

The merits and de-merits of self-regulating interest group management
are complex, and not at issue here. But their macroeconomic implications
are clear. Dilution of the private sector goal of narrow profit maximisation
further reduces the effectiveness of the price mechanism, and so further
reduces the likelihood of elasticities being high enough to justify monetarist
remedies for stagflation.

To summarise: the neoclassical model which underpins monetarism
assumes that all economic activity is co-ordinated by prices set in perfectly competitive markets. (Orthodox Keynesianism accepts the neo-

classical model minus only the 'auctioneer' whose job it is to call out different prices in the search for an equilibrium.) I have chipped away at this assumption with a sequence of five real-world qualifications:

(1)   Much economic activity, even in the private sector, takes place inside bureaucratic organisations co-ordinated by administrative *fiat*, rather than on the interface between organisations where they meet in markets.

(2)   Few of the markets that do exist meet the preconditions for 'perfect' competition — nearly all firms are of significant economic size relative to their market environment. Thus the price-taking behaviour of perfect competition is implausible.

(3)   Few market transactions are at arms-length. Buyers and sellers establish networks, which limit their readiness to respond to market forces, at least in the short-term.

(4) and (5)   Profit-maximising behaviour is constrained by both governmental and self-imposed regulation, with an eye to meeting a wider set of goals.

All this adds up to a lot less elasticity than would be needed to get the economy tolerably close to the self-adjusting neoclassical ideal-type. Networks and regulation reduce the flexibility of prices, and imperfect competition and bureaucracy reduces the effectiveness of whatever price movement we do get.

To complete the picture, we need to examine how the situation has *changed* over time. I have blamed poor macroeconomic performance on lack of elasticity (along with policy responses predicated on elasticity being plentiful). But the situation has, strikingly, *deteriorated*, as was documented in Chapter 2. So, we should be able to match the deterioration with evidence that the stock of elasticity has *diminished* over the post-war period, and be able to explain why this has happened.

These things cannot be measured with precision, but the trends support a depleting-elasticity thesis. Bureaucratisation has increased, as the importance of small firms in the economy has diminished.[13] The ability of firms to reduce elasticities by co-ordinating their pricing practices has probably increased as a result of the striking increase in the concentration of industry in the hands of the largest enterprises. From 1935 to 1968, for example, the share of manufacturing output in the UK that was accounted for by the 50 largest firms more than doubled, from 14.9 to 32.4 per cent.[14] The series of nationalisations of major industries in Britain since the war has probably had the effect of increasing the extent to which industry is in fact, or acts as though it is, regulated. (Against this, the breaking-up of the legal cartels that were encouraged during the Depression and the

Second World War must have given a once-for-all boost to elasticity. It seems though, that industries have, ever since, been getting better at operating informal collusive schemes, such as the price-leadership practices referred to above.)[15] Thus, there is plenty of evidence of elasticity-reducing trends to match up with the symptoms of the elasticity crisis – our steadily worsening performance on unemployment, inflation, and growth.

The last piece of the puzzle is to explain *why* all this has happened. What induces people to chip away at the elasticity that is necessary for their economy to function? It turns out to be a matter of the good of the all not being the good of the individual. If some firms can get together to reduce elasticity in their market, they can capture benefits in higher prices and profits, and/or in a more stable environment. Union members gain from negotiating contracts which secure privileges of pay and job security for workers with seniority. Bureaucracies win 'quiet life' benefits for their employees by wrapping their activities in red tape. In general, we can say that elasticity-reducing activities give those responsible more control over their economic situation, and so are, in themselves, rational and understandable.

What is bad about this, of course, is that in achieving more control over its own environment each agent necessarily *reduces* the controllability available to others. The merger of two firms into one means one fewer potential customer or supplier for all other firms; one fewer potential employer for workers, one less independent source of entrepreneurship and capital for the market. It reduces the number of choices available to everyone else, and, in a market system where people must more-or-less fend for themselves, choice of options is the only guarantee we have of being able to cope. Thus we suffer from a *planning paradox* – the efforts of firms and other organisations to control or plan their immediate environment makes the market system as a whole *less* stable; less conducive to successful forecasting and control.

The point may be summarised thus: the economy does two big things – it *creates* wealth, and then it *distributes* it. Participants in the economy are, on the whole, not concerned whether their personal prosperity comes from creating wealth, or from expropriating it later, at the distribution stage. If there is money to be made from altering the rules of distribution, then people will naturally enter into this, even if the wealth-creating capacity of the economy at large is thereby reduced. The great paradox of a system relying on the profit motive and competitive markets is that it consumes itself: to function effectively it depends on everyone accepting the constraints of perfect competition, but bending these constraints may be more profitable than working within them.

What can be done? Many elasticity-reducing activities are good in isolation. Increased concentration may lead to larger-scale and more efficient production methods; regulating an agricultural market may stabilize rural incomes at decent levels, for example. But the accumulated effect of decades of depleting elasticity is a serious loss of macroeconomic efficiency. We have moved far from the smooth, pliable ideal-type of perfect competition to what could be called a 'lumpy economy'. Each low-elasticity lump may or may not be a good thing in itself, but an economy full of them is nothing to be pleased with.

An approach to policy that reverses the trend to lower elasticity, whenever justifiable on the merits of particular cases, and that *compensates* (as conventional policies have failed to do) for the effects of the elasticity crisis on the business of getting the 'big numbers' of macroeconomic performance to add up, is needed. Ways of achieving non-inflationary full employment in a lumpy economy must be found.

Part II
Principles

7 The Possibility of Full Employment

'The first function of unemployment is that it maintains the authority of master over man.'

W. H. BEVERIDGE

It is time for some good news. Our economies, just two decades ago, were able to deliver unemployment and inflation rates of around two or three per cent. Now unemployment is at ten per cent or more, and inflation fluctuates wildly. Is the decline irreversible? In this chapter I will argue that it is not; that it is, in principle, *feasible* for us to match, or even better, the economic performance of the best years of the 1950s and 1960s. Establishing that this goal is feasible is not a trivial exercise, since the well-entrenched neoclassical orthodoxy within economics, and a good deal of prejudice among the public at large, must be squarely confronted.

Of course, feasibility is one thing; actually getting there is another. Most of the remainder of the book will deal with the policies needed to realise full economic potential. But now, in terms of the concepts introduced earlier, we wish to establish that it is, in principle, possible for the big numbers of economic performance to add-up satisfactorily. This chapter focuses on the biggest number of them all – unemployment. Chapter 8 then examines the links between this variable and the rate of inflation – another eminently large number.

In essence, there are just two sorts of reason advanced to reconcile us to high unemployment: people do not want to do the work or there is not enough work to be done. In economists' terms, there are 'supply-side' and 'demand-side' reasons. Naturally, economists differ in their inter-pretations of unemployment. Monetarists put most or all of it down to supply-side factors – to the unwillingness of the labour force to work. Keynesians usually concede something to the supply side, but are more impressed by inadequacies in the demand for labour. And opinions differ as to the extent that demand shortfalls are 'structural', and thus irrever-sible, or 'cyclical', and so temporary.

The basis of the monetarist position has been explained already (in Chapter 4). Recall that monetarists depend on unemployment actually being voluntary 'search' activity. People *choose* to become unemployed in order to invest time in seeking out a better job.

How does the search model deal with the persistent upward trend in unemployment over the last thirty years? In essence, there are two prongs to the explanation; one in terms of a switch in the composition of the labour force towards people who are inherently prone to search longer than average, and the second in terms of an across-the-board increase in search time. They add up to the proposition that actual unemployment rates have risen because the efficient or 'natural' rate has risen; this due to a voluntary or unavoidable reduction in the elasticity of supply of labour.

The composition argument invokes the substantial demographic changes that have affected the post-war labour market. The 'baby boom' lowered the average age of the labour force in the 1960s and 1970s. And the participation rate of women has been increasing fairly steadily. So? Well, both young people and women have higher-than-average unemployment rates. Therefore, an increase in the shares in the total labour force taken by these groups will increase the overall unemployment rate.

As a *description* of what happened to unemployment this has some validity. But it is intended by monetarists also to be a *justification* for higher rates, and as such is very dubious. For this depends on women and young people *choosing* higher unemployment rates for themselves, presumably due to some quirk in the labour market that makes it profitable for them to search longer and/or more often than men.

Chapter 3 presented evidence that runs overwhelmingly against the voluntary search model of unemployment. People do, of course, look for new jobs, but they sensibly prefer to do so from the paid security of a current position, rather than subsisting on unemployment benefits while searching.

A more plausible explanation of demographic differences comes from the demand side. Women and young people tend to be relatively low in the labour market pecking order. Accordingly, they tend to get the less desirable jobs – lower paid, less interesting, and less secure. That is, women and young people have higher unemployment rates because they lose their jobs more often. Also, they, especially young people, tend more often than adult men to be unemployed while trying to enter the labour market.[1]

What about the second monetarist hypothesis, that there has been an increase in voluntary search and leisure across all groups? This links an increase in the 'natural' rate of unemployment with increases that have occurred, from time to time, in the generosity of unemployment insurance benefits.

The fallacy remains. Higher benefits may allow someone who has lost their job to take longer and be more choosy about finding their next job. But this does *not* mean that the unemployed *chose* to be so in the first place. Search on-the-job, or no search at all, would still be preferred to unemployment.

No doubt there are always a few people who, not wishing to work at all, manage by fair means or foul to support their leisure by claiming unemployment benefits. Indeed, the story is told amongst my Canadian colleagues that one of the most fervent expositors of the increasing-natural rate doctrine had his initial interest in the topic stimulated when, on a skiing vacation in the Canadian Rockies, he came across a group with 'Unemployment Insurance Ski Team' emblazoned on their parkas. Personally, I have no objection to the unemployed joining university professors in having some fun on the slopes. But the point is that such behaviour is rare, which is why it makes for good anecdotes and newspaper stories when isolated instances do surface. There is simply no evidence that the problem of people enjoying being unemployed has reached significant proportions.[2]

Even on its own terms, the search model is apparently unable to explain a satisfactory proportion of the rise in unemployment. One of the leading Canadian researchers, Dennis Maki of Simon Fraser University, has admitted that the largest single contribution was made by the unexplained 'time trend' whose progress we charted in Chapter 2.[3]

So much for the supply side. Consider the factors affecting the demand for labour. The charts in Chapter 2 suggested that the greater part of current unemployment is the accumulated result of a trend beginning as early as the 1950s. Given that labour supply factors cannot explain this long-term trend, perhaps causes can be found on the demand side of the labour market. The question can be put thus: are there reasons why a significantly larger number of willing people cannot be profitably put to work?

There seems to be a deepening feeling, among the press and the general public, if not among economists, that there are inexorable and declining limits on the number of jobs. Jobs are 'disappearing', it is said, due to technological innovations – notably microchips – and due to competition from newly industrialising countries moving into traditional manufacturing markets. The structure of demand for labour has changed irreversibly.

From a long-run perspective, the disappearing-jobs argument is as fallacious now as it was when shouted-out by the machine-smashing Luddites 170 years ago. Getting rid of jobs — by labour-saving innovations or by finding cheaper sources of supply — is precisely the means whereby national productivity is increased, as labour is released to move into more productive activities. The result is the unprecedented level of prosperity enjoyed in Western economies.

Of course, when the economy is in a recession, it may well be rational for the workers concerned to resist losing jobs to computers or to Koreans, since the alternative can be no job at all. But the problem here is the failure to keep the *total* number of jobs at a high enough level; not the shrinking of the labour force in certain activities in accordance with long-run shifts in market forces. Indeed, I would bet (I do not know of studies of this matter) that more jobs are lost in declining industries in *boom* times than during slumps. This would be in part because booms tend to be set off by technological revolutions which necessitate radical changes in employment patterns, and in part because the more plentiful alternatives available when unemployment rates are low reduce workers' resistance to adjustment.

'But', the reader may ask, 'if everyone who wants a job had one — say, a ten per cent increase in employment — what would they all *do*?' To answer, you need only ask yourself what *you* would do if your income was increased by ten per cent. Or ask an unemployed person whether they could dispose of the increase in income that would come from being in work. I am sure that they would have a ready reply. The sum of all the answers to this question specifies what a fully-employed economy would be producing. The extra output and employment would be basically 'more of the same' — more of whatever goods and services employed people choose to consume now. The new jobs certainly need not be 'high tech'. I, for example, would probably make use of a 10 per cent increase in income to spend a month each year pottering around the Mediterranean in a yacht — a very old-fashioned, low-technology activity.

Thus the shortfall of demand is not 'structural'. Unemployment is due to a shortage of purchasing power in the economy; a shortage of what Keynesians call 'effective demand'. The people who want to work more have not got the money to buy the goods which would justify them working.

It might reasonably be asked whether there would be enough capital (machinery, equipment, factories) for additional employees to work with. In the present slump there is certainly plenty of spare capacity; enough, perhaps, to re-employ productively four or five per cent, at least, of the labour force. However, we are no longer geared-up to match the employment levels achieved in the 1950s and early 1960s. The economy has retreated along the path away from full employment, burning its bridges as it goes.

But the bridges can be rebuilt easily enough, paid for by savings from higher incomes and profits, and using best-practice technology, to the benefit of productivity. Although the short-run supply curve of the economy may become inelastic before full employment is reached — that is, attainable real GNP may fall short of full-employment GNP given currently available productive capital — the long-run schedule should be elastic, if it is basically a matter of adding rather similar plant and machinery to the current stock.

The amount of investment required for full employment would be reduced if the present capital stock were utilised more efficiently. For example, although the unemployed are not working as much as they would like, many currently employed people may be working *too much* — constrained by the rigidities in our system of employment into putting in more hours in a year than they would wish. This and other elasticity-reducing practices will be discussed later in the book, as well as the problem of how actually to *achieve* full employment — how to effect the necessary increase in effective demand. At this point, however, the concern is the feasibility of an economy running without unemployment. Having argued that the commonly cited constraints are not in fact binding, that unemployment is not due to the labour force's unwillingness to give up job search activities nor, to a shortage of capital, we can conclude that full employment is, in principle, possible.

The next chapter examines the *desirability* of full employment, by analysing important side-effects — on inflation and on the balance of payments — alleged to accompany low unemployment rates.

8 Inflation and the Curve

'Any economists who recommend unemployment as a solution to our problems should themselves be made the first unemployed.'

SIDNEY WEINTRAUB

The spy satellites monitoring our economies send back pictures which, suitably magnified, reveal about ten per cent of the labour force sitting idly in their backyards, and about ten per cent (or more) of our factories bolted shut and empty. The essence of the last chapter was the argument that there is no reason, in principle, why the idle workers and idle plants should not be brought together again.

'But', the sceptic could object, 'if we actually did succeed in putting all the unemployed back to work, the satellites would soon start sending a different picture. As well as humming factories and busy workers, you would see people pushing wheelbarrows laden with banknotes down to the shopping centres. We would have hyper-inflation!' This is the extreme of the Phillips curve hypothesis seen in action on the charts of Chapter 2. As the economy gets closer to full employment, inflation starts edging up at an increasing rate, until, at the almost inconceivably low level of no unemployment at all, inflation would be almost inconceivably high.

Why should inflation become a problem before *all* the potential for increased supply at current prices is used up? The monetarist answer — that unemployment is really voluntary or natural search activity, which workers have to be fooled into cutting-back on with inflationary wage increases — is empirically implausible, as shown in Chapter 4.

But Keynesians, who do not believe most unemployment to be voluntary, also expected an inflation-unemployment trade-off. It has recently been pointed out that Keynes himself, in a possibly rather pessimistic letter to *The Times* in 1937, worried about inflation resulting from further expansion when the British unemployment rate was still over 12 per cent, due to likely bottlenecks of skilled labour.[1] These concerns were formalised by Phillips' colleague at the LSE, the Canadian economist Richard Lipsey, who followed the 1958 Phillips article with a clarifying and extending analysis two years later.[2]

Lipsey's explanation is ingenious. It begins with the observation that the economy is made up of many distinct industries and markets. At any time, some industries will be expanding, and others contracting, as tastes and technologies change. Expanding industries have two potential methods of getting the extra labour that they need: they can hire from the 'pool' of readily-available unemployed labour, or they can, by offering higher wages, bid away workers from other industries. The lower the average unemployment rate across the economy, the higher the probability that the particular pools of unemployed available to the expanding industries will have dried up, forcing them to use wage increases as the means of attracting labour. With the additional, and very Keynesian, assumption that wages are 'sticky' (do not decline) in contracting industries, this means that lower unemployment will be associated with higher average rates of increase of wage rates, as predicted by the Phillips curve.

Lipsey's idea seems sensible and plausible, and was accepted as such readily by the economics profession, without much empirical testing. The trouble is that, plausible-sounding or not, the hypothesis does not appear to be supported by such empirical evidence as is available. Studies have found very little sign of wage increases being used to effect reallocations of labour between industries. Other instruments, such as recruitment expenditures, and notification of vacancies, appear adequate to do the job. A detailed analysis of three British labour markets — for teachers, bus drivers, and draughtsmen — found only a minor role for pay changes in adjustments to labour shortages.[3] For the US, Alan K. Severn found evidence that 'opportunity' (vacancies) explained 'a larger proportion of voluntary labor mobility than does wage position'.[4]

My own suspicions about the accuracy of the wage-adjustment hypothesis were aroused when, replicating an earlier analysis by Brian Reddaway, I found that in fifty-one British manufacturing industries over the fifteen years from 1958 to 1973, there was absolutely no sign of the faster-growing industries increasing wages more quickly than the average.[5] This was true in a sample which included some industries which had doubled their labour forces over the period while others were halved. That is, the price mechanism does not seem to play a large role in adjusting supply to demand in labour markets — other, non-price, instruments such as vacancies and queues take the major parts.

Why is this? Several factors may be involved. Wages are, of course, more than just the price of labour. They incorporate deep-seated social norms of the value of jobs, which may be impervious to the transitory buffeting of short-term market disequilibria. Wage changes can be a rather expensive tool for attracting new employees, since they normally must be paid as well to the firm's existing labour force. Expanding industries tend to be in modern, high-productivity sectors, which offer a relatively high *level* of wages, sufficient to maintain a queue of eager recruits whatever the cyclical state of the economy's labour market.[6] In any case, it seems that the unemployed should not have to put up with involuntary unemployment as a pool of reserve labour to facilitate non-inflationary adjustments to changing market conditions.

There is another argument for the social 'usefulness' of unemployment as an anti-inflation instrument which pre-dates Phillips and Lipsey, and which must be taken seriously. Keynes himself, as well as his distinguished contemporaries Michal Kalecki and William Beveridge, predicted what they called 'political' consequences of full employment. They expected that without the threat of being thrown into the pool of the unemployed, workers and unions might be emboldened to attempt to increase their share of national income by raising wage demands. If employers were not prepared to accommodate this, then what Beveridge called 'a vicious spiral of wages and prices' would result.[7]

This fear may have been behind the early resistance shown by business interests to Keynesian policies, which puzzled the first enthusiastic postwar generation of Keynesian economists. Since profits as well as wages would be higher with full employment, why wasn't this welcomed by capitalists? One leading Keynesian, Robert Solow, has attributed the hostility of business to stabilisation policy to 'mere obtuseness'.[8] But perhaps business leaders had a more fundamental concern about the very viability of the wage-profit system should full employment be sustained for an unprecedentedly long period.

This hypothesis has been offered to explain the sharp increase in inflation rates in the late 1960s, which followed twenty years of fairly low unemployment. To test it, Robert Gordon looked for evidence of an independent 'wage-push' in eight OECD economies, and for the opposing demand-side hypothesis that the increase in inflation was the result of a prior expansion of 'nominal' spending. He was not able to find empirical support for either proposition.[9]

It may be that the inflation was simply the result of labour trying to maintain the rate of growth of real incomes to which it had become accustomed over the period of unusually high and sustained productivity growth that accompanied the low unemployment and inflation of the 1950s and 1960s. As productivity growth rates began to slacken, an inflationary gap opened between money wage growth and the productivity that could validate it. Eventually, labour's expectations of sustainable real wage growth became more realistic — indeed, wage increases have fallen behind price inflation in several economies since the mid-1970s.[10] But it is certainly not true that the existence of a Phillips curve relationship between wage increases and unemployment over a certain period demonstrates that the low-unemployment years of that period were inflationary.

Why not? Inflation is the rate of change of *prices*, and prices are not affected by wages *per se*, but by unit labour costs — that is, by the cost of getting a unit of real output out of the labour force. These in turn are determined by the price of labour (the wage rate) *and* by labour productivity. If productivity rises by more than wages, then unit labour costs will fall, and so should prices. Indeed, this is just what happens when unemployment is low. The phenomenon known as 'Okun's Law' comes into play. With high demand for their output, firms are able to utilise their capacity more efficiently, so that the productivity of their workforces rises.[11]

It appears that, over the historical periods for which a Phillips curve relationship exists, the higher productivity associated with relatively low unemployment years exceeds the higher rate of wage increases in those years.[12] That is, the wage increases in these years have actually been *anti-inflationary* in their implication for unit costs.

This quite important point has been widely missed in the Phillips curve literature, where it is customary to assume, explicitly or implicitly, that wages and prices are linked rigidly. Economists of all schools have blamed the labour market, and unions in particular, for inflation, and for the unemployment that results from attempts to reduce it. This is, curiously, especially true of the 'post-Keynesians' and more radical British Keynesians, who, in most respects, look fairly left-wing politically. Because these economists tend to be particularly fond of the notion that prices are determined as a simple and unvarying mark-up on wages, they are led to focus on wage controls as an anti-inflation policy, even though such controls are, of course, highly unpopular with most workers and their unions.

But if not in the labour market, where does the Phillips curve originate? I suggest that we need look no further than the product market — the market for goods and services — where the prices that make up the inflation rate are actually set.

Recall from Chapter 5 the importance of elasticity in determining how a firm responds to an increase in the demand for its product. The lower it perceives its price elasticity to be, that is, the less the expected loss in sales from a price increase, the more likely it is to respond by raising price rather than increasing output. This suggests a link between elasticity and unemployment, or, more generally, between elasticity and the amount of underutilised resources in the economy.

Such a link is not hard to find. Elasticity, to a firm, is not a fixed number. How a firm's customers will react to a price increase depends largely on whether the firm's competitors match it or not, which, in turn, depends on how eager they are to pick up some extra business. The fuller their own order books, the greater the chances that they will go for higher profit margins rather than higher sales volume − that is, that they will match the price increase. Thus, the higher is demand relative to capacity, the lower will be elasticity as perceived by firms, and the greater the price changes − the inflation − that will result from a given increase in demand.

This may be the real Phillips curve − a relationship between capacity utilisation and price inflation in product markets. The orthodox correlation between wage-change and unemployment is then just a statistical artefact, which surfaces because there is *some* relation between price changes and wage changes, on the one hand, and capacity utilisation and unemployment on the other. The direct causal link is between prices and utilisation, not between wage changes and unemployment. This proposition seems supported by the increasing number of studies which have found a direct link between inflation and product market conditions.[13]

The worsening Phillips curve trade-off documented in Chapter 2 is easy to explain from a product market perspective, since it fits with the depletion of elasticity in our economies. As pointed out above, lower elasticity means that more of an increase in demand goes in higher prices, and less draws forth increased real output. From the point of view of the trade-off, lower elasticity means that more of some countervailing factor, such as excess capacity (and unemployment) induced by a recession, will be needed to hold price inflation to any given level. All this contrasts with the desperately strained attempts to rationalise the really dramatic deterioration of the trade-off by blaming rather marginal events in the labour market, such as changes in unemployment benefits or in participation rates.

So, we have the situation that inflation accelerates whenever demand is pushed above the level that has become customary. But it does not do so because it *has to*, as claimed by both monetarist and orthodox Keynesian theories, but because the people who set prices *choose* to raise them, in the (correct) expectation that others will do the same.

This does not mean that we should 'blame' the individual firms concerned. They are caught on a treadmill; in a process in which they must run harder and harder just to stay in the same place. If any one firm decided not to raise its prices, it would soon find itself losing money, not *because* its competitors would have raised theirs (it would, in fact, gain some market share from this), but because all its *suppliers*, of materials and labour, themselves locked into the inflationary process, would have increased prices and wages, and thus the firm's costs.

Indeed, business in general (and everyone else!) would gain from the larger sales and profits that would follow if, somehow, *all* firms happened not to increase their prices, and the economy translated money demand into higher output and employment instead. But inflation is the result of hundreds of thousands of individual pricing decisions, and no individual has an incentive to break the self-fulfilling process of inflationary expectations. Instead, there is always an incentive to try and get ahead of inflation by raising prices more than the expected average of others' increases, which, of course, duly worsens the trade-off. Such is the vicious circle in which our low-elasticity economies are trapped.

There are two important implications of this analysis.

(1)   Firms are forced into inflationary behaviour by the market structures in which they operate. Inflation does not do anyone any good, but individuals are powerless to act usefully on that information.

This model contrasts with both orthodox analyses, in which inflation is somehow an unavoidable or even desirable feature of the fundamental laws of the economic system. To monetarists, inflation is the price to be paid for tricking workers into holding unemployment below its natural rate. To the Keynesian, inflation results from the wage increases needed to reallocate workers between sectors, and is accordingly of some use.

(2)   Although unemployment is, as we have had re-emphasised in the early 1980s, one instrument which will eventually pull down inflation rates, it certainly is not necessarily the only anti-inflation instrument, and low unemployment is not *inherently* inflationary.

Indeed, such direct evidence as we have rather strongly implies the opposite. Very low unemployment is anti-inflationary, since it goes with high productivity gains. Okun's Law demonstrates this rather strikingly over the ups and downs of the business cycle, and there is evidence that permanently low unemployment rates, and the associated high levels of demand, would favour long-term productivity gains. This is because sustained pressure on the supply of labour generates incentives to invest in ways of using it more efficiently. Such can take the form either of upgrading the skills of the workforce — what economists call investment in human capital — or investing in plant and machinery as a substitute for scarce labour.[14]

What all this means is that we should be looking hard for an alternative to unemployment as the anti-inflation policy. If we could deal directly with the low elasticity-induced price spiral, we could, potentially, let the economy expand to output and unemployment levels which would at least match the performance achieved just twenty or thirty years ago.

The big thing is to shake off the fatalism inculcated by the macro-economic orthodoxies. In their different ways, both of these teach that the inflation that has followed whenever unemployment has been pushed below some critical level is unavoidable. To monetarists it is the penalty for encroaching on voluntary search unemployment — for tricking people into working more than they really want to. To Keynesians, inflation is the by-product of running down the pools of reserve labour needed to facilitate microeconomic adjustments between industries. Faced with the inexorable increase in the critical level — the 'non-accelerating-inflation rate of unemployment' or NAIRU, as it is sometimes called — neither school can do much more than shrug its shoulders, or offer some weak rationalisation blaming structural events in labour markets.

I submit that a NAIRU much greater than zero need not be accepted. Very high employment and capacity utilisation rates would lower unit costs through higher productivity, and so be inherently anti-inflationary. Job search and market adjustments do not need unemployment to function effectively, as is convincingly demonstrated both by Britain's own performance in the 1950s and 1960s, and by the even lower unemployment rates maintained until quite recently in Sweden, Switzerland, Australia, and New Zealand.

9 In Search of Band-X

The previous two chapters pointed out the potential for much lower unemployment, and argued that, in principle, this could be achieved without having to trade-off unemployment for higher inflation. In this chapter, it will be suggested that opportunities for improved economic performance exist at all levels of the economy.

Unemployment can be called a 'macro-level' inefficiency, because it represents failure on the part of the economy to utilise fully its *total* potential labour supply and capital stock. This is a very serious sort of inefficiency, but it is not the only one'. There are two lower levels at which below-potential performance is generated. As with unemployment and inflation, these lower-level inefficiencies can largely be blamed on lack of elasticity in the economy.

(1) The 'micro' level of individual firms can vary in the efficiency with which managerial and labour resources are utilised.
(2) In-between micro and macro is the 'market' level, at which the efficiency of the allocation between industries or markets of the economy's resources can be measured.

In a briskly competitive, high elasticity economy, sustained micro inefficiencies are impossible. When one firm gets an edge in lower costs on its competitors, it will cut its price in order to translate the advantage into higher market share. Its rivals will then have to find ways of matching the cost performance of the leading firm, or will lose their customers and be forced out of the market. Thus, the 'invisible hand' of competition ensures that the performance of all firms is kept on a par with that of the best operators. There will be micro efficiency.

However, in our lumpy, low-elasticity economies, the invisible hand atrophies. With lower demand elasticity, the pay-off in higher market share from cutting price is less, and the low-cost firm is more likely to take its reward in the form of a higher profit margin on its existing sales. This means that higher cost firms need not be forced to mend their ways or get out of the industry. Instead, they may shelter under what is called a 'price umbrella' held over the market by the high profit margin firms.[1]

Low elasticity may also be used to push prices higher directly, as firms take advantage of the implication of inelastic demand, namely that profitability is increased when price is increased because the loss of sales is small enough to ensure that total revenues increase. And behind the higher prices, costs may drift up too, as the threat of 'efficiency or bankruptcy' is lifted.

The various effects on costs of reduced competitive pressure have been summarised with the label 'X-inefficiency' by the Harvard economist Harvey Leibenstein.[2] Other names that turn up are 'monopoly slack', and the 'quiet life effect'.[3] They all stem from the fundamental paradox of market economies that was analysed in chapter 6 – the system as a whole needs plenty of elasticity if it is to function properly, but each individual and firm in the system has an incentive to try and reduce the elasticity of its own environment.

The consequences for efficiency are particularly serious, given the highly bureaucratised structure of modern business enterprises. The old-fashioned owner-operator may choose Wednesday-afternoon-golf (the 'quiet life') over squeezing the last ounce of productivity out of the workers. It may not be *fair* that the owner-operator is in a position to make a choice like this, but it is not necessarily *inefficient* – since higher costs mean lower profits, the owner must bear the consequences of a quiet life, and so, in economists' terms, can be presumed to make an 'optimal income-leisure trade-off'.

But most business is done by firms that are no longer run by their owners, who tend to be a diffuse group of shareholders. They are run by professional managers, whose interests do not necessarily coincide with those of the nominal owners. By 1972, the directors owned less than 2 per cent of the shares in 73 of the largest 100 UK manufacturing firms.[4]

In particular, the income of managers appears to be considerably dependent upon the number of people below them in the hierarchy of their firm, and even on the wages and salaries paid to these subordinates.[5] Since the firm's payroll is a large (usually the largest) element in its costs, the interests of owners and managers may here be somewhat in opposition, with managers having some incentive to let costs drift up, to the detriment of profits and efficiency. Cowling reports a 1973 study by John Palmer, which found that, in firms with a high degree of monopoly power – in our terms, firms facing low elasticities in the markets they sell to – profitability was about 30 per cent higher in the owner-controlled group than in those firms controlled by their managers.[6] The profit-sharing schemes available to many senior managers are intended to reduce the conflict of interest between them and the shareholders, but it is unlikely that the internal logic of the bureaucratic pecking order is thereby completely suspended.

The consequences of all this are worryingly evident in the effects of the most striking microeconomic event of the last twenty years – the great merger boom. At its peak, in 1968, 'expenditure on acquisitions (mergers) exceeded gross domestic domestic fixed capital formation and was almost double the net (of depreciation) figure',[7] and implied the takeover in that year of 27 per cent of the entire capital stock of British companies! The captains of industry spent more money (and, presumably, time) buying each other than they invested in new capital plant and equipment.

Why? Newbould's 1970 interview analysis of the managers involved in mergers revealed that their most important motive was the elimination of competition – the reduction of elasticity. Improved efficiency appeared to be a minor motive.[8] This is consistent with the findings of the many studies of the results of mergers, nearly all of which report lower profitability after the event.[9] Certainly, the merger boom and its results do not support the case of those who claim that mergers and takeovers are the market's means of ensuring the 'survival of the fittest'. The weaker firms get taken over, certainly, but their feebleness seems to be contagious.

Thus mergers seem to have served the interests of management, who get greater control over their market environment and so a quieter life, and/or the power, prestige, pay and perks that go with running a bigger bureaucracy, without the hassle of building market share through establishing technical or marketing superiority. Mergers do not appear to have served well the shareholders involved, nor the interests of the public at large.

Apart from bureaucratic empire-building, the salaried employees of firms have many well-established ways of purloining the fruits of monopoly slack. Examples are the erection of expensive and lavishly furnished office buildings, generous expense accounts and travel allowances, and, most prominent of all, the provision of a company car for the private use of the employee. In Britain, more than one half of the new cars sold each year are bought by companies rather than by individuals – a startlingly high proportion. These 'below-the-line' boosts to management compensation are inefficient because, typically, they cost more to produce than they are worth to the recipient. Most people offered the choice 'cash or car' would take the cash, and do something else with it. However, since the cash option is not available, because it would be too flagrant for the shareholders to stomach, the car is willingly but wastefully accepted.[10]

Thus, some of the profits that are fought over in a less-than-perfectly-competitive economy are dissipated during the struggle in the form of higher costs. Some economists have gone so far as to propose that, so long as any profits (or 'rents', as they are technically termed in this context) remain to be appropriated, the struggle will continue. According to this view, eventually all monopoly rents will be wasted away.[11]

Between the micro level of individual firms, and macro level of all firms, are the markets or industries into which firms are grouped. An economy could be 'macro-efficient' (have all its labour force and capital stock busy) and 'micro-efficient' (all firms operating at lowest possible cost) and still be inefficient overall because its firms were in the wrong markets. This can be called 'market inefficiency' because it is equivalent to some markets, or the industries supplying them, being too large, and others, therefore, being too small.

Unfortunately, there are plenty of examples. In agriculture, output may be kept too low by acreage or stock quotas designed to raise prices, or kept too high by restrictions on imports, such as those imposed by most countries on dairy products. Past policies on energy pricing, particularly in North America, have resulted in inefficiently extravagant consumption of certain energy sources. Public subsidisation of roads and airports may have distorted the transportation mix away from railways. The manufacturing sector enjoys tariffs and quotas which restrict cheap imports from developing countries, while export subsidies over-stimulate the industries receiving them. In 'high-tech' industries, vast sums can be wasted in the name of national prestige, as the Concorde exemplifies. Regional investment incentives lead to inefficiently located firms and industries. Many people believe that the armaments industry is too large.

The list could be extended. All these examples have in common that they result from a particular private sector interest group persuading politicians or government officials to divert resources in their direction, at the expense of the public at large. The effect is to reduce elasticities; to insulate the protected activities from the signals of market prices.

In a lumpy economy, it is also likely that some firms or coalitions of firms will be powerful enough to distort the allocation of resources even without explicit co-operation from government. The traditional example of this in economic theory is the 'restriction' of output that results when monopoly power allows prices to be raised above competitive levels, so that demand falls, and the monopolistic sector ends up being too small relative to competitive industries.

If the idea of big business being too small seems odd, the reader may prefer J. K. Galbraith's hypothesis that the marketing and advertising efforts of the corporate sector (the 'planning system', in his terminology) result in it squeezing out small business and the 'public goods' – health, education, urban and rural environments – contributed by government.[12]

Economists are unusually united in opposition to practices that lead to market-level inefficiencies. Perhaps unanimity in this (or in anything else) should trigger some suspicion. It is possible that we do not do justice to the complexities of the real world in which pressure groups and politicians operate. When there is macro-inefficiency (unemployment), for example, many market-inefficient policies may at least have the merit of saving some jobs. We probably underestimate, too, the value of stability in markets, even if achieved by protecting prices at 'wrong' levels, in aiding long-range planning and investment. We may not pay enough attention to our own 'second-best' theorems, which demonstrate that removing one market distortion may not improve matters overall if other markets remain distorted.[13]

Nevertheless, this does not justify the practices as good things in themselves. Their prevalence indicates the *potential* for significant improvements in efficiency. Thus we find, at all levels of the economy, economic efficiency below its potential. Taken together, these inefficiencies imply the existence of a *band* of economic performance over and above present levels. Given the multifarious origins of this band, it is probably appropriate to extend Leibenstein's terminology and call it 'Band-X'.

How broad is Band-X? We can do some back-of-an-envelope calculations to get an idea of its magnitude, focusing on real Gross National Product (GNP) as the performance or 'output' measure, and total employment as the input needed to produce output. These variables are shown on the vertical and horizontal axes of Figure 9.1.

Point *a* on the figure represents current levels of GNP and employment. Let us hypothetically eliminate the levels of inefficiency, starting with the macro-inefficiency of unemployment, which is currently running well above 10 per cent in the OECD economies. With a further 'discouraged worker effect' of two or three per cent,[14] it is reasonable to propose that employment could be increased by about ten per cent before unemployment was reduced to the levels of good years in the 1950s.

Opinions differ on whether a ten per cent increase in employment would add more or less than ten per cent to GNP. I would expect the former, due to the beneficial workings of Okun's Law. Take ten per cent as an intermediate position. Then moving to full employment (E_F) would increase GNP by ten per cent (to GNP_F), and take us to point *b*.

Now consider market-level inefficiencies. How much do they add up to? We will note in Chapter 20 that between 25 and 30 per cent of the economy is regulated. Studies of regulated industries typically find that they generate extra costs worth ten per cent or more of the value of output.[15] Manufacturing industries account for about 25 per cent of

GNP. They are usually not subject to direct economic regulation, but are bound around with various subsidies and tariff protection. In a study of Canadian manufacturing, I estimated the costs of import quotas and tariffs at 1.5 per cent of the value added (GNP) of the sector.[16] Adding on distortions induced by subsidies, location grants and so on, might well double that figure. Even if the remainder of the economy were assumed free of distortions, the numbers imply that total market-level inefficiencies cost around 5 per cent of total GNP. Eliminating them would effectively add this much to GNP_F (equivalent to 5.5 per cent of GNP_A). We would move to point c on Figure 9.1.

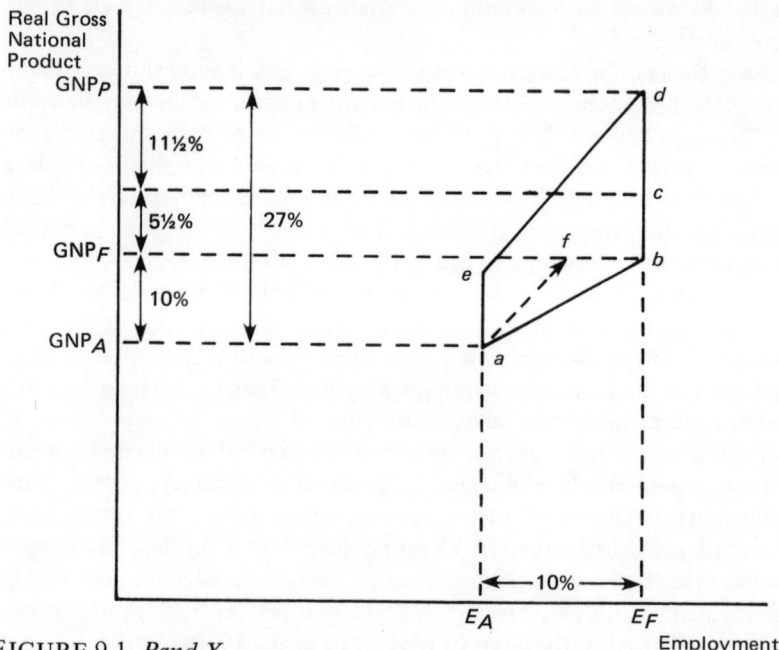

FIGURE 9.1 *Band-X*

What about micro-level inefficiency, due to firms operating at costs higher than they could get away with under competitive conditions? Until recently, information on micro cost inefficiencies has been either anecdotal, or based on limited case studies of particular firms or industries. The findings of such studies are usually rather interesting. For example, Primeaux found that electric power utilities competing with another utility in their market area had unit costs that were more than 10 per cent lower, on average, than the costs of monopoly power suppliers.[17] Steer and Cable found that adoption of the multi-divisional, or 'M-form' corporate structure in UK firms increased profit rates by six to nine percentage points.[18]

Recently, more comprehensive cost data have become available, for Canada and the US, for the many thousands of firms in each country's manufacturing sector. These data reveal striking differences in cost performance between firms in the same industry. In Canada, for example, the costs per unit output of the lowest-cost plant in an industry are, on average, *less than half* the unit costs of the highest-cost operators.[19]

This is a substantial number, at least comparable in magnitude to the better-known figures on differences *between* industries, or between more and less productive countries. It implies that the lowest-cost firms hold a generous 'price umbrella' over their weaker competitors. Should this umbrella be lowered, the highest-cost firms would be forced either to improve their cost performance, or, if this were not possible (because of bad management, or bad location, for example) to leave the industry and lose their customers to the lower-cost firms remaining.

If, say, the average cost difference between highest-cost and lowest-cost plants could be reduced from 100 to 50 per cent, and pro rata reductions achieved between the extremes, the cost savings would amount to about 10 per cent of the value of manufacturing GNP. (Put another way, with the same inputs of labour and capital, the sector could produce 10 per cent more GNP.) If it is reasonable to assume that the Canadian manufacturing sector is fairly typical in this respect of other industries and other economies,[20] then this 10 per cent number can be applied to our example. Accordingly, we would move to point *d* on Figure 9.1 representing a further 10 per cent increase in GNP (or 11.5 per cent of the original GNP_A).

By this stage, in our hypothetical example, inefficiency has been eliminated at all three levels – the economy's full potential has been achieved. Thus the resulting level of GNP is subscripted with the letter *P*, for 'potential', GNP_P is 27 per cent greater than GNP_A, the actual current level of economic performance.

The shaded area *deab* in the figure is our 'Band-X'. It delineates all the conceivable improvements that could be made to the current situation (point *a*) by reducing inefficiency on one or more levels. For example, a point somewhere on the line *ed* would imply full micro and market-level efficiency, with some macro-inefficiency remaining.

Now, an increase of Gross National Product of 27 per cent might be unrealistic. But how much is *needed*? Suppose that we managed to move within Band-X to point *f*, representing a 5 per cent increase in employment (improvement in macro-efficiency), and a 5 per cent improvement in market-level efficiency and micro-efficiency combined. This rather moderate-looking gain would imply a substantial improvement in economic performance. Unemployment would be down to 5 per cent (or a bit more if participation rates were encouraged to rise), which is still too much, but may be manageable. With GNP up by about 10 per cent, family incomes would receive a substantial boost. The larger tax base along with lower unemployment benefits and welfare payouts would wipe out the government deficit, and 5 per cent higher productivity would drive a big anti-inflationary wedge between wage and price increases. Higher productivity would also make exports more competitive on world markets, and discourage imports, to the benefit of economies like the British which are chronically prone to balance of payments problems when they attempt to expand domestically. The 'big numbers' would generally add up satisfactorily.

So much for potential economic performance. In these three chapters I have argued that, even in a troublesome economy like the UK, with its battered industrial sector, and relatively low productivity growth rates, highly satisfactory economic performance is quite possible. The rest of the book will suggest policies to realise the potential.

10 The Principles of Appropriate Policy-making

'The state has no business in the bedrooms of its citizens.'

PIERRE TRUDEAU

This chapter begins the search for a successful economic policy – for the means of realising the macroeconomic potential documented in the last three chapters. The sensible place to start is with present policies. Why are they failing?

The diagnosis focuses on low elasticity as the ultimate source of the problem. Low elasticity makes policy-making inherently more difficult. In addition, the effectiveness of orthodox policies has been reduced by stubborn reliance on economic models built on the assumption that the economy is highly elastic, that is, by dependence on neoclassical economic theory in either of its monetarist or Keynesian variants.

It is clear that *some* policy intervention by government is needed. The do-nothing, *laissez-faire* option, however understandable the disgust with conventional policy-making that motivates it, is itself invalidated by low elasticity, which prevents the price mechanism from doing the job unaided. What is needed, then, is not necessarily less (or more) policy intervention, but *smarter* policies.

The search begins with three criteria which must be satisfied if a particular economic policy is to be a success: (1) the policy maker must know how the relevant part of the economic system works; (2) the available policy instruments must be powerful enough to achieve the desired ends; and (3) the intervention must be properly consistent with the ideals of our pluralist democratic political system. These are the criteria of *knowledge, power*, and *propriety*. There are many – too many – examples of economic policies which fail to satisfy one or more of these criteria for success. To see what goes wrong, the policy-making process itself must be examined.

It seems that every policy has three important characteristics. There is

77

the *institution* initiating it, the *goal(s)* the policy is supposed to achieve, and the actual *instrument* used. Policies differ in the level at which each of these characteristics is specified. Institutions vary from the lowest, or 'micro' level of individual households and firms up to the macro level of national governments, with market-level institutions such as trade unions and industry associations in between. Goals range from personal advancement to the 'national good'. Instruments can be directed at particular firms, at groups of firms, at particular regions, or can apply to the citizenry as a whole.

These concepts are crucial to understanding where existing policies go wrong, and to designing more promising alternatives. It will be argued that a necessary condition for virtually all successful policy-making is that institution, goal, and instrument be at the same level. Such policies are *appropriate*. When policies are inappropriate – that is, when there is some distance between the levels of institution, goal, and/or instrument – it seems that at least one of the criteria for successful policymaking is invariably violated.

Consider the highest-level institution – the national government – and the goals it addresses. Obviously proper goals are the high-level objectives of full employment, stable prices, general prosperity, law and order, a secure environment, that is, getting what were earlier dubbed the 'big numbers' of economic and social policy to add up. We do not criticise our national governments for their concern with these goals on our behalf. Obviously improper is the very micro goal of enriching a particular individual – the prime minister, for example – though examples of this occur in our own economies, and are endemic to more corrupt societies. High-level governments are not supposed to be concerned with the affairs of individual citizens. More controversial are the in-between goals of policies aimed at the market level; at individual industries, regions, or even firms. In the post-war period, national governments have greatly expanded their market-level policy interventions. Generally, I will argue, such policies are bad.

Three problems keep recurring. First, there are chronic difficulties in specifying policy instruments that will achieve lower-level goals. National politicians and their officials are, in general, simply too far away from particular markets to possess either the knowledge or the power required for specifying instruments that can operate accurately and without side-effects. Economic life at this level is too complex and unpredictable for high-level policy-makers.

The second problem is more fundamental. Even if they could come up with a perfect policy for a particular market, national government policy-makers *should not* implement it. Why? Because just by being in the business of dealing with either market-level or micro-level goals, the policy-makers give an incentive to all interest groups at these levels to lobby government for policies in their favour. The resources used up in these 'rent-seeking activities', as they are called, are wasted because they do not result in any additional goods and services being produced. Instead of increasing the size of the economic pie, rent-seeking resources are funnelled into squabbling about how a given pie is to be divided up. Thus, it would be best for national governments to withdraw completely from the game of attempting to formulate and satisfy lower-level goals, even if this means giving up a few excellent projects. Government does not have the power to prevent rent-seeking, and other undesirable side-effects, from spoiling their micro-level and market-level policies.

Naturally, it is very difficult for politicians, however honourable, to refrain from indulging in lower-level policies when these would benefit their constituents. The consequences are most alarming in the US, with its system of weak party lines in the legislature, where the growth of special-interest lobbying, by 'PACs' (Political Action Committees) has reached near-epidemic proportions.[1]

And third, even if policies were perfect, and all lobbyists repelled, doubts could usually be raised about the goals themselves. Knowledge of how the economy works is generally not sufficiently fine-grained to justify much confidence that helping industry X or region Y will have benevolent repercussions for the wider goals which are national governments' ultimate legitimate concern.

As a concrete example of how things can go wrong, consider the dairy policy of the federal government of Canada.[2] The only really defensible goal of this policy is very micro – to assist the group of small, poor, dairy farmers on the fringe of the industry. The policy instruments are rather higher-level, being a system of supply quotas and subsidies applicable to all dairy operators. The policy is thus inappropriate for a national government, and it appears to violate all three of the criteria for successful policy-making.

First, because the policy is targeted at a rather small group, it is worthwhile for those affected to devote resources to 'capturing' the policy-makers. In this case, the farmers' lobby group, the 'Dairy Farmers of Canada', dominates more diffuse interest groups, such as the Consumers' Association, with the result that the policy is twisted to benefit all dairy farmers, needy or not, with the large producers gaining most. The farmers benefited (and consumers lost) to the tune of nearly $700 million in 1980.[3] Thus, government's willingness to pursue low-level goals has led to a clearly improper redistribution of income from the public at large to a small interest group.

But this is not all. It is very difficult to move around sums of money of this size with low-level instruments. The policy-maker does not *know* enough about the behaviour of the industry to precisely target the re-distributionary instruments without unforeseen and costly side-effects. The clumsiness of the system of quotas and price supports applied to the Canadian dairy industry has resulted in all sorts of distortions — too much industrial milk being produced (so that substantial quantities of skimmed milk powder have to be 'dumped' on the export market at a loss), inefficient location of production, even biases in the genetic selection of cows for breeding. The total waste has been put at more than $200 million a year.[4] This is the cost of delivering a low-level $700 million income redistribution.

And finally, there is the problem, endemic to micro redistribution schemes, of government's powerlessness to effect a permanent redistribution, because the value of the price supports, quota, and so forth, are quickly capitalised into farm values, such that only people currently in the industry benefit. Young would-be farmers find it even more costly than before to enter.

Some economists have suggested replacing the present policy with one targeted specifically at the poor farmers. But while this might eliminate the income spillovers to well-off producers, it would *increase* the distance between the policy-maker and the level of the policy instrument. It would be extremely difficult for the Federal Department of Agriculture to accurately (and inexpensively) identify the proper beneficiaries of the policy without creating perverse incentives for people to try to become 'poor dairy farmers', in order to qualify for handouts.

Best, then, would be for the federal government to abandon altogether this specific micro-level goal, and retreat to its proper territory of devising policies to ensure general economic prosperity. Such would provide the economic environment in which many small dairy farmers would be able to improve their own situation (either by upgrading their farm or by turning to something more rewarding). Certainly, *some* would remain in difficulties, but it simply is not efficient for a national government to worry about them. Chronically unlucky or incompetent farmers can only be helped by institutions at their own level in the economy — neighbours, or local community organisations, for example.

The moral of this example can be expressed in the maxim 'the best is the enemy of the good'. However noble and 'non-political' the motives, any attempt by a national government to reach down from its heights and attempt to clean out the little pockets of micro problems in the economy will be expensive, prone to undesired side-effects, and quite probably unsuccessful in the event after all. Much better to save the resources to help deal with the appropriate big-number goals, knowing that success with these is sure to ameliorate micro problems as well.

What about the other category of government's economic policy-making – its *macro*economic policies aimed at the big numbers of full employment, stable prices, and economic growth? There is no reasonable question that these are proper goals for national governments. But, on investigation, it turns out that, in most cases, the policies are inappropriately implemented with micro-level instruments. In this chapter, the example used is macroeconomic 'stabilisation policy': the attempt to keep aggregate demand for goods and services consistent with the economy's ability to supply, so that both unemployment and inflation are kept within satisfactory bounds. Chapter 16 will return to this topic in detail.

Stabilisation policy does not act *directly* on aggregate demand. It works indirectly, through the 'levers' of monetary and fiscal policy. These make use of government's own sizeable presence in the economy. Through the central bank, government has an important influence on the amount of money in circulation, and can use this to alter the quantity and cost of loanable funds. This, in turn, will affect demand through its impact on firms' and households' borrowing to spend on plant and machinery, buildings, and consumer goods. Also, government's own spending on goods and services is a large component of aggregate demand, and can, within limits, be varied, leading to additional 'multiplier' effects on private sector demand. And through changes in taxation, government can affect the disposable income firms and households have available to spend.

Thus, we can see that both monetary and fiscal policy rely on micro instruments. They work mostly by influencing the spending of individual firms and consumers (with the rest of the effect being through the spending of government departments). It is fairly easy to show that the distance between levels of institution and goals, on the one hand, and instruments, on the other, results in failure to satisfy all three of the criteria for successful policy-making.

First, there is the criterion of knowledge. How, it may be asked, does the government *know* how all the firms and households in the economy will respond to a change in taxes or interest rates? The answer, of course, is that they do not know. To cope, then, modern monetary and fiscal policy relies on two big simplifications.

First, individual spending is aggregated into categories, such as 'private sector investment', and 'household non-durables', to reduce the number of variables to a more manageable number. This amounts to assuming that behaviour can be approximated tolerably well by the notion of an 'average' consumer, 'average' firm, and so on.

The second simplification is to assume that the past can give a usable guide as to how people will behave in the future. This leads to the building of 'econometric models', which involve applying statistical methods to historical data in the hope of uncovering stable patterns of behaviour. The list of major errors made by policy-makers using aggregated econometric models is embarrassingly long. It begins with the very first attempt to forecast consumer demand, after the Second World War, when the strength of the urge to spend that had been pent-up through the war years was drastically underestimated.[5] It continues with the years of Keynesian ascendancy,[6] and on to the present age of monetarism, whose proponents have been disastrously optimistic on the effects of monetary policy on inflation. A particularly spectacular example of prediction error seems to be the application of the 'reaganomics' supply-side tax cut, though in this case, the policy-makers appear to have been motivated more by blind faith than by myopic econometrics.[7]

The failures of econometric models to supply the knowledge needed for accurate monetary and fiscal policy are well known and have been widely discussed. Reasons given range from the numerous technical problems with data and statistical methods,[8] to the more fundamental objection raised first by the conservative economist Robert Lucas, who pointed out that the private sector, if it is rational, will *alter* its behaviour pattens *in response to* government policy.[9] That is, econometric knowledge can only be valid if it is never used!

It must be admitted that policy-makers do often ignore the model-builders. As long ago as 1974 Gary Fromm counted some 650 mathematical models (not all of them econometric) constructed to influence social policy in the United States, and supported financially by the federal government. The median model size was 25 equations, and the average cost $140 000, but more than half were not used at all in any policy applications.[10]

On top of these problems of *knowing* what to do, the steady worsening of inflation and unemployment has now reached the point where even the cleverest (or luckiest) of stabilisation policies cannot be expected to restore non-inflationary full employment. Monetary and fiscal policy is just not *powerful* enough!.

Why not? Note first that in stabilisation policy government is almost always trying to get the private sector to do things that, as individual firms and consumers, they would rather avoid. An expansion of demand is supposed to lead to more output and employment, but firms would rather raise prices instead. A rise in interest rates is intended to cut back investment spending, but borrowers would rather build it into their costs and carry on as before.

Now, the government could deal with unemployment by simply *ordering* all employers to take on anyone wanting a job (and instructing the workers not to be choosy about who they work for). This, more or less, is what Stalin and Hitler did, so that Soviet Russia did not suffer a depression in the 1930s, and Nazi Germany increased employment by 8 million between 1932 and 1939.[11]

However, it is not our way to allow government to interfere so comprehensively and intimately in economic affairs. At the distance which our policy-makers must maintain between governors and governed, only what amounts to a limited subset of the potentially relevant policy instruments are available – the ragbag of incentives and penalties generated by changes in taxes, interest rates, and nominal demand. The trouble with this, as was noted in chapter 5, is that indirect price and quantity instruments need plenty of elasticity if they are to have much effect, and elasticity is precisely what our economies are running low on. 'Lumpy' firms and industries are getting better at translating demand into inflation rather than output; at shifting the burden of high interest rates onto small business and consumers. The instruments of orthodox monetary and fiscal policy have been enfeebled.

The same problems – inadequate knowledge and power – also ruin the attempts periodically made by desperate governments to *directly* control the wages and prices of individual firms and unions. Although the use of direct administrative *fiat* is more dramatic than the prods and pulls of stabilisation policy, it is still inadequate. In the 'battle of the loopholes', the private sector is always to be favoured.

As for the *propriety* of stabilisation policy: is it right that governments should attempt to influence behaviour by applying to us stimuli of alternate pain and pleasure, rather in the manner of Dr Pavlov and his unfortunate dogs?

The game of spotting inappropriate policies could be played on. We could look at institutions below the level of national government. For example, some provincial governments in Canada have attempted to contribute to the macro goal of fighting inflation by imposing rent controls in the regions under their jurisdiction. Since, however, these governments are unable to control rents in other regions, nor other prices in their own

provinces, micro-level rent controls have had costly side-effects in distortions of the relative prices of housing and other commodities.[12]

Subsequent chapters will document the policies that have been developed
in response to the major economic problems, demonstrating that nearly
all of the economic policy-making of national governments, at least, has
been inappropriate, and has failed to satisfy one or more of the criteria
for success. As a result, governments have failed to cope with the elasticity
crisis, and have, in many instances, actually exacerbated it.

It is important to ask *why* our affairs have been so badly mismanaged.
Are our leaders fools or are they knaves? Both failings no doubt have a
role. There is the natural knavishness of politicians playing along with
special interests at the expense of the national good, leading to the sort
of micro meddling exemplified by the Canadian Dairy Policy. And there is
the do-gooder foolishness of policy activists enthusiastically trying to
right the world's ills while lacking the knowledge or the power to technically handle the problems involved.

For the second failing, economists must take much of the blame. Our
perennial optimism about the amount of elasticity in the system not only
prevents us from perceiving the magnitude of our economic problems, but
has also led to unwarranted confidence in the effectiveness of our remedies
for such difficulties as are admitted. In a highly-elastic economy of small
competitive agents it really might be feasible to 'fine-tune' aggregate
demand with monetary and fiscal policy, so as to keep the economy on
a path of full employment without inflation.

What all this means is that any serious proposal for improving economic
affairs must offer more than a list of good, appropriate, policies. It must
also include the means of avoiding bad policies; of curbing the venality
of politicians and the incompetence of economists. That is, what is needed
is not a new economics, but a better political economy — a realistic appreciation of how both policies and policy-makers operate. This is the
subject coming up next.

11 Specifying Policy Instruments

I have pointed out the problems of those policies which are 'inappropriate' (that is, those for which the three defining characteristics – the implementing institution, its goals, and the actual policy instrument) are not at the same level.

Limiting ourselves to appropriate policies sharpens the focus of the search for solutions to the elasticity crisis. Given that the main concern is with the high-level big-number goals of full employment, price stability, and an efficient economy, the appropriate institution is, clearly, the highest-level national or federal government.' Less obvious are the appropriate high-level instruments – the actual means whereby national governments can get the big numbers to add up.

To put the problem in context, consider in general terms what a regimen of high-level, appropriate policies would look like. An economic policy is an attempt to get some agents in the economy to act such that the policy-making institution's goals are achieved. This can be done in three distinct ways:

(1) The policy-maker can try to create an environment – a market structure, in economists' terms – conducive to goal-fulfilling actions.

(2) The policy-maker relies on inducements, penalties, or administrative control to *directly* influence the behaviour of agents in ways believed consistent with goals.

(3) The policy-maker can, if powerful enough, simply *require* that agents perform well enough to achieve the goals, without specifying how they should actually do this.

I will call these, respectively, *structure*, *behaviour*, and *performance* policies. As an example to clarify the distinctions between the three types, consider the goal of a minimum wage, that is, the objective that nobody who is working be paid less than some given hourly amount.

This goal can certainly be achieved by legislative *fiat*. The government can simply enact a law making it illegal for any employer to pay less than

85

the minimum. This would be an example of a performance policy: it imposes on the system the requirement that the performance be satisfactory, without specifying how agents are to achieve this. Minimum wage laws are, in fact, the main explicit policy instrument used to achieve this particular goal. However, there are potential alternatives. Low wages could be increased by some sort of subsidy or tax concession system, whereby firms are encouraged to increase wages up to the desired minimum. This is a behaviour policy, which intervenes directly on the behaviour of agents in order to induce them to change their ways.

A third possible type of instrument would result from analysing those features of market structure that contribute to low wages, and changing them. Thus, it could be argued, rightly or wrongly, that various impediments to free competition (ie, contributors to low elasticity), such as trade unions and discrimination against minorities and women, lead to 'low wage ghettos' in the labour market, and that if these impediments were removed, the problem of unusually low wages would disappear. Such would be a structure policy.

The distinction between behaviour and structure policies may need clarification. The latter are long-range, inflexible, general measures designed to change market environments such that behaviour will *tend* to improve. Behaviour policies, however, contribute to the specific factors causing agents to act as they do. Since other specific factors are always changing, these policies must be short-range and flexible to react accordingly, and since agents differ in their responses, behaviour policies may need to be tailored to the particulars of specific groups of agents.

Thus, for example, a cut in the corporation tax rate designed to compensate for unusually high interest rates as a depressing factor in firms' investment spending would be classified as a behaviour policy. However, a permanent shift away from taxes on incomes (including corporate profits) towards 'indirect' taxes on goods, is a structure policy. The distinction will be useful in analysis of policy-making, but it is not necessarily always clear cut. For example, successive British governments have cut away at corporate taxes, in hope of stimulating investment, to the point where now relatively few revenues are obtained from this source. The cumulative effect of the behaviour policies looks very much like a major structural change in the tax system.

Another point to note is that performance policies will, in general, be structure or behaviour policies elsewhere in the economic process. A minimum wage law, for example, forms part of the economic environment determining firms' employment behaviour, and may have implications for how the system performs at delivering low unemployment rates.

A 'too high' minimum wage may result in young and unskilled workers being 'priced out of the market'.

For this reason, economists often criticise minimum wage legislation. But they would probably accept that this performance policy is an effective (if *too* effective) means of *achieving* the minimum wage goal, whatever its intrinsic merits. It is an appropriate policy for high-level government because it applies generally to all its constituents, with no micro-level special cases or exceptions.

However, examples of economic performance policies are still relatively rare. The post-war explosion of policy activism relied almost entirely on behaviour policy instruments to achieve its goals. Both the micro-economic intervention in the affairs of particular markets, as exemplified in chapter 10 by the Canadian dairy policy, and the macroeconomic business of monetary and fiscal policy, attempt to directly modify the behaviour of individuals, or groups of indivduals, by the use of various incentives and penalties. They were set up like this, as was noted in the previous chapter, because politicans and their officials, egged on by the confident new generation of Keynesian economists, believed for the first time that their understanding of economic behaviour was sufficiently sophisticated, and their means of influencing it sufficiently precise, for systematic behaviour-modification in the economy to be possible.

The widespread adoption of behaviour policies led to what has been called a 'managed economy' — an economy run by its elected and appointed officials rather as a firm is run by its managers, in an endless sequence of orders, threats, and enticements to the 'employees', aimed at inducing them to respond to changing economic circumstances in ways that achieve the 'managers'' goals.

Earlier chapters documented the disappointing and deteriorating performance of our managed economies. In the last chapter, it was argued that orthodox policies have failed not for more-or-less 'technical' reasons, such as inexperience or incompetence on the part of policy-makers, but because of *fundamental inappropriateness*. High-level government institutions cannot expect ever to achieve the knowledge and the power necessary to indulge in behaviour modification without chronic inaccuracy and unfortunate side-effects. The behaviour policies of the managed economy are inappropriate to high-level national governments.

It is important, however, to understand the reasons for the initial appeal of the managed economy. Behaviour policies seem to offer a prize which is not, in general, accessible to structure or performance policies This price is the lure of 'optimality'; of achieving the best of all possible outcomes. It can be demonstrated theoretically, under various restrictions, that should the economy not be able to find an optimal allocation of its resources under its own steam (because of 'market failures'), then there exists some set of taxes, subsidies, and other interventions – of behaviour policies, that is – which will guide it to the optimal path.

Now, it must be admitted that structural and performance policies cannot claim this optimality, even in theory. They are too blunt, too rigid, for this. For example, one of the oldest structure policies is the anti-trust legislation introduced first in the United States with the 1890 Sherman Act. This attempts to limit 'monopolisation' of markets, by, among other things, limiting the market share that could be taken by the largest seller, and resulted, notably, in the dismemberment of the Standard Oil Company and the American Tobacco Company.[1]

It is easy to object to the arbitrariness in this policy. In some situations (in the computer industry, for example, where economies of scale are important) firms may need to grow larger than the legal maximum in order to utilise the most efficient production technology. And in other markets (say, those with relatively high transportation costs, such as bakeries) leading firms may well be below the critical market share levels that attract anti-trust attention, and yet enjoy market power equal, in their own industry, to that objected to for big oil companies.

Why not treat each market on its merits? Do a cost-benefit analysis, trading-off the costs of monopolisation against the benefits of scale economies, to find the optimal structure for each industry, and then regulate the behaviour of firms in the industry to achieve this – that is, transform the policy intervention from a structure to a behaviour policy? This more or less describes the British approach to policy towards mergers. An immediately apparent practical consequence of adopting the cost-benefit approach is that not much gets done, since, as Hay and Morris point out, 'The difficulty with a piecemeal 'rule of reason' approach to mergers is that each investigation requires a major research effort.' Of about 800 qualifying mergers between 1965 and 1973, only 20 were referred to the Monopolies Commission for an inquiry.[2]

Non-optimality can also be raised against the minimum wage legislation given above as an example of a performance policy. Any rigid floor on wages must be inefficient from an economic point of view. If the problem is a market failure due to the benefits of on-the-job training received by young and unskilled workers being worth more to society than to the employers who bear the cost, then the 'optimal' response is to use subsidies (a behaviour policy) to make up the difference. If the problem is perceived politically as one of poverty – of the least productive workers being unable to earn a wage sufficient to maintain a socially acceptable standard of living – then the proper economist's response is: 'Fair enough; deal with poverty, if that is what the people want. But do so directly, with grants to the poor, rather than messing around with the price mechanism by distorting the market wage.' There is merit in these objections, with implications for the design of efficient structure and performance policies that will be drawn out below.

But first consider the behaviour policies offered as the optimal alternative. These require, as noted above, an unprecedented precision and power for their successful execution. How well-founded was the confidence of economists that such precision and power could be supplied? Much depends on the validity of the neoclassical model that underpins orthodox economics. In this highly elastic, competitive world, behaviour-modification policy-making is relatively easy, for three reasons:

(1) Since competitive markets work rather well by themselves, the number of problems to be dealt with by government is relatively small. (Extreme neoclassicists claim, indeed, that there is no need for *any* economic policy activism.)

(2) In a competitive economy it is relatively easy to predict how agents will respond to policy. This is because the competitive process, by driving out high-cost firms, and competing away above-'normal' profits, imposes a certain homogeneity on behaviour, limiting the options open in response to a tax change, or a change in interest rates. Our theoretical models of behaviour in perfectly competitive markets are much richer in predictive power than are the models of oligopolies (markets with just a few large sellers).

(3) High elasticities mean more effective policy instruments – more response to a deliberately engineered change in market conditions.

Unfortunately, if we ever did enjoy a high-elasticity economy, it is now long gone. As was documented in chapter 6, our economies are shot through with 'lumpiness' – with markets in which elasticities are low. This is not good news for the managed economy of behaviour policies. For one thing, low and diminishing elasticities have worsened the economic difficulties with which policies are supposed to deal.

Also, it is difficult to *know* how a lumpy economy will respond to policies. With a Band-X of slack capacity built up from all levels of the economy, the private sector has more potential to do surprising things than in the 'taut' economy of perfect competition. This point can be illustrated with the 'production possibility frontier' familiar to all consumers of first-year economics texts. The competitive neoclassical economy is always on or near the frontier, so that if it wishes to produce more 'guns' (the usual example), we know that some 'butter' must be sacrificed, and vice versa. The lumpy economy, however, is well inside the frontier (which represents the maximum potential of an efficient economy), and so could move in any direction, including moving towards producing more of *both* guns and butter, and towards producing less of both.

As an all-too-topical example, consider the use of unemployment and high interest rates as means of squeezing inflation out of the system. If the world were really neoclassical, then a small dose of recession would have spurred a drastic bout of competitive price-cutting. In fact, though, much of the economy (both private and public sector) is large, or lumpy enough to face elasticities too low to make price-cutting appear a profitable response, and may even (as did the US auto-makers in 1974) attempt to *increase* prices, so as to maintain total profits on a smaller sales volume by increasing profit margins per unit. It is difficult to know now if recessions are deflationary or inflationary.[3]

It is true that the current recession has, at great cost, finally pulled down inflation rates. But because of its effect on investment in both physical and human capital, the long-term consequences for productivity and supply elasticities have probably been to make our economies more prone to inflationary outbursts in the future. This example also illustrates a third point that can be made against policies relying on behaviour modification: their toolkit of penalties and incentives may simply be unable to exert sufficient leverage to bend the lumpy economy to the desired ends.

All this serves to reinforce the argument of the previous chapter, that 'inappropriate' policies do not work. Behaviour policy instruments are inappropriate to high-level institutions with high-level goals, because they operate down at the level of individual agents. This is true of the instruments of 'macro'-economic monetary and fiscal policy, which depend on manipulating accurately individual behaviour (albeit aggregated for computational tractability).

The point made, I should then concede that there is certainly some role for intelligent monetary and fiscal policy. After all, governments have had responsibility for collecting taxes and printing money for a long time, and have no doubt developed considerable expertise about the effects their actions have on the economy at large.

However, the fundamental inappropriateness of these policies, magnified by the increasing lumpiness of the economy, means that we cannot — as recent experience so clearly demonstrates — *rely* on them to do the job unaided. Something else is needed, perhaps structure and performance policy instruments. Note at once that these can be as 'micro', and thus inappropriate, as behaviour policies. The Canadian dairy policy described in the previous chapter, for example, is a sort of structure policy aimed at a specific industry. The now enormously complex tax system, with lists of special cases and exemptions, represents structural fine-tuning run riot.

Such policy instruments are therefore subject to the same problems — of knowing what to do, and having the power to do it — of inappropriate behaviour policies, to which they add the difficulty of being supposedly rigidly fixed, and so unable to be adjusted in response to surprises. (For this reason, micro-level structure policies tend to degenerate into behaviour policies. The confident or hopeful declamation of the 'right' structure crumbles in the face of unforeseen side-effects and altered circumstances, so that revising the policy becomes an 'ongoing' process.)

Similarly, performance policies can go astray if aimed too low. Even minimum wage laws may be too micro, since they are directed at a particular subset (the young and unskilled) of just one factor of production (labour). As a result, they can result in the substitution of capital and skilled labour for unskilled workers, possibly to the extent that the latter are left *worse off* than without the legislation.[4]

But, as we raise our sights to higher-level policy instruments, the situation begins to look better, Economists may not now, or ever, be able to specify the 'optimal' structure for a particular industry. But we are on much firmer ground with a proposition such as, 'in general, competitive markets are better than monopolistic markets, because they result in a more elastic economy'. That is, if we could devise and apply policy instruments increasing elasticity overall, then economic performance for the economy as a whole would, we may be fairly sure, improve (even though some *particular* markets could, conceivably, be made worse off).

As for performance instruments — those which simply mandate that goals be met, without attempting to specify the actual behaviour that will make this happen — it is possible to feel confident that deploying them in the cause of high-level goals such as full employment, stable prices, and national prosperity, will be relatively uncontroversial, compared with the uncertain impact of a policy such as the minimum wage law, which may not achieve its own goal of reducing poverty, and could interfere with others, such as increasing productivity. That is, it will be easier, in general, to satisfy the 'knowledge' criterion for successful policy with high-level structure and performance instruments; easier, that is, to know *what* we want policies to do, than with either behaviour or low-level structure and performance instruments.

The 'power' criterion — the 'how' of policy — is also easier to meet at high levels. The means available to national governments applying structure and performance policies offer them an advantage over the private sector which, in a lumpy economy, they do not enjoy with behaviour policies. And because high-level instruments are, by definition, *general* in their application, they give less of an incentive to the sort of special-interest pleading which has so twisted the results of governments' often well-meaning attempts to sort out behaviour at the micro level.

All these assertions require documentation, which they will receive in later chapters dealing with particular policy issues. The purpose of this chapter has been to establish guidelines that will direct the search for successful policy instruments to help the economy achieve its high-level goals. The allure of instruments manipulating economic behaviour is their promise of optimality; of potentially offering the best of possible worlds. In a lumpy economy this potential is not realisable in practice, which leads on to structural and performance policies. Although offering only improvement rather than optimality, these policies appear to be, in principle, feasibly modest in their requirements for success.

The next chapter specifies in more detail a regimen of high-level policy instruments.

12 Proposal for a Governed Economy

'The rule of law, not of man.'

F. A. HAYEK

This is the third of three chapters concerned with building a foundation of principles on which successful economic policies can be built. In chapter 10, it was argued that policies should be 'appropriate' – that is, the policy-making institution, its goals, and its policy instruments must all be on the same 'level' in the economy. This implies that national governments should confine themselves to high-level instruments and goals. Examples of the latter are easy enough to identify. Appropriate and important goals are: full employment, price stability, and the productive use of all the economy's resources. These are the 'big numbers' that we all wish to add-up better.

The difficult part, of course, is actually devising high-level policy instruments. Governments have mostly relied on inappropriate instruments; notably those operating (as do monetary and fiscal policies) on individual agents, and so making unrealistic demands on policy-makers' ability to understand and control market behaviour. What are needed are high-level structure and performance policy instruments. Such instruments would directly constrain the big numbers to add-up satisfactorily, whilst doing whatever is feasible to the economic environment (in particular, working to increase elasticity) to *facilitate* adding-up behaviour. The trick is to ensure that the economy gets the job done, while making the process as painless as possible.

What would these policies look like? A clue is given by the examples of (low-level) structure and performance policies from the previous chapter – those concerning monopolies and minimum wages. One of these is a structure policy, the other deals with performance, but what they have in common – and what distinguishes them from macroeconomic monetary and fiscal policy, and from microeconomic regulation – is that they make use of the legal system. That is, they are *laws*. Behaviour policies are backed ultimately, it is true, by the government's legislative authority, but their day-to-day operation is an administrative, discretionary business, depending on decisions made by cabinet and government officials.

Now, the drafting, debating, enacting, and enforcement of laws – the *governing* of the citizenry – is a traditional and proper function of governments, along with their responsibility for running the various nationalised activities, such as post office, police, armed forces, and so on. Certainly, governments' involvement in law-making has a much firmer basis in historical precedent than their comparatively recent attempts to systematically manage economic affairs.

This chapter investigates the theoretical desirability of extending the use of laws to meet big-number economic goals. What is proposed here is a shift from our present, unsuccessful efforts to 'manage' the economy; towards what could be called a governed economy.

Of course, there are already many examples, in addition to the two already noted above, of laws either aimed directly at economic goals, or impingeing on the economy. Laws define property rights. Laws set the minimum working age, and maximum working hours. The nineteenth-century laws allowing businesses to incorporate with limited liability have perhaps been as important as any other government intervention in the economy before or since.

How do economic laws differ from the behaviour policies of the managed economy? In five important ways:

(1)   Laws specify the environment in which people act, whereas behaviour policies work on the actions themselves. Thus, some laws affect institutions (in our terms, 'structure') such as limited liability and anti-trust legislation, and others simply specify performance (that certain goals be met) without suggesting *how*. Examples of these are minimum-wage laws, and laws limiting the emission of pollutants. In contrast, the goals of the managed economy are approached indirectly, by attempting to suitably modify behaviour or actions, accepting as given the environmental framework.

(2)   The second difference follows from the first: laws are, in essence, *orders*, defining the terms under which people must act. Behaviour policies, on the other hand, must rely, in non-totalitarian societies, on penalties and bribes – the stick or the carrot – to attempt to *persuade* people to act as desired by the policy-maker.

(3)   Laws are the expression of basic principles, and so are *permanent*, at least in intention. Behaviour policies, in contrast, are necessarily flexible or *temporary*, since the actions which will achieve given goals vary according to economic circumstance.

(4)   Since laws embody principles, they are *universal* in their applicability. No-one is to be excused from doing what is right. Policies must be *particular* in their incidence, if they are to be sophisticated enough to effect desired ends without wasteful spillovers.

(5)   Good laws are *popular*, in that they express a consensus on how things should be done. Even successful behaviour policies, however, are likely to be unpopular, in the sense that their effect on individuals is to induce them to do things that they would not by themselves choose. One example is expansionary stabilisation policy, which can only succeed in its goal of increasing output and employment if individual firms can be persuaded not to raise their prices, the latter action being the more profitable.

Now, if we go through this list of differences, applying the previous two chapters' analysis of appropriate and inappropriate policies, laws emerge as superior to behaviour policies as means of achieving economic goals.

First, we have seen how the 'distance' between national governments and private agents makes it very difficult to achieve goals indirectly through behaviour-modification, especially in a low-elasticity lumpy economy. Laws that mandate directly that goals be met avoid this problem completely. Specifying the appropriate behaviour is left to the experts – the private agents themselves. Laws and behaviour policies thus operate in opposite directions: laws begin with the goal, and let the behaviour fit in, while the policies specify behaviour in the hope that this will achieve the goals. Of course, the goals themselves must be feasible and desirable, but since they are common to both laws and policies, so too is the problem of goal selection. Chapter 7, 8 and 9 argued that our big-number economic goals are certainly desirable, and are, in principle, feasible. Structure laws do affect behaviour, but in a general way that does not require the degree of accuracy and control needed by direct behaviour-modification policies.

The second difference, in methods of enforcement, also seems to be resolved in favour of law-making. The rule of law invokes national government's trump card – its unquestioned monopoly over the legislative process and over the legal system that implements it. No-one else, in our non-feudal societies, is allowed to make laws, or to employ judges and police as enforcers. (Certainly, there are many subsidiary authority relationships — between local government and ratepayer, employer and employee, adult and child — but their formal legitimacy is granted and defended by the national legislature.) National government is therefore the 'big cheese' in the law-making business. This is not so in the managed economy. There, government becomes just another player in the market, attempting to alter behaviour in its interests by making use of the set of instruments at its disposal.

The limitations of this approach have been examined. Government cannot, it seems, expect to *know* how best to deploy its policy instruments, and finds, in any case, that their effectiveness is blunted by the lumpiness of the low-elasticity economy.

The third difference, the permanence of laws, is probably also to their advantage. Of course, laws are often amended or even repealed, but they are *expected* to be durable, and do in fact last much longer, on average, than the budget-to-budget existence that is about the maximum for fiscal policies. This means that laws can be much more thoroughly prepared and discussed than is possible for economic policies. No-one expects a ruling that is to last for decades to be pushed through in weeks or months, which is all the time available to economic policy-makers in their never-ending battle against the unforeseen vagaries of macroeconomic events. This is particularly important for laws altering the institutions of the economy (such as limited liability), which, like all policies, must embody an attempt to predict their effect on economic behaviour.

The durability of laws, once in place, can be expected to benefit the poorly-understood goals of economic growth and high productivity, by providing a stable economic environment for the private sector's long range investment decisions.

The fourth difference was the universality of laws compared with the uneven and discriminatory impact of behaviour policies. The principle of 'equality before the law' is powerfully attractive. It certainly has a finer ring than 'equality before the bureaucrat'. In any case, the opportunities for special pleading that open up when governments show themselves ready to descend to the market and micro levels of the economy ensure, in practice, that the managed economy does not even achieve this limited sort of equality. Behaviour policies have 'name tags' on them, and, inevitably, these name tags become negotiable — to be bought and sold.

Finally, the popularity of laws expressing a general consensus gives them an obvious advantage over meddling policies. A popular law is largely self-enforcing, and the minority of renegades can be dealt with by the legal system. There is no need to bribe people to obey the law. On the other hand, policy-makers in the managed economy must either use bribes (grants, subsidies, tax breaks), or unpopular and therefore vulnerable penalties (taxes, tighter credit, incomes policies) to induce the private sector to act so as to achieve policy goals, however widely approved they may be.

Certainly, governments have shown themselves capable of enacting laws which did not command enough of a consensus. In such cases, the results (if the matter is important enough) have been most unpleasant — disagreeable side-effects, and breakdown in respect for laws in general. Good examples are the attempt to prohibit alcohol in the United States in the 1920s, and the current absurd and counter-productive attempts to prevent the use of marijuana and other drugs. But the high-level goals of macroeconomic policy are highly popular. The real debate is about their feasibility, and about the best means of achieving them.

To summarise the discussion so far: I have contrasted the temporary, discretionary system of policies acting on behaviour, which our governments now use to regulate economic affairs, with the permanent, non-discretionary structure of laws on which, for a much longer time, governments have relied to intervene in wider social dealings. On all points of comparison, laws seem better, in principle, than policies.

No doubt I have over-simplified the concept of a legal system, relying as I do on the everyday knowledge of the lay consumer of laws. Certainly, I have neglected the imperfections of the system. All citizens may be equal before the law in theory, but things often work out better in the courts for the rich and privileged. And laws are formulated which, openly or otherwise, achieve the goals of special interests rather than those of the public at large. But these failings result from the normal venality of people; from the inherent imperfectability of society. The proper question is whether we do better at *containing* the consequences of our failings with laws or with discretionary behaviour policies.

My vote goes to the former. I would loathe to be a citizen of one of those many states in which my social and legal status would be a matter of somebody's 'policy', with little or no appeal to the impartiality of the law. Yet this is just what we all put up with in our economic lives. We are continually buffeted by ever-changing policies, imposed on us by institutions from the national government down to the boss at work. These policies may seem arbitrary, even whimsical. Certainly, those of national governments are not notably successful.

Thus, I am proposing an alternative to the managed economy. Why not have government actually *govern* the economy as it does the rest of our social activities? That is, let government replace its system of behaviour policies with a system of economic laws, operating on the structure and performance of the economy. Translated to the macroeconomic problems with which this book is concerned, these laws would require, first, that economic agents be *required* to act in such a way that the big numbers add-up satisfactorily – ie, that the economy performs well – and, second, that market structures be such as to *facilitate* as far as possible the behaviour that results in adding-up.

What would these economic laws look like? It is easy enough to envisage structure policies, because we already have many examples of them in place. Examples noted above are commercial law and anti-trust legislation. In addition, much of the regulatory activity suffered (or enjoyed) by industries falls somewhere between structure and behaviour policies, depending on the extent to which it relies on fixed rules as opposed to day-to-day intervention. Of course, existing structure policies are not necessarily *good* policies. I have argued that elasticity is the most important structural factor, and in later chapters some policies presently affecting structure will be blamed for contributing to the decline in elasticity that is behind our deteriorating economic performance. In general, elasticity will dominate our evaluation of appropriate structure.

It is more difficult, however, to envisage the concrete form of performance policies. Social laws specify simple rules (do not steal, do fasten your seatbelt) which can be followed by individuals. Economic laws would, in general, be more complicated. It is not obvious what they would look like.

As an important example, consider the goal of a stable price level. This goal must be expressed in terms of a formula – the consumer price index – which is the aggregate of several thousand prices, all set by different agents in the economy. A stable consumer price index could be achieved by enacting the law 'nobody raise their price' – a price freeze – but the inefficiencies of such a rigid law would soon become intolerable. Something rather more subtle is needed.

It is a similar story for unemployment. A 'full employment law' could take the form of a Stalinist edict, making it a crime for anybody to be found without a job, but this would not be very popular. A less obtrusive means of implementing the goal is needed.

Indeed, economic laws which directly limit individual behaviour only seem proper where society's moral goals are involved. It is acceptable to have laws setting the minimum age at which children can join the workforce, since we accept a moral responsibility for the well-being of minors. It would not be acceptable, however, to have a law specifying the *maximum* working age, since this discriminates against a fully-enfranchised section of the adult citizenry (and private sector regulations on retirement age may thus contravene these persons' civil rights).

Thus, the performance policies, or economic laws, of a governed economy would not necessarily look like laws as we usually think of them. But they would incorporate the same principles that make social laws fundamentally different from the behaviour policies of the managed economy. That is, they would act *directly* on economic goals, rather than indirectly through attempts to suitably influence behaviour. They would be *permanent*, reflecting the stability of our goals, in contrast to the ever-changing reactions of policy-makers in the managed economy. They would be *non-discriminatory* in application, unlike the necessarily name-tagged behaviour policies. And they would rely not on the bribes and penalties of taxes, subsidies, grants, etc, but on the *fiat* authority of the legal system.

If feasible in practice, then, the governed economy approach has much to recommend it. The big numbers of economic performance would add-up satisfactorily, leaving the private sector maximum room to achieve this as best it can. And by transferring the excellent principle of the 'rule of law not of man' to the economic sphere, it could ensure economic rights to go along with our other civil rights.

With all these fine features, why has the governed economy not been adopted already? In fact, most of the specific policies that will be proposed in this book have already been tried, with success, in some economy at some time. All of them have been seriously suggested by respected economists. What is offered in this chapter is an analytical framework — the governed versus the managed economy — which can enable us to *distinguish* good from bad policies.

I should note a near-precedent of the 'law-making' approach to economic policy — what the Yale economist William Nordhaus calls 'creeping economic constitutionalism'.[1] This is the movement to impose rules or laws on government itself. The three major examples of economic constitutionalism are the monetarist prescription of fixed growth in the money supply; the proposal that government be required to balance its budget; and the advocacy of a return to the gold standard. These policies have been suggested as ways of coping with the untrustworthiness of politicians when they are given discretion over the levers of the managed economy. Such is also one of the justifications given above for the economic laws of the governed economy. But economic constitutionalism differs in that it operates not on the performance, or goal variables, but on the *behaviour* of one sector of the economy — government itself.

None of the constitutionalists' objectives — stable money growth, balanced budgets, gold standard — are true goals in themselves. They are, rather, all *means* of achieving the goal of eliminating inflation. As such, they are exposed to all the problems raised by the complexity and fickleness of economic behaviour that are faced by conventional managed-economy policies, and are even less suited than the latter, on account of their rigid simplicity, to deal with these.

We are now living through the failure of the monetarist experiment, which foundered on the difficulties of defining just what is this 'money' that is to have its supply controlled precisely, and on the volatility of the demand for money in response to policy.[2]

The gold standard and balanced budgets are old ideas, pushed aside by the triumph of Keynesianism in the 1950s and 1960s, but now enjoying a resurgence on the tide of disillusionment with activist policy-making. It is very difficult to make sense of them. The gold standard would tie our currencies to a metal of which the marginal supply is controlled by Russia and South Africa. Balanced budget edicts face enormous conceptual problems — distinguishing current from capital expenditures, sorting out the different levels of government, even settling the time period over which balancing is to occur.

The moral is that economic rules or laws, with their essential simplicity, are only appropriate when their objectives are equally simple. Such is true of the proposed performance policies, which deal with relatively straightforward and uncontroversial concepts like full employment and a stable price level. However, laws acting at a lower level on some particular facet of economic behaviour are mismatched against the variety of microeconomic life.

To summarise; I have urged the desirability of a fundamental change in economic policy-making, a shift from the managed economy of direct intervention in microeconomic behaviour to a *governed economy*, in which the state 'governs' through economic laws to determine the environment of economic activity. These laws would fit into two categories. There would be performance policies, to ensure that the goals of policy-making are met; that the big numbers of economic performance add up. And there would be structure policies, designed to increase elasticities in markets so as to facilitate the sort of behaviour conducive to getting satisfactory performance.

Perhaps a simplistic analogy is helpful. The governed economy would be like a race in which the organisers specify the finish line, and do all they can to make the route as smooth as possible, but rigorously refrain from directly 'assisting' the runners by pumping them full of stimulants.

Subsequent chapters put some meat on the bones of the governed economy concept by specifying the actual form of the appropriate policies.

Because performance policies are less familiar than structure policies they are dealt with first, beginning with the most difficult – the system of retail-level price controls proposed for achieving the goal of a stable price level.

Part III
Policies: Getting The Big Numbers To Add Up

13 Price Controls and Inflation

'Two cheers for the civil service!'

WASSILY LEONTIEF

The worst thing about inflation may be that powerful people *believe* it to be so bad. Prime ministers and central bankers are willing to subject the economy to the miseries of deep recession in order to slice a few points off the consumer price index. Prosperous economists sit around large conference tables and announce that 'we' – meaning the rest of us – will have to 'tighten our belts' (ie face bankruptcy or the dole queue) in order to exorcise the inflationary demon.

Their concern is surprisingly difficult to rationalise, at least in terms of their own neoclassical theory. As the Keynesian James Tobin has pointed out, the theoretical cost of anticipated inflation results from a distortion due to the impossibility of paying interest on cash, and cannot amount to a significant sum to be compared with the costs of unemployment:

> I suspect that intelligent laymen would be utterly astounded if they realised that *this* is the great evil economists are talking about ... Extra trips between savings banks and commercial banks? What an anticlimax![1]

However, as we all know in practice, inflation *is* a considerable nuisance, for at least two big reasons:

(1) Inflation blurs the mental measuring rod that everyone uses when they accept or spend money. Except when a 'big ticket' item like a car or home appliance is involved, it is not worthwhile exhaustively searching the market for the best price every time we buy something. Instead, we rely on past experience of buying and selling to inform our assessment of

whether a given deal is a good one. If the price level has remained stable over time – that is, if inflation has been low – then past experience in the market will be relevant. If not, then our painfully assembled store of market information will be devalued, and our capacity to make reliable judgements reduced accordingly. Inflation erodes consumer expertise.[2]

(2) Inflation reopens old wounds. In the real world, most prices are not set by the anonymous 'auctioneer' of neoclassical theory, but by buyer and seller getting together and *bargaining*. This is a costly business, in terms both of the valuable time spent negotiating, and the 'psychic costs' of the stress of conflict resolution. Inflation means that old bargains become obsolete more frequently – the pace of costly negotiating must be stepped up. This is particularly obvious with the wage-bargaining process between firms and unions, but is likely also to be a factor in the millions of deals between firms, and even in the 'implicit bargaining' that goes on between firms and private consumers.[3] The latter may be annoyed every time the price of a brand they consume goes up, even if the prices of other products (and their own incomes) have also risen.

Further, inflation may introduce or exacerbate inequities in the distribution of income, as the need for more frequent changes to prices strains the adjustment processes whereby weaker groups in the community tag along behind the more powerful firms and unions who set the pace of price and wage changes.

Thus it is quite right to be upset by inflation. It serves no useful purpose, and appreciably reduces living standards. But this does *not* justify the much larger costs of mass unemployment. The willingness of the monetarist types who currently control economic policies to use unemployment as an anti-inflation weapon can only be plausibly explained by their ideology – a dogmatic commitment to the neoclassical model in which unemployment is largely 'voluntary'. Amongst the more prosperous, another factor may be loyalty to the class whose interests may, if only temporarily, be served by disciplining workers and their unions.

But unemployment is not necessary to control inflation. Chapter 8 argued that although there is at present some sort of trade-off between inflation and unemployment, there *need not be*. That is, it is potentially feasible for our economies to operate with non-inflationary full employment.

The trick lies in somehow short-circuiting the process whereby increases in nominal demand are translated into higher prices rather than increased output and employment. Recall that there is a paradox in this process: while other firms – both competitors and suppliers – are raising prices, it would be foolishly unprofitable for any particular firm to refrain from doing so itself. Yet, all firms would gain if *all* of them refrained from inflationary price changes, and increased output instead. With other prices steady, each firm's profit margins would be maintained, and total profits would increase with the increase in volume of output and sales. The paradox follows from the elasticity crisis. Low elasticity makes each firm more prone to increase price, and less to raise output and employment, in response to an increase in nominal demand.

Therefore, we are led to look for a two-pronged anti-inflation policy. The present shortage of elasticity must be prevented from resulting in inflationary behaviour, and, over the longer term, something must be done to replenish the stock of elasticity, so that the economy is better able to deal with macroeconomic problems by itself.

Elasticity-increasing structure policies are available, and will be discussed later. However, we should not expect the lumpy economy ever to be broken down into the smoothly self-adjusting perfectly competitive ideal of neoclassical theory. Market imperfections are a *fundamental* feature of the real world, caused by the intrinsic differences between all the participants in markets, and by the awkward gap between uncertain future and present actions emphasised by Keynes.

For this reason, and because of the time that any significant structural change would take, a *direct* anti-inflation policy is needed now. In terms of the governed-economy concepts introduced in the previous chapter, we need a performance policy to *ensure* that the big numbers of aggregate supply and demand add up to the same total, so that peoples' spending is matched by real output increases rather than just higher prices. It is not too hard to identify such a policy. If inflation is rising prices, then price rises must be stopped. Government should invoke an 'economic law' to control prices directly.

Now it is difficult to think of a quicker way of upsetting a group of orthodox economists than by tossing the phrase 'price controls' into a discussion of anti-inflation policies. No other concept seems to assail more brutally the neoclassical ideal of 'free' markets, nor, it must be admitted, provide more historical examples of unsuccessful attempts by governments to intervene in the economy.

Yet an effective system of price controls is entirely feasible. Inflation could be controlled directly. Furthermore, starting as we must from the real economic world of lumpiness and the resulting 'Band-X' of under-utilised potential, price controls would actually push markets *towards* the competitive ideal. That is, price controls could be not just a performance policy dealing with inflation, but also an elasticity-augmenting structure policy of beneficial consequences for other goals such as productivity growth.

The proposal is as follows: government would pass legislation setting up a price control agency with a mandate to hold some acceptable measure of inflation – say, an augmented consumer price index – to an acceptable rate of growth – say, zero. The system would have these features:

(1)   *Only retail prices would be controlled*. Inflation is a general increase in retail consumer prices (that is, in the prices of goods as they finally leave the economic system and are consumed by households) and, with the exception noted below, only these prices need be subject to direct intervention. The prices of the dozens of intermediate transactions that go into each consumer good – prices of raw materials, goods in process, and the cost of capital and labour – would be left as they are now; set by bargaining between buyer and seller. Of course, buyers and sellers would need to take into account the controlled final prices, lest their inter-mediate deals result in unprofitable final products.

(2)   *Not all retail prices would need to be covered directly by controls*. Price controls would be a lot simpler (though also redundant) if the economy really were 'neoclassical' – that is, made up of markets each with thousands of small firms selling identical commodities, like prairie wheat farmers. Instead, sellers in most markets are 'heterogeneous', they produce goods and services recognisably different from those of their competitors. This is true for almost all industries, from corner stores differing at the very least in their location, to giant multinationals using advertising to claim the superiority of their product over that of their rivals.

   Now it would be ridiculously expensive and inefficient to try to control every dimension, every nuance of quality differential, of all the products of every firm, even with the simplification that controls be restricted to retail commodities. Fortunately, such comprehensive coverage would not be necessary. So long as the prices of the major characteristics shared by products in a market were set, competition for market share would 'keep the sellers honest' with respect to differences in minor and less tangible quality differences. Such competition would probably be en-couraged by higher quality elasticities under a price control system. That is, with the prices of major characteristics set, consumers would be able to focus their attention on intangibles, and hence become more know-ledgeable and thus more responsive to differences in quality.

   What this amounts to is that the 'price' of a commodity would actually be given as a formula, calculated as a function of the various measurable physical characteristics embodied in it. Such formulae, which are called 'hedonic price indices', have been found capable of matching a very high proportion of the price differences actually found in markets, even of complicated products like automobiles.[4] These price formulae would allow sellers to vary the amounts of each characteristic to suit their own capabilities and the changing tastes of consumers. The formulae would be adjusted over time as some characteristics became obsolete, and new ones were added.

In general, competition – high elasticities – would control prices wherever possible. There would be, in most instances, no need to specify prices for fringe products taking a small market share, since the price that can be charged for these is controlled by the prices of mass-produced substitutes in the market.

Nor would genuinely new products (that is, products whose characteristics did not fit into an existing hedonic price formula) need to be controlled. Most such goods disappear before ever achieving significant sales. As for the few successful ones, these are usually subject to 'learning curve' decreases in costs as output increases, along with vigorous competitive pressures to keep price changes close to costs. Only when the new product showed signs of reaching maturity – a flattening-out of the learning curve – would the controllers need to take a formal interest.

There are some industries producing products of which price differences are almost entirely due to intangible quality differences. Wine is a good example; fashion clothing another. However, in these markets there are plenty of sellers; plenty of competition to restrict price increases. This is because the technologies involved in creating highly heterogeneous products require small-scale firms to apply them.

Although firms in industries which are highly competitive in structure can be relied on to keep each others' profit margins from getting out of line, they cannot be expected to prevent price increases by their own suppliers. In these cases, therefore, an exception would have to be made to the general rule, and prices controlled below the retail level. Thus, for example, the prices of inputs such as glass bottles used by the wine industry would be controlled. The clothing industry would have prices of its textiles, thread, and machinery set for it. Many small-scale service sector industries, competitive themselves, would require protection by controls on the prices of the main appliances and materials that they use.

The principle, then, is to control as few prices as possible, and these as close to the *end* of the economic system as possible, taking advantage of whatever high-elasticity markets and corners of markets exist (with these elasticities to be augmented, of course, by pro-competition structure policies, discussed in later chapters).

(3) *The controls would be at the industry or market level.* In keeping with the principles of appropriate policy-making, controls should be as

high-level as possible. Practically, this means operating at the level of the industry rather than of the individual firm. That is, the agency would announce price formulae for commodities, to be satisfied by all producers. In contrast to wage and profit margin controls, there would be no grubbing around by government in the affairs of individual firms.

(4) *The profitability of individual firms would not be subject to control.* So long as the price and quality constraints built-in to the price control formulae were satisfied, firms would be welcome to increase profits by finding means of increasing productivity. Nor would firms be prevented from cutting prices below the controlled maximum in order to take full advantage of lower costs by increasing market share at the expense of lagging competitors, who are then forced either to match the productivity improvements, or lose their place in the market. Such is the 'engine of growth' of competitive capitalism, and one of its main justifications. If anything, the 'engine' would be speeded-up by price controls, since these, by removing the possibility of price increases as a means of increasing profitability, focus firms' attention on the alternative of finding ways of reducing costs.

(5) *It must be permanent.* This is perhaps the most difficult thing to accept about a direct anti-inflation policy. Inflationary behaviour is not, as monetarists assume, due to more-or-less arbitrary and unstable expectations of future price increases, which could, conceivably, be jolted downwards by a short, sharp bout of controls. Instead, the tendency to respond to demand increases by nudging up prices rather than by increasing output is by now deeply entrenched in our low-elasticity economy. To escape from the unattractive choice between inflation and unemployment offered by the Phillips curve trade-off, we must accept, albeit without joy, the necessity of a permanent policy dealing specifically with inflation.

It is more urgent that this point be widely taken by economists and policy-makers, than that agreement be reached on the specifics of the anti-inflation policy. These chapters urge the advantages of a performance policy to control prices directly, consistent with the notion of a governed economy, which I believe to offer the best hope for successful policy-making. Others have supported wage and profit controls, or tax-based incomes policies — known as 'TIPs' — which will be criticised in chapter 15. But most important right now is to get agreement that *something* serious must be done; that it is worth considering seemingly radical proposals in the quest for non-inflationary full employment.

(6) *If controls are to be permanent they must accommodate the long-term changes in relative costs that are the result of trends in technology and prices of raw materials.* Even with no inflation – that is, with no increase in prices on average – some commodities should go up in price, and others fall, as exogenous supply-side conditions change. For example, products made with new technologies, such as the word processor used to type these pages, tend to get relatively cheaper as production costs fall with scale economies and the learning curve effect.

On the other hand, labour-intensive activities, such as domestic service and housebuilding, as well as most assembly-line processes after their scale economies are fully exploited, have become relatively dearer as the accumulation of capital has made this factor relatively abundant, and labour relatively scarce.

During a temporary price freeze – say, extending no longer than six months – these changes in long-run costs may be ignored without intolerable consequences. But a permanent price control system must be able to mimic the market forces that generate changes in the structure of prices. It appears that, on average, individual retail prices move around 3 per cent up or down relative to the consumer price index each year.[5] That is, even with no inflation, we would observe particular price changes, with the size of these averaging plus or minus 3 per cent. Thus, permanently freezing the price structure would result, in a year or two, in intolerable distortions, with some commodities being sold at a loss, and others generating sizeable windfall profits.

However, it should not be beyond the wit of price controllers to deal with relative price changes. Precisely because they are long-term, cost-changing trends in technology can be monitored. Already available analytical tools (statistical sampling of firms' costs; a mathematical input-output model of price formation; econometric specification of price formulae) would be combined and developed into a routine procedure for managing changes in ceiling prices.

The market itself would provide much of the information needed. In falling-cost industries, leading firms would show the way, as they do now, by under-cutting existing prices. All the controllers would have to do is tag along behind, formalising the new price structure as its pattern settled down. And for many commodities, especially those which are labour-intensive and so increasingly appropriate for production in newly industrialising countries, prices paid for imports are a good guide to the path market forces are taking.

It should be emphasised that the controllers would *only* include truly exogenous (uncontrollable) events in their calculations of relative price changes. Such include changes in technology (that is, in the knowledge of how things are best made) and changes in the prices of raw materials determined by supply and demand in world markets. They would not, in particular, allow price increases for intermediate goods (that is, semi-finished commodities) to be passed on into price increases further along the stages of production. Such prices are 'endogenous' – they are determined within the system. So, they should be set by the buyers and sellers themselves, subject to the crucial constraint that all intermediate transactions must be consistent with the controlled final retail price.

Thus this proposal turns traditional wage and profit margin controls on their head. Whereas these attempt to control prices by controlling costs, retail price controls would work in the opposite direction – they would control costs, by setting a ceiling on the price that could be charged for each good at the final stage of production. Such price controls would, in effect, *simulate* perfect competition by imposing the discipline of price-taking behaviour on firms. The essence of this is that, with the ultimate market price of a good to be taken as given, firms (and their unions) have to turn their attention towards reducing costs and increasing output as the means for increasing incomes.

How would incomes – wages and profits – be determined within a price controls system? In a zero-inflation economy with no change in the shares of labour and capital, the change in wages would be equal to the average rate of productivity growth (the rate of growth in per capita real GNP). To match the market, the price controllers should build this rate of wage change into the price formulae, so that prices in activities with slower-than-average productivity growth would rise, and prices in relatively high growth industries fall. Such adjustments in relative prices are necessary, both to avoid windfall profit losses and gains, and to encourage demand to move towards those activities making the most economical use of society's resources.

But how would *actual* wage changes be made to conform to the theoretically appropriate rate? We could continue to rely on the present system, based on collective bargaining between employers and unions. The key requirement is that wage increases be approximately the same in *all* industries, no matter what their particular rate of productivity growth, and our basically decentralised wage determination system has shown itself, historically, quite good at achieving this. In particular, and perhaps surprisingly, wage increases in fast-productivity growth industries have tended not to exceed the national average. (If this were not so, then differentials would have opened up between the rewards paid to similar labour in different industries which would be both unjust and inefficient.)[6]

If it were felt necessary to give collective bargaining a helping hand, price controls could be supplemented by a general wage order system, under which *all* wages would be compulsorily adjusted periodically (perhaps annually) by an amount equal to the whole economy's 'ability to pay'. That is, wages would follow increases (or decreases) in real per capita GNP. Such schemes have been tried before, and with some success.[7]

What about non-labour income — profits? Profits pay the return needed on the capital tied up in an industry, and compensate the entrepreneurs who set up and run firms, for their energy and nerve. Profits also reflect luck, and, more sinisterly, the pay-off from achieving a degree of market power over one's suppliers or customers. The net result, as a number of researchers have discovered, is that substantial and often persistent differences in profitability exist between industries, and between the firms inside industries.[8]

Until more is known about the determinants of profit differences, price controllers should probably adopt a rather cautious strategy, such as making an allowance in the price formula of each product for a profit rate equal to the average of that earned by the firms producing it over the previous few years. The important thing is that whatever formula is used should apply to the commodity, not to the individual firm producing it, so that if any firm can better the average cost performance of its competitors by improving productivity, the resulting profit gains would not be snatched away.

To summarise the chapter: I have proposed, as the 'performance policy' part of an anti-inflation program, a system setting ceilings on the prices of products sold at the retail level. For various reasons, this system differs from the wage and profit controls usually put forward when a direct anti-inflation policy is being mooted — it would be permanent, it would operate on commodities, not on individual firms, and, most importantly, it would control costs by controlling prices, not the other way around. This proposal may sound rather radical, but it is in fact consistent with two fundamental and sensible principles:

(1) As an 'economic law', price controls would fit the idea of *governing* rather than managing the economy, as is appropriate to national governments concerned with high-level goals.

(2) These price controls would, in effect, *impose* the price-taking discipline of perfect competition on firms and unions, with the beneficial consequences for economic performance that have been urged by economic theorists ever since Adam Smith.

This granted, the practical problems of implementing a price controls system are likely to be considerable, and probably more numerous than I have recognised. However, the pay-off for a successful policy would be huge — a chance to achieve non-inflationary full employment.

The case for controls should not be obscured by the smokescreen of unthinking prejudice that has always seemed to choke off open-minded debate on the topic. Accordingly, the next chapter counters eleven of the fallacies often used to discredit direct anti-inflation policy.

14 Eleven Fallacies about Controls

'Rail travel at high speed is not possible because passengers would die of asphyxia.'

REVD DR DIONYSIUS LARDNER

It is not necessary to love price controls to accept them as an anti-inflation policy. Submission to rules and laws is unpleasant when it conflicts with personal inclinations, but, so long as laws are fairly applied across society, their application generally leaves us all better off. So it is with the system of economic laws proposed here to deal with inflation. Permanent retail price ceilings would often be irksome for individual participants in the economy. They would be quite costly and difficult to operate. Mistakes would no doubt be made. But no policy is perfect and costless. The real point is that the benefits from beating inflation would justify a lot of inconvenience.

This chapter challenges a number of statements commonly made about controls, demonstrating that while many of these have some validity for the various wage and profit margin policies that have been attempted before (on which more in chapter 15), they are fallacious when applied to price controls as proposed in this book.

Fallacy 1

Price controls distort the allocation of resources, by interfering with free market forces.

This is probably the most deep-seated misconception, depending on the cherished neoclassical myth that the economy is really a perfectly competitive system, with prices set by invisible but super-efficient 'auctioneers'. In such a taut, efficient world, where prices are just sufficient to yield every firm a 'normal' profit – no less and no more – intervention by heavy-handed bureaucrats would obviously mess things up.

115

But (to repeat a point stressed throughout this book), if the real world really were neoclassical, neither price controls, nor any other direct anti-inflation policy, would be *needed*. The monetary squeezes begun a few years ago in the UK, Canada, and the US, would have had the auctioneers slashing prices at the first sign of excess supply (unemployment). Instead, unemployment on an enormous and tragic scale has only just managed to bludgeon inflation rates down to the levels of a decade or so ago. This is because the economy is really a lumpy, low-elasticity thing, far removed from the textbook ideal of perfect competition.

And this is why another policy is necessary, and why a sensible policy could work. Chapter 9 pointed out that a by-product of low elasticities is economic slack – a 'Band-X' of underutilised potential, meaning that prices are often not at theoretically correct levels without serious ill-effects. In the real world there is room for manoeuvre, unlike the knife-edge situation of perfect competition. Price controllers would accordingly have some leeway to make mistakes, just as the private sector does at present.

Indeed, there is substantial evidence that it is actually better for prices to have some stability, even if this rules out achieving the theoretical optimum. Many farm commodities have prices controlled by government marketing boards, at the request of the farmers, on the grounds that stable prices are necessary to encourage investment in new crops and techniques.[1] In the business world, it seems that efficiency is well served by explicit or implicit contractual arrangements binding buyers and sellers, and limiting price flexibility.[2]

The important thing is that long-run trends in relative costs due to technological change and changes in primary input prices be matched by changes in relative prices, so that distortionary profits or losses do not occur. But there is nothing mysterious about this. Precisely because they are long-run trends, relative cost changes could be monitored and matched by price controllers, as suggested in chapter 13.

What about the short-run? Part of the myth about markets is that auctioneers are busy in them every day, adjusting prices up and down to compensate for temporary fluctuations in supply and demand. In fact, the use of price changes to clear markets in the short term is confined to a few perishable agricultural commodities, and to the 'paper markets' for assets (stocks, bonds, foreign exchange, futures, etc) which are not included in the consumer price index. In the great majority of consumer goods markets short-term variations in supply and demand that result in mismatches between the two are adjusted to by allowing stocks of inventories or orders to vary, not by price changes, which are costly and upset customers.

Indeed, there seems to be a rather strong social norm disapproving, as 'profiteering', of price increases to clear short-run excesses of demand over supply: in the free-enterprise United States a great fuss is always made when auto dealers respond to a shortage of a popular new model by charging more than the manufacturer's 'recommended' retail price.[3] What does happen is that the more 'negotiable' dimensions of deals respond to temporary mismatches of supply and demand. Car salesmen do not normally gazump their own sticker prices, but they do vary the price they will pay for a trade-in. This sort of thing would not be of concern to price controllers.

No such social norm discourages price *decreases*, when supply exceeds demand, and nor would the price controllers, whose concern would be only to maintain price ceilings, not floors.

To summarise: by keeping a careful watch on long-term trends in relative costs, and by leaving to existing market institutions the job of handling short-term fluctuations, price controllers should be able to avoid distorting the allocation of resources.

Fallacy 2

Controls would require a huge bureaucracy.

The British employed seventy-seven inspectors (twenty-seven of them qualified accountants) to enforce their price control legislation in 1942.[4] The Price Commission disbanded by Mrs Thatcher's government soon after it came to power in 1979 employed about fifty professionals, in a total staff of 600, who dealt with 8000 'notifications' each year, many of these involving large numbers of individual price changes.[5]

These are not huge numbers, given the size and value of the job. After all, even 'market' price-setting is not costless. The Walrasian auctioneer must be paid. The City of London and Wall Street employ thousands, most of them involved in price-setting, many of whom are substantially rewarded for their labour. Retail prices are set, for the most part, by lower to middle-level private sector bureaucrats. Under a price controls system, these jobs would be partially transferred to similar people working in a public sector bureaucracy. This work would be simplified by restriction to the market or industry level, in comparison with wage and profit margin control schemes, which require dealing with individual firms, and incur the associated compliance and/or avoidance costs.

Hence, although the bureaucracy needed to run a permanent price controls program would not be petite, there is no reason to expect it to be inflated out of proportion to the job it would be doing.

Fallacy 3

Controls dilute quality.

It is true that for many, perhaps most, commodities, it would be unfeasible for price controllers to include all the relevant characteristics in their pricing formulae. Matters of 'taste' cannot be measured objectively.

I have suggested that prices of the relevant measurable characteristics be set explicitly, and the remaining intangible factors be controlled by the market – that is, by competition for customers between sellers. If consumers were assured of value for money on most characteristics of competing products, they could then focus their attention on the remaining differences, with a consequent increase in elasticity – that is, in the responsiveness to perceived quality differentials – that would discourage sellers from diluting quality.

Note that many intangible quality factors are not 'produced' at a cost, so that there would be no pay-off to cutting back on them. Things such as the brand name and 'image' of Coca Cola, the 'flair' of Olivetti, the experience and reputation of an industry leader like IBM, the location of a corner store (all sources of what economists call 'rents', and accountants 'goodwill') are valuable assets, which it would serve no purpose to devalue.

It is in the routinised parts of the production process that there exists scope for cutting costs by lowering quality: by using inferior materials, or by reducing the number of quality control inspectors on the assembly line, for example. But precisely because they have become routine, these dimensions of quality could be specified in the controllers' price formulae. Even reliability can be effectively controlled by specifying the warranty offered by the seller.

Fallacy 4

Controls lead to shortages.

Shortages can be seen as an extreme version of quality dilution. With the latter, sellers cut back on some of the characteristics of their product that they are prepared to offer at the going price; whereas shortages mean a cutback in *all* characteristics – that is, in the total availability of the good.

The fear that price controls will lead to shortages seems to be a legacy from wartime conditions, under which rationing was needed to help divert about half of GNP to military uses. Such concerns are hardly relevant now in times of national and international mass unemployment and under-utilisation of productive capacity. Business could profitably increase production at going prices, if the demand were there. That is, there is potential in our economies to control prices, expand demand, and not run into shortages.

Fallacy 5

Controls should be temporary.

On the grounds that a little of a bad thing is better than a lot, it is often suggested that, if some sort of controls program is to be imposed, it should at least be short. Then a break in inflationary expectations may be achieved, without a buildup in costly distortionary side-effects.

This view is quite mistaken. Far from breaking down expectations, a controls program that is known to be of limited duration encourages firms and unions to 'hold their breath' — to refrain temporarily from inflationary behaviour in the expectation of a great rush of 'catching-up' price and wage increases after the controls are taken off.

The distortions that result from this behaviour offer some of the more celebrated examples of problems due to controls. In the six-month price freeze of 1973, the US consumer suffered unprecedented and alarming shortages of the great American staple, beef. This happened because farmers did not slaughter their stock, speculating that, by holding on a few months, they would be able to cash in on higher post-controls prices.[6] In the event, the speculators were wrong, as speculators often are. The frenzy of slaughtering that followed the lifting of controls resulted in a glut, and prices actually fell a little. But the damage was done.

I have argued that inflationary behaviour is deep-seated in our low-elasticity economies, and will require a sustained effort to root out. Only a permanent controls program can turn-around expectations, so that instead of saying: 'Here is a temporary policy. How shall we ride it out, or circumvent it?', firms and unions believe: 'The policy-makers mean business. The retail price level is not going to rise this year, or next year, or the year after. How best do we adjust our own planning and contracts to fit in with this new fact?'

That is, controls should establish a permanent, and thus reliable, *long-term* framework for non-inflationary decision-making. It should be emphasised that these retail price controls would not be punitive. No-one is to be 'blamed' for inflation. Inflationary behaviour is a rational response to an irrational situation — the low-elasticity economy. We would all benefit from an injection of rationality into the system at large, basically by replacing 'price-making' with 'price-taking' as the market rule of the day.

Fallacy 6

Controls should be flexible.

Flexibility is a good-sounding word, but it has been the ruin of the micro-meddling in our managed economies. Flexibility means that the outcome is up for grabs. It encourages 'rent-seeking' behaviour – the employment of lawyers, accountants, and lobbyists to turn the flexible policy-maker in the desired direction. All this uses up real resources (in both private and public sectors) to no productive end.

The essence of the governed economy approach is that it would rely on *rules*, on economic laws, which, in principle anyway, are not negotiable.

The point of economic laws is that they apply widely, which dilutes the incentive of individuals to lobby against them. The scope of price controls is limited by the need to have relative prices change, but at least the program here proposed would apply at the industry level, to commodities, rather than to individual firms. And, as far as possible, the controllers would be adjusting prices up and down by the application of fixed rules, rather than through discretionary decisions. That is, they would be *governing* prices, not managing them (even if, as a result, 'mistakes' would sometimes be made with individual prices).

Of course, even laws are, in practice, variable in interpretation, and in the intensity with which they are enforced. The price control agency would be subject to lobbying, complaints, and attempts at political interference in its day-to-day business. If, as I claim, it is possible to specify a fairly inflexible set of rules under which controllers would operate (these rules to be themselves variable only through parliament), then their resistance to interference would be higher than that of the typical regulatory agency.

Fallacy 7

Controls never work, anyway.

Wage and profit margin controls have not had more than moderate success, but when genuine price controls were imposed during the Second World War, they were remarkably successful, despite the very unfavourable economic circumstance of general shortages of consumer goods. The cost-of-living index in the UK, having risen 30 per cent from the start of the war to the end of 1941, then rose only 1 per cent over the next four years, to December 1945, under the price controls program.[7]

Orthodox economists, though normally not much interested in history and its lessons, are always ready to reach back through the centuries in the search for examples of unsuccessful price controls. A Roman emperor named Diocletian attempted for thirteen years to 'command cheapness', with the death penalty for transgressors, and gave up. A thousand years later, Kublai Khan had a try, and also failed in due course.[8] (No doubt these men were trying to suppress the effects of an irresponsible monetary policy, something that no serious advocate of controls would now recommend.)

It is a pity that opponents of controls do not look closer to their own times for precedents. The lack of interest in the success of wartime economic management in general, and price controls in particular, is odd. The great applied economist Lord Beveridge had no doubts, and in an almost offhand way, as though the point were obvious, included controls in his proposal for achieving non-inflationary full employment after the war:

> Adoption by the State of a price policy is a natural and probably inevitable consequence of a full employment policy.[9]

The full employment part was written into legislation; controls were quietly forgotten.

Fallacy 8

Price controls are unpopular.

In fact, Gallup polls in inflationary periods have found majorities in support of some form of anti-inflation controls, despite experience of the mis-handled wage and profit margin controls.[10]

These polls pose a dilemma for modern monetarists and devotees of the so-called 'rational expectations' doctrine, since this depends, as we have noted, on two assumptions: (1) that everyone in the private sector *knows* how the economy works; and (2) that the economy they know about is neoclassical — that is, perfectly competitive. This pair of postulates is inconsistent with people voting for controls, since these would be harmful and redundant in the monetarists' neoclassical world. I expect that the proper resolution of the dilemma is to accept assumption (1), and drop the other — people know how the economy works, and they know well that it isn't neoclassical!

Fallacy 9

You cannot control all prices.

It would not be feasible or desirable to bureaucratically set all prices of all commodities, given the multidimensional nuances that distinguish even closely competitive goods in most markets. But nor would it be necessary to do so. The controls proposed in Chapter 13 would take advantage of the fact that most of the price differentials between goods in each market can be accounted for 'by a quite small number of objectively measurable, and thus controllable, characteristics. Remaining, less tangible differences would be 'controlled' by competition between sellers, with this sharpened by a likely increase in the keenness of consumers to 'shop around' on intangibles, given that value for money would be safely controlled on tangible features.

There are some industries, as noted in the previous chapter, in which intangibles dominate the reasons for price differences between sellers. These are probably to be found most often in the service sector. Hairdressing is a good example: it would be tedious indeed to work out and quantify all the reasons that a haircut costs twice as much in one establishment as in another.

But, by their nature, such industries are highly competitive, with many small, labour-intensive sellers. Only small firms, with their freedom from the rigid rules of bureaucratic big business, can generate large amounts of intangible diversity. Thus competition, perhaps supplemented initially by a simple price freeze, could be relied on to keep small firms from inflationary hikes in their profit margins. Formal controls would then be moved back a stage, to the suppliers of materials to the small business sector.

Fallacy 10

Inflation cannot be controlled internally, because world inflation rates cannot be controlled.

Over the long term, the exchange rate must adjust to compensate for differences between the domestic inflation rate and the inflation of our trading partners. The actual mechanism of this adjustment is quite controversial, but the end result is not. When these adjustments do not take place, there are distortions right across the economy – in the prices of imports relative to competing locally-produced goods, and in the prices received for the latter at home and abroad.

Thus, if the UK had zero inflation, and its trading partners averaged five per cent, its exchange rate would have to appreciate by 5 per cent. The pound would move from, say, $2 each, to $2.10. Then, even though the US dollar price of American-made goods had gone up by 5 per cent, their landed price, in sterling, in the UK market, would be unchanged.

Similarly, the price received by UK exporters, again in pounds sterling, would not alter.

It is true that changes in particular world market prices cannot be adjusted away by the exchange rate. If a country exports manufactures, and imports raw materials, such as oil, then an increase in the price of the latter requires an increase in domestic prices relative to wages, since the country is, in real terms, worse off than before. In technical terms, it has suffered a deterioration in its 'terms of trade'. Such would be allowed for in the price control formulae, which respond to truly exogenous price changes of raw materials.

In general, the presence of a great world market over which the domestic policy-maker has no control would be of assistance, not a hindrance, to running domestic price controls. The world market provides useful information on trends in prices, technologies, tastes, and so on, and it also gives competition to local sellers — it is an important source of elasticity in markets.

Fallacy 11

You cannot control prices without controlling wages.

The trickiest fallacy has been saved till last. I have suggested that if final prices were controlled directly, then costs (prices of intermediate goods, and of factors of production, most importantly labour) will fall into line.

The validity of this depends on how the trade unions would respond to price controls. If they so wished, they could push wage demands up against prices, resulting in massive bankruptcies and unemployment, and even the demise of the capitalist market system. In this case, we may as well get the revolution over with as soon as possible.

But, it is my judgement that the labour movements in our economies are, for better or worse, at most reformist in their objectives, and, in many matters, really rather conservative. In particular, the recent econometric evidence supports the hypothesis that wage increases are aimed at no more than compensating for increases in the cost of living.[11] Thus, if the cost of living were controlled by retail price controls, wage controls would be redundant, and thus undesirable, given their intrinsic unpleasantness (on which more in the next chapter).

Note too that price controls are here proposed as part of a policy package to enable us to reach non-inflationary full employment, and the increase in employment and productivity that this would yield would allow substantial improvements in real household incomes.

The fruits of higher productivity might most efficiently be distributed to the workforce by means of *general* wage orders, applying to all employees, as suggested in the last chapter. But micro-meddling in particular pay structures is not likely to do any good. The next chapter reviews the evidence on this and on other 'incomes policies' that have been proposed.

15 Incomes Policies: How to Not Control Inflation and Get Everyone Mad

'If there was a gimmick that would solve it, this would unquestionably have been discovered long ago'.

SIR RICHARD CLARKE
(on the problem of controlling incomes to contain inflation)

The idea of supplementing macroeconomic monetary and fiscal policies with some more specific anti-inflation instrument is certainly not new. Frustrated by the failure of orthodox policies, and stirred by the politician's natural activist impulse to 'do something' about a problem, British governments of both parties attempted some sort of direct anti-inflation policy about once every six years in the post-war period up to the mid-1970s.[1]

But they never re-introduced the direct price controls which had been a permanent and highly successful feature of wartime economic policy. It was hoped that something temporary, something apparently less 'draconian' in its implications for government's role in the economy, could squash the inflationary spiral. We know now that these hopes were unjustified. With more than thirty years of hindsight, it is clear that none of the policies adopted was able to halt the decline in economic performance documented in chapter 2 of this book. Why not?

None of the five programs tried to control prices directly. (A partial exception was the first intervention, by Sir Stafford Cripps, between 1948 and 1950, which has been judged 'the most successful of the post-war period'.)[2] Instead, they took a step back, to the ingredients of prices. The price realised when a good or service is sold is divided up amongst all those who had a hand in its production. For all but the simplest of personal services, this involves paying-off hundreds or thousands of workers and firms involved at some stage of the production process. The typical end result is that about 80 per cent goes in wages and salaries – payments for labour – and about 20 per cent in profits – payments for capital and entrepreneurship (including taxes and depreciation).

That is, prices are incomes. Now, most of us are keen for our incomes to increase. What happens when claims for higher incomes add up to more than the total current value of the goods being produced in the economy? The prices of goods have to rise to accommodate the increased income claims made on them – there is inflation.

Responses differ. The monetarists who are currently in command in the UK and the US try to frighten wage and price setters into cutting back by threatening bankruptcy and unemployment. Such tight-money policies have had some success in reducing inflation, but at an appalling cost.

Some Keynesians – those of more interventionist bent – have looked for more direct ways of influencing incomes. Three methods for implementing 'incomes policies' have been tried or suggested. First is the 'moral suasion' or 'jawboning' approach, which involves the government *asking* the private sector to keep its wage and profit increases within some guideline. Moral suasion was the instrument relied on in the Conservative government's policies introduced in 1956 and 1961. A second approach to incomes policy was tried by Harold Wilson, in 1966, and Edward Heath, in 1972, who used direct *administrative controls* to limit wage increases and profit margins. The third approach, as yet unapplied, but increasingly discussed by economists over the last decade, is the 'Tax-based Incomes Policy' (TIP), which would use *incentives and penalties* – taxes and tax concessions – to encourage non-inflationary behaviour.

Moral suasion, alas, has not been a success. Certainly government should announce its targets for inflation, but more than exhortation seems to be necessary if targets are to be met. Harold Macmillan's 1956 'price plateau' led to the joke that he had 'persuaded firms to hold their prices steady between rises'. There may be exceptions. The Canadian government's current '6 and 5' program, which asks that wage and salary increases be limited to six per cent in the first year (1982–3), and five per cent in the second, seems to have mobilised some enthusiasm amongst the public and with lower-level governments. But moral suasion does not appear to have been permanently successful at reducing inflation in the past, and is not widely expected to do much better in the future. Apart from its general feebleness, moral suasion is unattractive in that the well-behaved folk who comply are penalised in favour of the antisocial types who do not.

Thus, desperate governments in many Western economies have resorted from time to time to imposing direct administrative control over incomes. Typically, such programs are in two parts, reflecting the division of income receivers into labour and capital. One part controls wages and salaries, the other profits. Typically, too, such policies are called 'wage and price controls'. This is a serious misnomer. Although the *goal* of the policy is always a reduction in the rate of price inflation, the *means* is never to directly control prices; rather, it is to control the costs or incomes that are the ingredients of price. Thus, an accurate name is 'wage and profit controls'. It is not pedantic to insist on this distinction. Casual misuse of the phrase 'price controls' is annoying because it tars the concept with the failure of incomes policies, and so makes the case for true price controls needlessly harder to put across.

Wage and profit controls involve government in the affairs of individual workers, unions, and firms. They are thus extremely 'inappropriate' in the sense of the analysis of chapter 10: high-level government is 'micromeddling' in the private business of its citizens. The history of these policies offers classic examples of nonfulfillment of the three criteria for success, that the policy-maker should *know* what needs to be done; should have the *power* to achieve it; and that the whole business be *proper* in the first place.

Consider first the 'knowledge' criterion. The policy-makers must know enough about the inflation process to be able to specify actions to deal with it. That is, they must have a valid and usable *theory* of inflation. The usual theoretical basis for wage and profit controls is the doctrine of 'cost-plus pricing'. This has prices set by firms as a mark-up over their costs, which are made up of the wages and salaries they pay their own employees, and prices of materials and other inputs bought from other firms. This much is tautological, since all profits can be seen as a mark-up. So, the theory is operationalised and made suitable for policy analysis by two restrictions:

(1) It is suggested that mark-ups are rather constant, being set to yield a 'normal' or 'customary' profit margin over costs.
(2) The actual business of setting wages, and marking them up into profit margins, is supposed to be routinised into easily controllable procedures.

These propositions imply that it will be administratively feasible for a government agency to control costs, and that the result will be to control inflation too.

Taken to its logical extreme, the cost-plus model implies that only wage increases need be controlled. This is because all elements of cost divide ultimately into either wages and salaries or profits, and so if profits are set as a constant margin over wages and salaries, only the latter need be controlled to control total costs. Accordingly, the more hard-line advocates of incomes policies (in the UK to be found notably in the Cambridge Department of Applied Economics, and in the US amongst disciples of the 'Post-Keynesian' school) tend to concentrate on the need for wage controls. Their position was summarised by one of the leading American Post-Keynesians, the late Sidney Weintraub:

> Wages and depreciation are about 85 per cent of the costs of production and if you keep them in line, then it follows that prices will also come into line . . . the mark-up has been constant for the past 80 years, so I guess there's a fair chance that it will continue . . . thus . . . you don't need price controls, because they will be controlled through controlling wages.[3]

The constant mark-up model appears to exclude 'market forces' (ie supply and demand) as a determinant of price. It thus annoys neoclassical economists, who hate the idea of abandoning profit-maximising, 'rational', behaviour.[4] The idea of relying on wage controls also enrages trade unions, who tend to be sceptical about the constant-mark-up assumption. For this reason, incomes policies have usually been introduced with controls on both profit margins and wages.

Neoclassical economists and trade unionists are not always in agreement: in this case they seem to have good grounds for joining forces. The fallacy of incomes policy is the same one that undermines the Phillips curve trade-off between inflation and unemployment (chapter 8); the assumption that because something *is*, it *must be* — in particular, that because a simple 'mark-up on wages' model appears to explain pricing behaviour before an incomes policy, it will continue to be valid after the application of controls.

The assumption is clearly invalid. Take attempts to control increases in labour income. Historically, it is true that these are mostly achieved by negotiated increases in hourly or weekly rates laid down in contracts between employers and unions. Accordingly, the pay control part of phase II of Edward Heath's incomes policy brought into effect in April 1973 (phase I was a five month pay freeze) restricted wage and salary increases to 'one pound plus 4 per cent'.

However, although an increase in formal rates may be the simplest way for employers and employees to increase pay, it certainly is not the *only* way. Even before phase II had gone into effect, the union leader

Clive Jenkins had distributed '24 hot tips' – ways for unions and employers to more-or-less legally dodge the intent of the wage control.[5] These included various improvements to fringe benefits, pensions, benevolent funds, more generous 'merit' awards and 'promotions' to higher-paid jobs, and cash bonuses. Some idea of the difficulty in stopping this sort of thing is given by Sir Alec Cairncross's observation that 40 per cent of manufacturing workers in Britain are on some sort of 'payment by results' system.[6] The problem is a typical consequence of an inappropriate policy. High-level government officials just cannot expect to know enough about the complex business of income determination to prevent an 'unholy alliance' of employers and employees from circumventing the relatively simple rules of pay control. Employees, believing (correctly, as it turns out), that the incomes policy will not control inflation, have a strong, and, indeed, legitimate incentive to find ways around wage controls. Employers, not wishing to put up with a strike to 'do the government's dirty work', and confident that increased labour costs will be passed on under the terms of the incomes policy into higher prices with no loss of profitability, have an incentive to connive with their workers. No government agency can be expected to outwit such an alliance.

What about profit margin controls? If anything, these are even more difficult to specify than wage controls. The simple-sounding rule 'let the percentage that profits are of costs not increase' quickly turns into a tangle of ambiguity and special cases when applied to an unco-operative and cunning private sector. Gardner Ackley – a very experienced Keynesian economist who is not unsympathetic to the idea of controls – has given a sample of some of the difficulties that arise:

In computing the firms' margins over materials plus labor costs, how are inventories to be valued? What operating unit is to be used (if less than the entire firm, how are joint costs to be allocated)? If overhead costs should be excluded, what are overhead costs? Won't there have to be provisions for adjusting abnormally low base-period margins, due to special sales, close-outs of unprofitable lines, and many other unusual circumstances?[7]

The controllers' dilemma is that if they don't attempt to deal with all these fine points and special cases, costly distortions will arise; and if they do, they inevitably create loopholes through which price increases can escape. As just one example, the UK Price Commission found that, when tea prices rose, blenders priced their inventories on a replacement cost basis; when they fell again, the blenders switched to historic costs. This was perfectly legal under the controls rules, and it evaded their intent.

The lesson is clear: planners and administrators of wage and profit controls can never *know* enough about the enormous variety of micro-economic behaviour to deploy these controls so that inflationary pressures are permanently suppressed. Some temporary respite may be obtained, but effectiveness is soon diminished as business learns how to play the game to its own advantage.

There are side-effects, too. To the visible costs of running the controls bureaucracy must be added the hidden costs incurred by the private sector in complying with the regulations – all the head-scratching and form-filling. There are the wastes of 'paper entrepreneurship', the high-paid labour diverted to finding ways around the regulations, or putting pressure on the controllers to change them. Ackley was involved in the vastly complicated profit margin controls in the US during the Korean War. He reports

> We found that a difference of a few words in a definition could mean millions of dollars to a large company; thus its lawyers and lobbyists could easily earn their pay by getting the definition changed or an exception made.[8]

Perhaps worst of all is the insidiously perverse incentive implied by all cost-plus pricing rules: if the *percentage* margin on costs is limited, then the way to increase total profits is to let costs rise. That is, it pays to become *less efficient*, especially as one of the easiest avenues to higher costs is to pad managers' fringe benefits, an option always attractive to them. It is difficult to precisely document cost-padding amid the short-lived confusion of profit controls, but economists who have been involved in these programs do not doubt that it is a problem.[9]

What about the *power* criterion – the ability of policy-makers to get their own way, once they have decided what they want the private sector to do? With the profit margin part of incomes policies there does not seem to be a major problem: most firms will obey an edict issued by a legitimate government authority. The real difficulty is knowing what edicts to issue. Wage controls are a different matter. Unions bitterly oppose them. They fear, with some historical justification, that the wage control part of an incomes policy will be more effective than the profit margin part, with the result that prices will rise more than wages, and real incomes fall. Determined trade union resistance can be more than most governments can handle, as Mr Heath found out with the miners' strike of 1973–4.

For this reason, politicians of both the left and the right are now very cautious about their ability to impose an incomes policy.

The third criterion by which a policy should be judged is of its *propriety*: is it the sort of thing government should be doing to its citizens? Incomes policies are not proper in this sense. Micro-meddling in the detailed affairs of firms is bad enough; interfering with wage determination even worse. With the latter, the problem is not that wage controls interfere with market forces — there is nothing *improper* about that, since 'market forces' are only a means, not a sacred end in themselves. Rather, the problem is that the wage structure seems to be tied in with intrinsically more important things than the market. Wages are the major source of income for the great majority of the population, and as such embody complex and deeply-felt views on what people and jobs are 'worth'. Against the strength of these feelings, mere 'economic' forces may be subservient. The economist J. R. Crossley writes of economic change being

> constrained by a strongly conservative tendency for the wage structure to re-establish itself along lines which the social psychologist would not hesitate to describe as a classic example of social normative behaviour.[10]

New industries tend to offer a premium to build up their work-forces, but the premium is not eroded after growth slows; rather it is 'fossilised' by custom and tradition into what has been called the 'geological' wage structure.[11]

There are, of course, all sorts of problems generated by the process of establishing and evolving earnings differentials. Government may have a legitimate role in this process, setting up commissions and tribunals to examine incomes and relativities in particular industries and occupations. But the accidental and arbitrary implications of wage controls for incomes are not welcomed.

So much for wage and profit controls. One should not expect much credit from attacking them, since they do make an easy target, and one which few economists would care to defend with any vigour.

Nevertheless, some Keynesians, demonstrating a commendable unwillingness to abandon anti-inflation policy to the cruel monetarists, have looked around for a more economically sensible means of implementing an incomes policy. What they have come up with is now known by the acronym 'TIP', for 'Tax-based Incomes Policy'. TIP proposals differ in many respects, but all share the notion that firms and unions should be *induced* — by incentives or penalties — to act in a non-inflationary way, rather than being *ordered* to do so as in orthodox wage and profit controls.

The original idea (the TIPoff, one might call it) seems to be due to H. C. Wallich and Sidney Weintraub, who suggested in 1971 that inflationary wage increases (that is, increases above the rate of productivity growth) be taxed.[12] Variants have included Abba Lerner's plan to issue freely negotiable permits to increase wages, with the total amount issued equalling the economy's capacity for non-inflationary increases; and Arthur Okun's idea of giving tax rebates to employees accepting non-inflationary wage rises, and to firms holding their profit margins constant.[13]

The theoretical appeal of TIPs is their apparently sensible flexibility. If a firm really needs to pay a higher-than-average wage increase, say to attract labour to a productive new industry, then, under a TIP, it could do so if the increase were worth more to it than the tax it would pay (or rebate it would lose).

But the usual problems with 'cute' schemes for engineering economic behaviour remain:

(1) The significant 'lumpiness' of the economy means that some firms would be able to absorb taxes by passing them on in higher prices, thereby increasing the burden to be born by the more competitive sectors, and diluting the anti-inflation impact of the TIP.

(2) 'Flexibility' is not unique to TIPs. Old-style wage and profit controls, as noted above, are flexible, too. The more a firm wishes to avoid them, the more it spends on lobbyists, lawyers, and accountants. The theoretical distinction between 'rigid' rules and regulations, and 'flexible' taxes and subsidies just doesn't stand up in the real world. With both sorts of policy, the impact can be deflected by anyone wishing to devote enough resources to 'paper entrepreneurship'.

(3) TIPs in no way avoid the administrative difficulties of direct wage and profit controls. Before a tax can be levied, or a rebate assessed, the same business of defining and measuring a wage increase, a profit margin, or a cost, must be gone through. In fact, the passages from Weintraub and from Ackley cited earlier in this chapter were actually taken from articles on TIPs. Opinions differ on the size of these administrative problems. Weintraub claimed that a TIP could be applied to the 500 largest Canadian corporations by 'three or four people working in the taxation department' — which seems absurdly optimistic.[14]

Since these criticisms of TIPs and wage and profit controls follow my vigorous defence of price controls, which certainly would not be trivial in their administrative requirements, it is worth concluding with a brief comparison of the two approaches.

Note first the fundamental difference between incomes policies which try to deal with inflation by controlling costs, and price controls which would deal directly with inflation, while letting costs sort themselves out within the non-inflationary constraint. This difference stems from (1) a different theory of the inflation process; and (2), a different theory of economic policy – of the 'governed' versus the 'managed' economy.

Incomes policy advocates have a cost-push model of inflation: prices are pushed up by increases in costs resulting from attempts by labour and capital to increase their incomes. To restrain inflation, therefore, incomes must be restrained; in particular, the incomes of members of trade unions, which are usually seen as the chief instigators of cost-push. (Indeed, fear and resentment of the trade union movement seems to lurk in the hearts of many supporters of incomes policies, despite their typically 'leftish' stance on other matters.)

In contrast, my reading of the evidence is that inflation is due to a mixture of 'demand-pull' and inchoate but unstable expectations about future inflation rates. Firms raise prices because they expect that other firms will be doing it too, and because it is temporarily more profitable to do so than to expand output when nominal demand increases. Unions tag along, trying desperately to maintain their members' standards of living. Allegedly 'powerful' unions are almost invariably found to be riding on the back of powerful employers. The good jobs are in industries with large and profitable firms, and in the public sector.[15]

People do not believe that it is their own greed which fuels inflation, and they will not accept incomes policies implying this to be so. They would welcome the stability in the cost of living that would be the result of successful price controls, and would have no difficulty in fitting wage claims and lower-level prices into a retail price ceilings framework.

What about differences in the policies themselves? Price controls would require specification of the characteristics of a large number of retail-level goods and services, and a mechanism for altering the relative prices of these in line with long-term trends in technology and exogenous material prices. Prices of goods-in-process, and the incomes received by firms and workers, would not be controlled explicitly.

Incomes policies require that every firm (above a certain size) and every collective agreement be controlled individually. In essence, the administrators of incomes policies need to develop a 'theory' – a special knowledge – of each union and firm. Price controls thus appear to be less demanding than incomes policies both in their administrative require-ments, and in the theoretical knowledge needed to put them into opera-tion. A Ford Fiesta is a simpler thing than the Ford Motor Company, and a Fiesta and a Mini Metro are more alike than are Ford and British Leyland.

An important side-effect of incomes policies is the incentive they offer to let costs drift up. In contrast, price controls would encourage produc-tivity improvements, because the firms and workers concerned could pocket the resulting profits.

Price controls should be easier to enforce. They rely on high-level government's trump card – its monopoly over the legal system. They would have millions of consumers as unpaid monitors, and, in any case, are not punitive in their impact on firms and workers. Incomes policies, on the other hand, require government to 'mix it' right down at the micro level of the economy, trying to out-manoeuvre firms and unions at their own game.

Price controls would not involve government in unseemly and trouble-some intervention in the distribution of income, as must attempts to control individual wage settlements and profit margins. The retail price of a good is divided up into hundreds of slivers of income, accruing to each of the firms and workers who had a hand in its production at some stage. Thus a 'mistake' in price setting (and mistakes would occur) would be widely shared, and so less likely to be a significant problem for any one firm or group of workers.

Finally, price controls, being higher-level, offer less inducement to the private sector to engage in wasteful 'rent-seeking' lobbying, and to politicians to respond to this.

The bottom line for any policy is how well it works. Incomes policies have been tried many times, and have failed, or disappointed, as often. Price controls rather like the system I have proposed were deployed in several countries during the Second World War and worked well under very difficult circumstances. They should be given another chance.

16 Achieving Full Employment: The Case of the Faint-hearted Entrepreneurs

It would be good to beat inflation. But perhaps the biggest benefit of a direct anti-inflation policy would be its contribution to an even more important goal — reducing unemployment. In sharp and welcome contrast to monetarism, which has used *increases* in unemployment to bludgeon down price increases, price controls would set the stage for drastically reduced unemployment rates.

First we must face up to the scale of the problem. In chapter 7 I argued that the truly 'natural' rate of unemployment, when this is properly defined to exclude people choosing leisure or resting between jobs, is approximately zero. Now, zero unemployment probably seems an impossibly optimistic target, except perhaps to someone who grew up, as I did, in an economy where unemployment was in fact only a decimal point or two away from zero most of the time. So let us aim for 2 or 3 per cent, at least as an interim goal. Such has been achieved in all the Western economies, in the lifetime of all but the most precocious readers of this book.

But even this would require at least a 10 per cent increase in the number of jobs, when allowance is made for the 'discouraged workers' who would like to work again, but no longer find it worthwhile to register as officially unemployed. These people probably add two or three percentage points to a measured 10 per cent unemployment rate. Thus enormous numbers of new jobs are needed — at least two and one half million in Britain; ten million in the United States.

It is clear that governments cannot achieve increases on this scale by themselves; neither with direct public sector employment programs, nor by 'buying' jobs from the private sector through subsidies and tax breaks. Apart from other objections (for example, concerning what all the public employees would *do*), it would be prohibitively expensive. Even if the jobs could be bought for an amount equal to the average wage of people already employed, something like a 30—40 per cent increase in government expenditure would be required. Although some of this would eventually flow back from increased tax revenues, the increase in government deficits would almost certainly be intolerable.[1] So the bulk of the jobs must be provided by the private sector on its own. We need a 'bootstrap' theory; a plan for the economy to pull itself up to full employment.

Now there is certainly no shortage of *potential* demand for the goods and services that a fully-employed economy would produce. The problem is to make this demand *effective* — to translate the 'money votes' of consumers and investors into real output and employment. This is where the big pay-off would come from a successful direct anti-inflation policy, such as price controls. What has been happening is that too high a proportion of each year's money votes have been siphoned-off into higher prices — into inflation. Price controls would block the inflationary detour. By removing the 'raise prices' option, controls would force firms to consider the alternative of increasing production as their response to the money votes being laid on them.

But would they *do* it? I argued in chapter 7 that full employment is, in principle, possible. That is, there is not (despite monetarist claims to the contrary) any immutable barrier to the economy operating at a significantly higher rate of real GNP. In technical terms, the long-run supply curve is, or could be, flat.

But we still must get there from here. The early stages of recovery are relatively straightforward, since the recession leaves a sizeable margin of excess capacity (idle plant and machinery) on which a larger labour force can be put to work. If the fall from full employment had been sudden, then the spare capacity on hand would be sufficient to re-employ most or all of the unemployed. But the decline in economic performance has been going on for so long — from the very beginning of the post-war boom, as documented in chapter 2 — that business has long since abandoned the scale of investment need to maintain a capital stock sufficient to give every willing person something to work with. A major re-investment effort is needed.

Now the key characteristic of investment is that it is long-term. It takes years to recover the costs of expenditures on new plant and machinery. This would not matter if investment decisions were fully reversible, but usually they are not. Once a new plant has been built and equipped, it cannot normally be easily altered to some other use. You cannot bake bread in a ball-bearing factory. This means that investing firms have to deal with uncertainty. They must feel reasonably sure that a market for their product will exist at least up to the pay-back horizon of their investment.

For a few lucky firms uncertainty is not a problem because their markets are guaranteed. Examples are to be found in the armaments industry, with its 'cost-plus' contracts, in nationalised industries, and perhaps amongst those very large corporations whose size is sufficient for their collapse as a consequence of bad luck or bad management to be politically unacceptable – Chrysler being the most conspicuous recent case.

But most markets are not guaranteed. Most firms must face the possibility of failure; of their investments not returning a profit. Even in basically buoyant industries the size and taste of the market can alter in unpredictable ways. So investors must be risk-takers. For all the money it spends on business school graduates and computer models, the modern corporation must basically allocate its investment funds on faith. In the famous phrase used by Keynes, investment depends on the 'animal spirits' of entrepreneurs.

Our problem is that the animal spirits are burning low. As a class, the captains of industry are a cautious lot, a few well-publicised exceptions (Freddy Laker, Clive Sinclair) notwithstanding. They draw in their horns quickly when they sense any weakening in market conditions. And because of the multiplying linkages that make one firm's spending another's income, cautiousness is contagious.

Now the courageous investor was not at a premium during the two decades of the post-war boom. With the national market growing almost everywhere at between 5 and 10 per cent each year, and international markets expanding even faster, it didn't take a lot of guts to invest in new capacity. Even too large an expansion was soon validated by the brisk growth rates of those days.

But that happy era ended ten years ago. The countries that lost the war (if not all of the ostensible winners) have rebuilt their capital stocks. Europe and Japan have by now caught up with Britain and the United States and joined them as slower-growing, 'mature' industrial societies. The enormous growth in world trade seems to have reached its limits. There may even be fewer exciting new products and technologies around, outside the computer industry, to stir up the entrepreneurial juices.

It is hard to sort-out causation, since the prospect of lower growth rates induces investment cutbacks which then ensure that growth *will* slow, but the problem is by now manifest – a 'de-industrialisation' of our economies; a shortage of the up-to-date capital needed to equip our still-growing labour forces for productive work. American business, once the undisputed role model for capitalists everywhere, is now being criticised for its alleged bias against the sort of long-term, slow-payback investment in new markets and technologies that has apparently typified much of Japan's industrial effort.

So what can be done to restore entrepreneurial nerve? We need first to identify the factors that cause animal spirits to soar and sag. A lot of research has been done on this, and has succeeded in establishing one important proposition, that the single measurable factor that contributes most to investment decisions is the pressure of demand on capacity. When business sees its inventories falling, and its order books fattening, it can see the pay-off from investing in new plant and machinery. Other factors seem much less impressive. Interest rates measuring the cost of borrowing investment funds are not normally very important. It took the extraordinarily high interest rates of 1982 to generate signs of a significant relationship with investment. In particular, prices do not seem to influence investment very much, outside of markets for primary products, such as food and minerals. That is, for all their doctrinal support of 'free markets' and 'the price mechanism', the captains of industry do not pay price signals much attention when making their most important investment decisions.[2]

This is not difficult to justify. Price signals are usually not very clear. An increase in the market price may indicate a shortfall in supply relative to demand, but it does not reveal the *size* of the discrepancy. That is, it does not inform prospective investors how much capacity needs to be added before price will fall to its equilibrium level. To know this, firms must know as well the elasticity of demand — that is, the *amount* price will fall when supply is increased — and data on elasticities are notoriously sparse.

In contrast, a firm with falling inventories and increasing order backlogs can *see* what the supply shortfall is, and so can calculate directly and quite accurately (at least over the short-to-medium time horizon) what extra capacity it needs. No elasticity information is needed.

Here, then, is the place for price controls. By ruling out inflationary price rises, controls would divert demand to press against capacity, and so encourage investment. This pressure, if maintained, should be sufficient to trigger an expansion of investment and output leading eventually to the restoration of full employment. All that government would need to do would be to maintain the growth of aggregate demand at a rate about equal to the rate at which the economy was able to increase capacity and output. The process would get a kick along from the multiplier effects of an initial boost to incomes in the sectors where investment goods are produced, leading to further increases in demand through all sectors of the economy. The private sector would be doing the job itself; investing and increasing employment for the most persuasive of reasons — a healthy profit.

How long would it take? I do not know; nor do I believe that this matters much. So long as progress is being made (a point or two off the unemployment rate each year, say) we should all be pleased. There is a lot of work to be done. Not only must the stock of physical capital be rebuilt, but the supply of 'human capital' – the knowledge and skills of the workforce – has been seriously eroded by persistent and high unemployment. All activities, including work, need constant practice if they are to be performed well. Many skills, including the basic ones of reliable performance and working in teams, can only be learnt 'on the job'. The total value of human capital has been estimated as worth about as much as tangible plant and machinery.[3] It may take many years to create and re-create the skills that a high-employment economy needs.

Suppose, then, that we do eventually succeed in pulling down unemployment rates to satisfactory levels; to, say, the 1 or 2 per cent that was last enjoyed in the 1950s. Could this be *maintained*? Is it possible to avoid the peaks and troughs of the business cycle that were a feature even of the best decades of the post-war boom? It is not likely to be possible, or even desirable, for a national government to stamp out all sources of fluctuations in aggregate economic activity (many of which are international in origin). But policy in a governed economy should be able to do two things: it should achieve a significant smoothing out of the cycle, and, most importantly, it should be able to prevent the troughs from showing up as unemployment.

What is the nature of the problem? The high-growth decades ending with the first big oil price increase in 1973 can be seen as a period of favourable 'supply shocks' – investment booms to replace obsolete plant; diffusion of new technologies; access to cheap world market sources of commodities. Shocks like these allow an economy temporarily to bypass the Phillips curve. That is, because they increase national productivity, 'good' supply shocks are anti-inflationary, and so permit the economy to get closer to full employment without price increases. But as the effects on productivity growth of each shock wear off, the latent inflationary pressures reassert themselves. Government then has to deliberately contract the economy – which has always meant increasing unemployment – in order to keep inflation from taking-off. As noted above, it is not reasonable to expect another run of pleasant supply shocks to match those of the 1950s and 1960s. We can dream about them (discovery of an abundantly cheap oil substitute; world disarmament; a big increase in trade with developing economies) but pleasant surprises cannot be counted on in economic strategies.

But, with price controls to deal with the Phillips curve inflation/

140 *Getting the Big Numbers to Add Up*

unemployment trade-off, there is no reason why the economy should not be kept permanently at full employment. Recall from Chapter 8 the arguments about the role unemployment plays. In an old-style managed economy it is used as a sanction, as a stick to beat down inflationary wage and price increases. *It is not useful in itself.* In particular, the old rationale that a 'pool' of unemployed people is needed to facilitate the continual process of structural adjustment is a myth. Indeed, a 'tight' labour market probably *facilitates* the necessary movements of workers from declining to growing occupations and industries. This is because turnover rates are higher when unemployment is low – more workers pass through the labour market when people have the job security that encourages voluntary mobility. It is in recessions that the pressures to protect jobs in dying industries and firms are greatest.

Once they settled down to the full employment level of GNP, firms would build up margins of spare capacity and inventories of materials and goods, just as they do in any equilibrium situation, in order to cope with the unforeseeable twists and turns of the market. Some firms may 'hoard' some labour (employ more workers than are currently needed) for the same reason. All this makes good business sense. But it makes no sense for society as a whole to hoard labour; to maintain a stock of millions of idle and unhappy unemployed workers.

Still, some policy action would be needed. Events such as changes in demand for exports as a result of other economies' business cycles cannot be controlled, and so must be compensated for. The goal of policy should be to stabilise aggregate demand at the level that will keep output at full-employment rates. There is nothing novel about this suggestion, of course, given that governments actually legislated such a responsibility upon themselves at the end of the Second World War, and that they did set out to use the available tools of monetary and fiscal policy to fulfill it.

The relative mildness of post-war business cycles (until the current one) is probably evidence of some success in the application of stabilisation policy. The problem, though, has always been that two goals – inflation and unemployment – were being aimed at with the single instrument of aggregate demand management.

But with inflation under control, central bankers and treasury officials should be sufficiently expert to keep aggregate demand close to full employment levels. They might need some help. There are problems with orthodox demand management policies: in a lumpy economy they often impact unevenly on different groups; they take time to work, and sometimes induce surprising side-effects. Thus, a more direct means of adding a bit to aggregate demand one year, and taking some off the next, could be useful. Some attention has been paid recently to the Swedish Investment Funds system. This allows firms to place up to one fifth of their profits in tax-free funds from which the authorities can release them to finance investment during recessions. The scheme seems to have been quite successful.[4]

Other policies have been devised.[5] Government could set up a fund for making grants or low-interest loans to local authorities and voluntary organisations for labour-intensive activities, with the amount disbursed varied counter-cyclically. Shrewdly designed wage subsidies can encourage employment, though these are a little too 'micro' for my taste.[6]

What do not work well are job creation schemes aimed at 'disadvantaged' members of the labour force. Such programs do succeed in making work for the middle-class types who run them, but are not a cost-effective tool for lowering unemployment rates.[7] This is not surprising – from a governed economy perspective targeted job-creation is hopelessly inappropriate, with high-level government trying to reach down to mop up specific pockets of unemployment. Indeed, by focusing attention on particular classes of workers, these programs may actually *reduce* their chances of employment, since employers may, rightly or wrongly, associate assisted workers with low productivity.[8] In any case, the bureaucracy needed to run job creation programs generates a ratchet effect – it is administratively easier to expand these programs than to contract them. This makes them unsuitable as stabilisation policies, which must be flexible enough to reduce employment as well as increase it.

By far the best that government can do for high-unemployment groups would be to keep the big number (the average unemployment rate across the economy) small, so that employers have the best incentive of all, a labour shortage, to take on unattractive workers and upgrade their skills on the job.

Stabilising aggregate demand in a full-employment economy would not be trivial. The authorities would need to monitor the 'queues' of unfilled orders and unsold inventories, and react to changes in these. If orders build up and inventories run down too far, the economy 'overheats', which under a price controls regime would mean the emergence of shortages – of real queues of consumers in the shops. At the other extreme they would risk the re-emergence of queues of unemployed workers.

But the normal margin of slack in the economy should give enough room for a stabilisation policy to operate successfully, facilitated by two factors:

(1)   Elasticity-augmenting policies that are part of the governed economy approach would help the system deal with unemployment by itself. Higher elasticities mean more response to price cuts in markets where excess supply appears. Full employment would itself increase elasticity, by easing the process of structural re-allocation of resources between declining and growing industries.

(2)   Stability is self-perpetuating. If business comes to believe that full employment will be maintained over the medium term, then it is less likely to react to a short-term slackening of demand by cutting inventories and laying-off workers. That is, it is less likely to exacerbate fluctuations; to make expectations of a slump or boom self-fulfilling. It has been noted that most of the observed ups and downs in GNP are in fact accounted for by swings in inventory investment, much of which is due to de-stabilising swings in business expectations.[9]

To summarise: a governed economy could achieve and maintain full employment. The key is to have inflation looked after by a separate policy: retail price controls. Demand then induces higher output rather than higher prices, and the tools of stabilisation policy, including orthodox monetary and fiscal management, can be focused on keeping aggregate demand approximately sufficient to maintain full-employment output levels.

What this amounts to is a transformation of demand management from an awkward, low-level behavioural policy to an appropriate adding-up policy. With the former, the authorities need to know and worry about just how the economy will split aggregate demand between inflation and real output. With the latter, they need only react to changes in orders and inventories to ensure adding-up. If inventories fall, demand should be reduced, and vice versa. It may not be quite this simple, but it seems appropriate to try.

17 Trade and Exchange Rates

'How innocent we were!'

RONALD MACKINNON

(on the benefits expected from floating exchange rates in the early 1970s)

The biggest of the big numbers of economic performance are certainly unemployment and the inflation rate. But related to these two, and of considerable importance in their own right, are the numbers measuring the economy's performance on foreign trade and in its public sector. We look at trade in this chapter, and the public sector in the next.

The importance to an economy of its dealings with other economies is related to its size. As a rule of thumb, the bigger a country the smaller the proportion of its gross national product traded abroad. This is simply because in a large economy, there is more room for internal trade – for shipping goods around within the borders of the country. Thus, exports of goods and services from the United States are about 10 per cent of GNP, and from Canada, which is about one tenth the economic size of the US, more than 30 per cent.

There are many trade-determining factors other than size, however. These include the economy's need to pay for raw material and food imports, and its economic history as a colonial power. Britain, as a result, though a larger economy than Canada, exports and imports a similar proportion of its GNP. All these are big numbers, which have increased in the post-war period. The United States, in particular, has raised its exposure to world markets, in part unwillingly due to its need to pay more for oil imports in the last decade. Imports into the US were only 3.5 per cent of its GNP in 1946.

So, we live in what are called 'open' economies – economies in which domestic events are very much exposed to influence from what goes on in other economies and in world markets. This complicates policy-making, for two reasons:

(1) It brings in another adding-up requirement. To full employment and a stable price level we must add the constraint that, over the long-

143

run, anyway, the value of an economy's exports must equal the value of its imports (plus or minus the position with respect to foreign investments, which are not of concern here). This is because it is from exporting that we earn the foreign currency needed to pay for our imports.

(2)   The trade situation has implications for inflation and unemployment. The cost of imported goods enters directly into the consumer price index, and has an indirect influence through competition with local producers. Exports have a multiplier effect on domestic output and employment. And imports are a 'leakage' of domestic spending out of the domestic economy, which can frustrate attempts to expand the economy to full employment.

This last complication is particularly familiar to the British, who have had the brakes applied to most of their post-war expansions not so much because of inflationary pressures, but due to alarming build-ups in the trade deficit, with imports outstripping exports and so requiring the Bank of England to dip into its reserves of foreign exchange to make up the difference. This led the economist Samuel Brittan, a leading sceptic of the efficacy of Keynesian stabilisation policy, to complain

> In the 1950s and early 1960s the Treasury behaved like a simple Pavlovian dog responding to two main stimuli: one is 'a run on the reserves', and the other is '500,000 unemployed'.[1]

Times have changed. North Sea Oil has dampened concern about the balance of payments, and it is a long time since anyone grumbled about half a million being unemployed. But the underlying difficulties for Britain are worse now — what is needed is a strategy that will increase aggregate demand by enough to raise employment by at least 10 per cent without having this leaked away by a manufacturing sector already gravely weakened by the recession and the high value of the oil-backed pound sterling. With its much smaller import/GNP ratio, the leakage problem is less severe for the United States. I will focus, then on the British situation.

Fortunately, the problem is not fundamental. Given time, domestic industry could gear-up again to produce the goods. But in the short-term, supply elasticities are higher for imports. The great world market can respond more quickly to an increase in demand. And once they get an extra bit of market share, importers tend to hold onto it, since domestic capacity adjusts down to the new market situation. Thus, import penetration has ratcheted upwards in the UK.[2]

In the economics of trade, a key variable is the exchange rate – the price of the local currency in foreign currency units. The exchange rate affects both imports and exports. Suppose that the pound sterling rate falls, or 'depreciates'. This means that it takes fewer marks, francs, US dollars or whatever, to buy one pound; or, equivalently, that it takes more pence to buy one dollar. As a result, the amount of their own currency that a foreigner has to give up to buy a given number of pounds, in order to pay for a British-made good, falls. That is, British goods are cheaper on the world market, and so the demand for them will increase, to an extent determined by the elasticity of demand. As for imports, if the number of pounds British consumers must give up to buy the foreign currency needed to purchase foreign-made goods has gone up, so, then, will their price on the UK market, leading to a reduction in demand, the extent of which depends on the price elasticity of demand for imports. The import and export effects of a depreciation are mutually reinforcing in their implications for the balance of trade – both result in an 'improvement' – an increase in the surplus of exports over imports, or a decrease in the deficit, depending on where the economy is starting from.

An 'appreciation' of the exchange rate naturally works the other way. Thus, we have a price variable which should, in theory, be able to compensate for the fluctuations in the other factors that influence trade (notably the level of GNP at home and abroad, which determines the incomes available to buy goods and the productive capacity to produce them) to keep exports and imports in balance; to ensure that these big numbers add up as they should.

However, following the Second World War, most countries 'fixed' their exchange rates, holding them constant for long periods until forced to change by persistent trade surpluses or deficits. This system worked well enough at first, but strains began to develop in the 1960s, when inflation began to increase at different rates in different countries. The pound became a 'weak' currency, as Britain's lower productivity growth caused its domestic price level to rise more quickly than that of its major trading partners. There was often pressure for a devaluation (the word used for a depreciation when the rate is set by government) to restore relative prices of domestic and foreign-made goods.

For some reason 'defending the pound' became a matter of national pride, or was interpreted as such by the politicians. Instead of devaluing, they would deliberately induce some unemployment in order to reduce incomes and thus the demand for all goods, including imports. The 'fundamentals' were still wrong, however, and by 1967 the speculators had sold so much sterling that devaluation became unavoidable. The pound was cut from \$2.80 to \$2.40 in November, giving the speculators an instant profit at the expense of the Bank of England, and so ultimately, of the British people.[3]

This would not do. Pressure for reform grew, in Britain and in other countries, and culminated in the introduction of 'floating' exchange rates in 1973.[4] These allowed exchange rates to rise and fall on the tide of market forces. It seemed a good idea at the time to eliminate the rigidities and distortions of the fixed rates system, and allow countries to regain some independence in their domestic economic policies.

But it has not worked. After ten years of floating rates, it is almost unanimously agreed that they have been a disappointment. Exchange rates have fluctuated much more than expected, with destabilising effects on domestic economies. And persistent balance of payments disequilibria have not been eliminated. The 'surplus' countries — Japan, West Germany, Switzerland — have stayed that way; the economies which began the period with chronic tendencies to run deficits (Britain, the US) still have problems. Central banks have actually intervened more in foreign exchange markets than they did under the previous fixed rate system.[5]

What has gone wrong? Once again an overdose of neoclassical economics is to blame. Neoclassical faith in the existence of optimal prices, and in the market forces that will find them, has proved as optimistic in the international sphere as it was for inflation and unemployment in domestic economies. Specifically, the floating rates model is inadequate on two points.

First, it misses the speculators and money managers who buy and sell currencies in the expectation of future exchange rate changes, and in the search for the highest short-term rates of interest. Economists are still not sure whether speculation is ultimately stabilising or destabilising. Keynes at first thought that it was a good thing, and he was very good at it; making fortunes for himself and his college by speculating on the stock market. Later in his life, apparently his views altered.[6] It is undeniable that speculation can result in large short-term swings, and that, when what is being speculated on is not just a paper asset but also a price of considerable importance to economic decision-making, these swings are a sizeable nuisance. So it has been with exchange rates.

The second problem is with the equilibrium price toward which speculators may or may not be swinging. If markets were perfectly competitive, then such a price would exist. But the reality of trade seems to be different; more 'structured' than the smooth homogeneity of neoclassical theory.

It turns out that we may need, in effect, *two* exchange rates — one for exports, the other for imports (and perhaps a third for capital flows).

Why? Countries tend to specialise in making the things that they are good at, and import as much as they can afford of the rest of their needs. This is obviously true of primary produce-exporting countries like New Zealand and Canada, but it holds too for a manufacturing economy. Firms concentrate on whatever special products they have some advantage in, then look for export markets to enable them to take full advantage of scale economies in producing these goods. Reciprocally, a country's imports are made up of a large variety of many other countries' speciality products. Any economy's detailed trade statistics reveal the number of products exported in significant quantities to be smaller than the number imported.

What are the implications of this for exchange rates? For exports, it is preferable that the exchange rate be *stable*, for two reasons:

(1)   Specialist exporters have a lot at stake. They must plan marketing and investment with the foreign market in mind. If they make a mistake, the domestic market will not be large enough to absorb it. But swings in the exchange rate of plus or minus 10 per cent a year (which have been quite common) can easily wipe out trading profits, and make it very difficult to plan. As a consequence, investing in exports is discouraged.

(2)   Some of the income from selling a specialised commodity goes as 'rent' to the owner of whatever it is that provides the special touch. This may be land, in the case of agricultural products, or it can be some special entrepreneurial flair, or design skill, encapsulated in a manufactured good. Changes in exchange rates often result in large changes in these rents, which have accidental and therefore undesirable implications for the distribution of incomes in the economy. For example, about half the 1979—80 profits of the Canadian pulp and paper industry were due to the 20 per cent fall in the Canadian dollar since 1976. These profits were paid for by Canadian consumers in general, for whom the depreciation has meant higher prices for imported goods.

So, a stable exchange rate would be good for exports. It may not even matter much what *level* the exchange rate is stabilised at, within limits, since the rate, if stable, is eventually capitalised into the market value of rent-yielding assets, leaving other prices unaffected.

But imports are a quite different story. After some year-to-year averaging, we should spend on imports no more and no less than we earn from exports (and receive in net foreign capital inflows). A persistent discrepancy means an accumulated running up or down in the country's reserves of foreign exchange (and/or in its short-term borrowing and lending), and difficulties in maintaining non-inflationary full employment.

Now, even with a stable exchange rate, export earnings fluctuate considerably. World market prices change, and so do supply conditions in the exporting country. In addition, other factors important to the domestic demand for imports have their ups and downs – world market prices, again, and domestic incomes. This means that if one variable – the exchange rate – is to keep imports in balance with exports in the face of uncontrollable variations in all the other factors, it should be able to alter a lot. For example, when export receipts are down, or domestic demand pressure high, we will need a sizeable depreciation of the exchange rate to make imports more expensive, and thus discourage them. It probably takes a 10 per cent change in the exchange rate to get as much as a 5 per cent change in imports.[7] How could these conflicting requirements be resolved? I suggest a two-pronged policy.

For the sake of export stability, the exchange rate should be set by government on what is called a 'crawling peg'. At any time, the exchange rate is fixed, or 'pegged' to a certain value relative to other currencies, but this rate is changed periodically to compensate for international movements in relative prices. Amongst economists there is some support for crawling pegs. They avoid the rigidities of simple fixed rates, and the volatility of floating rates, and are less attractive to speculators than either of the other systems.

The peg should be adjusted frequently, according to a simple and well-known rule. Then it would be a good governed economy policy – an economic law setting a stable framework for private sector decision-making – not susceptible to the 'fine-tuning' itch of the managed economy, nor to the lobbying of interest groups.

What precisely should the simple rule be? There is quite a substantial technical literature on the 'optimal peg'.[8] I would conjecture that a good rule would keep the home country currency value of the average of prices received for exports and paid for imports equal to the home country's consumer price index. For example, suppose that the country had successful retail price controls, so that the value of the CPI did not change. Then if all foreign prices (of exports and imports) rose by 5 per cent, so too would the exchange rate, leaving the local-currency price of exports and imports unchanged. This is as it should be, since nothing 'real' has altered – we have just compensated for differences in inflation rates.

However, because the structure of a country's exports and its imports usually differ, export prices and import prices typically change at different rates. In particular, primary product prices in world markets fluctuate rather more than do prices of manufactured goods. Suppose, for example, that the price we receive for our exports goes up by 10 per cent, while that paid, on average, for imports only rises by 5 per cent. This is called an 'improvement in the terms of trade', and is obviously a nice thing to happen to us. Under the crawling peg rule, the exchange rate would be appreciated by 7½ per cent. Thus, in domestic currency, exporters would receive 2½ per cent more, and purchasers of imports would pay the same amount less. The benefits of the terms of trade improvement would be divided equally between exporters and importers.

Of course, such a rule would be to an extent arbitrary, and therefore not generally 'optimal'. But a major point of this book is that the private sector will adjust comfortably to any approximately sensible policy rule, so long as it can *rely* on it staying the same. In the long-run, stability of policies is much more valuable to the economy than is the futile chasing-around for the precisely optimal response to every economic problem.

What about controlling the quantity of imports, to keep them in line with the economy's capacity to pay with the foreign exchange earned from exporting? A slow-changing crawling peg will not handle this. What is needed is a means of putting a 'wedge' between the official exchange rate and the price paid for imports. Some countries actually do set different exchange rates for exports and imports, and even for sub-categories, such as overseas investment and tourists. Mexico and Brazil are current examples. But these require all sorts of exchange controls and other bureaucratic interventions to make them function, and are probably not to be seriously considered for the developed, open economies that we are concerned with here.

The developed countries do in fact have a system of wedges in place. They are called tariffs. But these seem largely suited to the microeconomic purposes (of dubious validity) of protecting individual industries. They are costly to alter frequently, and susceptible to political meddling. And, as with any low-level behavioural policy, there is a knowledge problem to setting tariffs — we need to know all the elasticities to predict how market demand will actually respond. In any case, most of the developed economies have signed the GATT (General Agreement on Trade and Tariffs), which commits them to further reductions in tariffs, and rules out their use as a flexible macroeconomic policy.

One possibility, urged in particular by some Cambridge (England) economists,[9] is direct controls on imports. Comprehensive controls would limit imports. But they represent micro-meddling on a grand scale. On what grounds would each of the thousands of commodities imported be assigned its particular quota? How would the lobbying of powerful industrial interest groups be resisted? Satisfactory answers to these questions are not likely to be forthcoming.

We need a governed economy approach — a performance policy which ensures that imports 'perform' satisfactorily — that is, that they add-up to the desired total, while staying clear of the microeconomic business of the economy. Such a policy has already been suggested, notably by Lord Kaldor and Wynne Godley.[10] The idea is that government sell off licences to import to the highest bidder. A licence would specify a certain *value* of imports, but not the actual nature of these. The total amount of licences put on the market would equal the desired value of imports, given the economy's earnings from exports.

The licences should be fully negotiable, that is, able to be bought and sold privately. Thus a market price would be established which would economically allocate imports to those to whom they were worth most, ie, those prepared to pay the price. Formally, this price would be equivalent to a tariff, but the great advantage of the scheme is that the policy-maker need not have to guess in advance what the value would be: the market alone would establish that. Negotiable import licences would ensure adding-up, while not preventing the efficient use of imports at the micro-economic level. The actual number issued would be subject to revision, as export market conditions altered, and as policy-makers corrected mistakes in their forecasts of these conditions. But 'mistakes' at this high level do not much matter, so long as they are not cumulative, since the private sector is left plenty of room within which to adjust.

A negotiable import licence system would be useful at both stages of the economic strategy to achieve and maintain non-inflationary full employment. In the recovery stage, it would give domestic industry a breathing space in which to build up its capacity and output without demand leaking away to quicker-off-the-mark importers. And once full employment had been reached, the licences would allow policy-makers to concentrate on keeping aggregate demand matched to potential output, without having to worry as well about the side-effects of monetary and fiscal policies on the balance of payments.

It is often argued that direct controls on imports are 'protectionist', and so contrary to GATT rules and liable to provoke retaliation. But this misses the point of these policies, as the Cambridge economists have pointed out. They are *not* designed to *reduce* imports, but rather to prevent an increase in imports, beyond an economy's capacity to pay with exports, from stifling efforts to expand to full employment, as happened in so many post-war British expansions. Indeed, the larger capacity and higher productivity of a full employment economy would no doubt lead to an increase in exports, and so permit an increase in the quantity of import licences issued. In an economy with full employment, the market value of these could drop to zero.

The International Monetary Fund, and other guardians of proper economic behaviour, seem to believe that the only good medicine for a sick balance of payments is a nasty dose of mass unemployment. In this case, the cure may be worse than the disease. A more equitable and efficient antidote is available.

18 Government: the Deficit and What to Do About It

'A billion here, and a billion there, and pretty soon it adds up to some real money.'

SENATOR EVERETT DIRKSEN

The largest single lump in the lumpy economy is government itself. In the OECD economies, government spending averages around 40 per cent of Gross National Product. This is a large number, and one that has grown about fourfold since the end of the First World War.[1]

There are three aspects to the government budget: what the money is spent on; where the money comes from; and the gap between spending and tax revenues – the surplus or deficit. All three are controversial.

Government spending can be divided into three categories:

(1)   Government undertakes various activities which the unorganised citizenry cannot be expected to handle for themselves. These include the provision of 'public goods', which are shared by all: national security, law and order, infrastructure, dealing with spillovers or 'externalities', and running 'natural monopolies', such as water and sewage systems, and the post office. Such are the traditionally approved state interventions in the economy, and they raise numerous problems of scope and detail. Some of these will be relevant to later chapters on regulation, but on the whole public goods, externalities, and natural monopolies are not central to the concerns of this book. They currently consume about 28 per cent of government budgets in the UK, of which nearly half is absorbed by the armed forces.[2]

(2)   The largest category of spending is *handouts*, which took about 65 per cent of the total budgets of governments at various levels in 1980. These can be cash in the hand – 'transfer payments' – such as pensions,

152

unemployment and welfare benefits, and family allowances; or payment in kind, such as free education and health care. In an honestly administered liberal state, handouts are normally designed to assist people whose incomes from private sector sources are judged too low to enable them to achieve a socially acceptable standard of living. Other motivations are possible (for example, to buy votes, or to impose cultural uniformity through state control of education) but amelioration of economic inequality is the primary and most respectable goal of handouts.

(3) The remaining cheques written by government officials support various economic activities: agricultural subsidies; regional investment and employment grants; assistance to exporters. In most European countries the bulk of these expenditures are now made by the European Economic Community. It is quite difficult to know just how much is involved, because a good deal of the money is disbursed in the form of 'tax expenditures' (that is, as exemptions from paying tax rather than as a direct cash grant) which do not show up in conventional accounts of government spending. However, direct subsidies from British local and national governments added up to about 6 per cent of the 1980 budgets. To put this in perspective, it has been calculated that the cumulated subsidies and tax expenditures to business in the UK since the early 1950s have been equivalent to about half of the taxes collected from companies in that period.[3]

Together, the various government expenditures make a substantial sum. Is it all justified? I will argue that in a successful economy government expenditures would take a significantly smaller proportion of GNP than they do now.

The key is full employment. Unemployment was by 1980 directly responsible for transfer payments of about 25 per cent of total expenditures (and a lot more by 1983). Most of these would be unnecessary in a fully-employed economy. Full employment means higher incomes, which means higher revenues for business, including subsidised state-run enterprises. Full employment would eliminate the macroeconomic justification — more jobs — for propping-up the more uneconomic nationalised industries, such as British Leyland and British Steel. This would save a few billions.

Indeed, a government restricting itself to appropriate policies would eschew completely 'micro-meddling', including the whole panoply of industrial and regional subsidies and grants. The point I have stressed is that, although some such programs turn out successfully, the system of micro-meddling as a whole is inappropriate for high-level national governments. The tools available are too clumsy for low-level intervention to be generally successful. As well as the policies that turn out badly, micro-meddling generates wasteful incentives to the private sector to engage in 'rent-seeking' efforts to influence the policy process.

Thus, the only appropriate solution is for high-level government to 'tie its own hands'; to extricate itself completely from the micro-meddling business, and to resist the temptation to get involved in even the most promising and deserving situations. 'If it is such a good deal, why won't the private sector do it by themselves?' should be the attitude, even (perhaps, especially) of a socialist government. The above-the-line savings from an end to microeconomic expenditures would be at least 5 per cent of current government spending.[4] Added to this would be substantial savings from elimination of tax expenditures, and in adminstrative costs, and in the private-sector resources devoted now to lobbying and other-wise dealing with government.

Finally, full employment would provide a decent environment within which government could put its own affairs in order. A strict 'adding-up' constraint on total spending could be imposed by the legislature. This would mean that politicians and bureaucrats yielding to their natural urge to introduce new social programs would have to find existing pro-grams to cut. Adjustment within government would be facilitated by eliminating the job tenure rights of public servants. Such would increase the elasticity of the public sector.

In times of more than 10 per cent unemployment, there is resistance to this sort of thing. Such is understandable, if unfair to the already unemployed and new entrants to the labour force, whom the combination of job security and hiring freezes is keeping out of public sector employ-ment. But with full employment, the legitimacy of objections to more flexibility in government spending would evaporate. There would be plenty of job opportunities for everyone.

What about the other side of the public sector accounts — its revenues? There can hardly be a more vivid example of the pitfalls of our present attempts at running a managed economy than is provided by the taxation system. The simple and respectable revenue-raising rationale for taxes has been overlaid with two less straightforward objectives. One is to help implement the social goal of income redistribution. The other is to use taxes as an instrument of economic policy. In both cases the goals may be entirely worthy, but the instruments are inappropriate.

It is a familiar story. Government introduces a tax which requires both precise knowledge of how the private sector behaves, and the power to bend it to the policy-maker's will. There are almost always surprises and side-effects which confound the good intentions of the tax, and eventually necessitate some sort of corrective action. This has now reached the point where a good proportion of the initiatives proudly unveiled by finance ministers in their annual budgets are no more than efforts to undo the damage done by their predecessors.

A major example is the attempt to redistribute income with 'progressive' tax rates: rates which increase for taxpayers in higher income brackets. Do the wealthy actually pay anything like the taxes implied by the progressive schedule? Of course they do not. There are loopholes, exemptions, shelters; most of them the unintended result of past efforts to 'tune' the tax take. And there are clever lawyers and accountants to steer their clients towards the best deals.

This means, first, that progressive taxation has failed to effect a significant redistribution of incomes and wealth. Though people on low incomes pay little or no tax on incomes (they do pay indirectly, through sales and value added taxes), there is little difference in the proportional burdens of middle and upper income groups.[5] The ease with which the rich slough off their nominal liabilities has led one American researcher to describe his country's estate tax as essentially 'voluntary'; serving 'no purpose other than to give reassurance to the millions of unwealthy that entrenched wealth is being attacked'.[6] In Britain, there used to be a 98 per cent maximum rate on investment income, which was only paid by people who 'choose to do so'.[7]

The second unfortunate consequence of the present tax system is an inefficient allocation of resources. Taxes jam a wedge between real returns on projects and the returns actually received by investors. This may not be distortionary if wedges are of the same thickness, so that the ranking of projects is not affected by taxation. But our highly complicated system results in tax rates that differ widely, and so play topsy-turvy with rates of return. Thus, in Britain, the tax structure diverts about 80 per cent of personal savings to the big institutions (pension funds, insurance companies, building societies) who in turn invest the money mostly in government securities, property, and 'blue chip' shares. Where the funds do not go is into small businesses and innovative but risky new firms and industries.[8]

Thirdly, high marginal tax rates on upper income earners probably do not discourage work, as is sometimes claimed, but they certainly do discourage paying taxes. Hard data are obviously lacking, but the size of the 'underground' or 'black' economy has been estimated at anywhere from 5 to 20 per cent of measured GNP.[9] Underground activities range from out-and-out crime to the barter of services between respectable professional people; what they all have in common is that they are untaxed.

Illegal evasion (and legal but unsporting 'avoidance') forces government to compensate by squeezing more out of the unfortunate wage and salary earners who are not in a position to dodge taxes. Such is unfair, and ultimately likely to erode the effectivenss of the whole system, by destroying the public's perception of its legitimacy.

Finally, the 'paper entrepreneurship' that goes into avoiding and evading taxes is pure waste. It creates no new wealth, but just contests the division of the existing pie. There must be more productive things for all those clever tax consultants to do.

These complaints are not novel. Pressure for tax reform has been growing for some years, and the matter has been extensively studied by Task Forces and Commissions in a number of countries. The general direction for reform is clear. The tax system must be *simplified*. There are different views as to how this should be done. In Britain, the Meade Committee has recommended moving to an 'expenditure tax', as have also a US Treasury group, and a Swedish Royal Commission.[10] This would involve taxing individuals and firms on what they *spend* (on their cash flow) rather than on what they *earn*. There are theoretical pros and cons to expenditure taxes, but their main virtue may be their relative simplicity. The mood has changed from the hopeful fine-tuning of 'optimal' tax theorists, to a more sensible appreciation of what a tax system can, in practice, be expected to deliver.

Between one quarter and one half of government revenues in most economies are already collected by expenditure taxes in the form of sales taxes levied on most goods and services.[11] A disadvantage is that these taxes cannot be made progressive in order that the rich pay relatively more, except by the value-laden singling-out of 'luxury' goods for higher rates. Thus, sales taxes should probably be supplemented by returns filed by individuals, as at present. But these should be a lot simpler than they are now, with an absolute minimum of loophole-widening special cases and exemptions. The choice between home-owning and renting should no longer be distorted by interest-deductibility. The extraordinary British custom of selling more than one half of new cars to companies, rather than to the individuals who will use them, should no longer be profitable.

Nor should the tax schedule be more than mildly progressive. Opening up a gap between average and marginal tax rates induces inefficient avoidance and evasion activities. The tax system just is not a very good instrument for effecting a substantial redistribution of income. If the government thinks that some people are getting too rich, they should do something about the *source* of the wealth; not try and snatch it back after it has been earned. Some of the policies proposed elsewhere in this book would help. A stable non-inflationary environment would discourage speculators. Anti-monopoly laws should be strengthened, as should those concerned with the exploitation of women. De-criminalising drugs would impoverish organised crime. A high-elasticity economy would have fewer niches for privilege and protected interests.

In summary, the motto of tax reform should be *For simplicity without exceptions*. Taxes can be a tolerable method of raising revenues. They are not well-suited to micro-meddling with the distribution of income, or with the allocation of resources.

A final note: although they have already been discredited by events, the Reagan administration's supply-side tax cuts deserve a mention. These were ostensibly based on the premise that the US economy is so far up its 'Laffer curve' that a reduction in tax rates would encourage a spurt of effort sufficient to expand the tax base enough to maintain total revenues. Available research on the relationship between work and taxes gives absolutely no support to the supply-side premise, and even back-of-the-envelope calculations demonstrate its implausibility.[12] J. K. Galbraith, James Tobin, Emma Rothschild and others have concluded that the whole exercise is a thinly-veiled effort to redistribute income from the poor to the rich; a 'counter-revolution' against the welfare state.[13]

Having discussed separately the expenditure and revenue sides of government's ledger, the last step is to put them together, and examine the budget deficit or surplus.

The traditional Keynesian recommendation was that finance ministers should stabilise aggregate demand by running deficits in recessions, and surpluses at peaks in the business cycle, so as to lean against swings in private sector spending. There was some political innocence in this pre-scription. The problem is that politicians, once given a legitimate-sounding excuse for deficit spending, wish to do so whatever the situation of the economy. It seems now that political reluctance to cut spending programs or increase taxes, coupled with steadily-deteriorating economic performance over the last decade, have resulted in deficits becoming an apparently permanent feature of the macroeconomic landscape.[14]

This has encouraged cries for a statutory requirement that government balance its budget. From a governed economy point of view, these cries must strike a chord of sympathy: as a participant in the economy, govern-ment should be subject to economic laws just as the private sector is, and a balanced-budget constraint would reduce the scope for micro-meddling and for the political business cycle of election-year largesse.

However, it is extraordinarily difficult to specify precisely how such a statute would be written. It is difficult to define just what a 'balanced budget' even means. The Yale economist William Nordhaus has demonstrated that a $100 billion deficit can be turned into a surplus of more than $100 billion by taking due acount of capital spending and correcting federal debt for inflation.[15] Government could also dodge the statute by relying on non-expenditure programs, such as regulation and loan guarantees. And over what period should the budget be balanced? One year is generally assumed, but why not five years, or one month?

In any case, the arguments for a balanced budget statute lose much of their force in a successful economy. Full employment would swell the tax base, and thus tax revenues, by at least 10 per cent, with no change in the average tax rate. As noted above, expenditures would shrink – perhaps by as much as 20 per cent – with fewer unemployment and welfare payments, and with severe pruning of micro-meddling programs. Government literally would not be able to spend all the money allocated in its budget, and would have to give some of it back to the taxpayer.

To conclude: I have argued that the economy would work better if government's own presence in it were simpler and smaller. The specific suggestions offered here have all been made before, often by people of a *laissez-faire* bent, who are keen to reduce public involvement in the economy at all levels. My reasons are rather different: government should, indeed *must*, be involved in economic policy, but its involvement should be through *laws*, rather than by the exercise of its own bulk in the market place.

Part IV
Policies: Increasing Elasticity

19 Against Monopoly

'If you owe $1000, your bank manager has you in his power. If you owe $1,000,000, you have your bank manager in your power.'

J. M. KEYNES

The point of a governed economy is to ensure that the big numbers of macroeconomic performance add-up satisfactorily. Previous chapters have shown how these adding-up goals can be met despite the loss of microeconomic elasticity that is responsible for present poor performance.

However, it is sensible to look for ways of doing something directly about the elasticity crisis. Although it is most unlikely that the economy could ever be transformed into the super-elastic ideal-type of neoclassical perfect competition, this still leaves plenty of scope for improvement. The decline in elasticity documented in Chapters 5 and 6 is largely endogenous to the economic system. That is, we did it ourselves; and what has been done can presumably be undone.

The economy would certainly benefit from an infusion of elasticity. The more flexible and responsive are economic agents, the easier it would be to put them on the path to non-inflationary full employment. And a more elastic economy would do better on one very important goal that is not, because it is open-ended, susceptible to adding-up policies – namely higher national productivity or GNP per capita. More elastic markets are leaner, smarter, more efficient markets.

Recall how the process works. In the product market where firms sell goods to each other and to consumers, elasticity is largely a matter of the extent of competition. If there are plenty of sellers, no one will have the power to increase price without losing customers. That is, demand elasticities will be high. And the potential for improvements in market share when a firm has only a small part of the market encourages finding ways of cutting costs and thus prices to take advantage of high elasticity.

But the great paradox of capitalism is that individual firms have an incentive to reduce the elasticity of their markets, even though the consequence of all of them so doing is that the system as a whole deteriorates.

One way to make money is to devise a better product, or to find a better way of producing it. But another is to twist the demand curve to permit the same product to be sold for a higher price – to attain some monopoly power. The latter involves a loss in elasticity; a reduction in the choices available to buyers, which contributes to the decline in the power of the price mechanism and leads eventually to the emergence of discontinuities in the system manifested as unemployed labour, idle plant, and inflation.

The dangers inherent in the private sector's quest for power over its markets have long been recognised. Adam Smith (a perceptive critic of free enterprise capitalism) warned in a famous passage about the risks in letting competing sellers consort with each other.[1] More recently, Hugh Gaitskell and G. C. Allen argued (in 1943) that the growth in market power that had occurred even by then was incompatible with post war full employment because of its 'adverse effects on efficiency, the demand for labour, and new enterprise'.[2]

Yet governments have not acted decisively to preserve market forces from the erosion of elasticity. In part, no doubt, this is due to the political power of big business. But there are technical difficulties too in designing suitable policies: our knowledge of elasticity-reducing behaviour is not sufficiently precise to unambiguously support enthusiastic policy activism.

Take the core proposition of traditional anti-monopoly economics; that elasticity-reducing market power is the result of concentration of an industry in the hands of a few large sellers – an oligopoly. This supposedly allows firms to co-ordinate their pricing to avoid competing with each other, and to maintain higher prices and profits without attracting new competition from outside firms.

There is empirical support, from dozens of studies, for the oligopoly model,[3] and it provides the intellectual justification for anti-trust and anti-merger policy. But the doctrine has recently been vigorously challenged by a group of economists led by Harold Demsetz of the University of Chicago. Demsetz points out that the concentration-profitability correlation could be due not to relatively large firms charging higher prices, but to their producing more efficiently at lower costs, due perhaps to scale economies, or to some intrinsic property of 'excellence' that pays-off in both profits and market share.[4] If this interpretation is correct, then applying old-style anti-trust policy to break up big firms could worsen market performance by destroying efficient units, and by diluting the rewards that are the incentive for achieving superiority.

There are other cases of market practices that are difficult to interpret. 'Predatory pricing' – unusually low prices charged to drive out weaker rivals and pave the way for high prices in the future – is tough to distinguish from praiseworthy, may-the-cheapest-seller-win *competition*. Another example surfaces when all the firms in a market (say, tenderers on a contract) quote the same price. This is sometimes taken to be prima-facie evidence of collusion. But in their defence, the firms' lawyers – if they have done first-year economics – can point out that identical prices are a distinguishing characteristic of textbook perfect competition, when no individual seller has the power to charge a price different from the going rate.

The moral that emerges is that rather simple rules-of-thumb are in-adequate. The problem is that orthodox pro-competition policies are *inappropriate*. There is too much 'distance' between policy-makers and the minutiae of real-world markets for the latter to be successfully regu-lated by rigid rules.

In reaction, there have been suggestions that competition policy should shift to a case-by-case, rule-of-reason approach, enforced through the civil code rather than in criminal courts. The European Community has moved in this direction.[5] The idea has some merit, but its application is likely to be ponderous and expensive, and still subject to fundamental doubts about the ability of even the shrewdest economists to reliably specify just how a particular market should operate, and to convince a judge accordingly.

An approach appropriate to the governed economy is needed: high-level goals and policy instruments to match the high-level institution (national government) which must design and implement them. The suitable high-level goal is surely that elasticity in the economy as a whole be increased, whatever happens in particular industries and markets. Then the economy will work better.

What about the instruments? The key is to make use of general and well-established propositions about how the economy operates, without depending on an unattainable degree of reliability and precision in this knowledge. I suggest a two-pronged policy package, with one part acting on the structure of markets that determines performance on elasticity, and the other working directly on performance itself.

First, performance. Firms may try to expand to obtain the market power to push up prices and reduce elasticity; or they may do it for the sake of scale economies and efficiency. The policy-maker cannot expect always to sort-out the two motives. But presumably the firms themselves know what they are doing. If, then, the *pay-off* from market power (higher prices) could be eliminated, one big motive for undesirable elasticity-reducing behaviour would disappear. This effectively turns around the traditional approach to competition policy. Rather than attempting to predict and tinker with the sort of industrial structure and behaviour that leads to poor performance, the governed economy approach would deal directly with performance, and let structure and behaviour look after themselves.

The appropriate instrument for doing this is the retail price controls system proposed in previous chapters to deal with inflation. Recall that the formulae used by the price controllers to adjust relative prices would allow only truly exogenous changes in technology and raw material inputs to result in price decreases and increases. In particular, a deliberately engineered reduction in elasticity would not be an acceptable rationale for a price increase.

Thus, price controls would remove this incentive for further increases in market power. In addition, it is possible that the controllers would develop sufficient expertise to identify past efforts to reduce elasticity, and roll them back. This would mean that big firms whose size was motivated by the desire to gain control over their markets would become relatively unprofitable, and be forced to scale-down their operations. On the other hand, market leaders whose position was won by superior cost performance would not be penalised and could even gain from the reversals suffered by unwieldy rivals.

An anti-inflation policy would no doubt help boost elasticity by imposing 'price-taking' behaviour on firms, and so diverting their attention to lower costs and higher output as the means of increasing profits. But sellers are very clever at devising ways of avoiding price competition, as I found in an analysis of sixty case studies undertaken by the late UK Price Commission.[6] Usually one firm, which often but not always is the biggest in the market, is tacitly nominated as industry 'price leader', and is followed obediently by its 'competitors'. In all but a few markets, there was clear evidence of this or some other form of successful coordination of price among firms.

It would be unrealistic to expect price controllers to pick up and counter all these practices. We should expect that any group of established firms is eventually going to find ways of eliminating 'wasteful' price competition from its markets, given that it is so clearly in its interests to do so. Also, price controllers cannot be expected to have expertise in other important dimensions of elasticity and competition — the speed with which an industry recognises and adopts new products and techniques.

This leads on to the second prong of the pro-competition package, focusing on the *structure* of markets. Can market environments be fostered that encourage good price and productivity performance?

There has been a resurgence of interest in the old notion that established firms should be kept on their toes by the threat of competition from outsiders. In the jargon of what has become a hot new field of microeconomics, markets should be 'contestable'.[7] This means that it should be possible for new sellers to move quickly and cheaply into an industry (and, just as important, be able to move quickly out again) to pluck any excess profits left lying around by incumbent firms, be these due to too-high a price, or to failure to adopt the latest cost-reducing technology.

The big implication of contestability is that the present make-up of an industry may not have much bearing on how well it performs. Even a monopoly could be constrained to be cost-efficient and price-competitive if it had always to contend with the threat of another seller contesting its market. Thus the theorists of contestable markets are trying to revolutionise competition policy by shifting attention from the firms actually present in an industry, to their *potential* competitors lurking in the wings.

In the United States there have been forces pushing towards more contestable markets. In many markets imports now provide a credible competitive threat. And the 'deregulation' of the last five years or so (on which more in the next chapter) has made incumbents in the transportation and communications industries more vulnerable to competition from domestic firms. The net effect, according to the economist W. G. Shepherd, is that the American economy has become more competitive in the last two decades, despite increases in size concentration in most markets.[8]

The effects of greater competition were vividly demonstrated by the accommodating behaviour of two of the most powerful unions in the US, the United Auto Workers and the Teamsters. Faced with increased competition for their employers' products, due, in one case, to Japanese car imports, and in the other to deregulation of the trucking industry, these unions accepted unprecedented real wage losses in efforts to keep their once-mighty employers in business. Although the quantitative importance for the economy at large of these well-publicised events may have been exaggerated,[9] they probably do illustrate a difference between the US economy and the British. The latter is already more concentrated than the United States, or, indeed, than any other major industrial nation. Whereas the largest 100 industrial firms account for 33 per cent of total output in the US, in Britain the equivalent figure is 41 per cent.[10]

Concentration on this scale is likely to limit competition; first because it increases the likelihood that big firms will be able to agree not to contest each others' territory too vigorously, and secondly because it reduces the size of the small-firm sector which, in all economies, is a primary source of new competition. By the early 1970s, just 32 per cent of British industrial workers were in firms with fewer than 500 employees. Corresponding figures for other EEC economies were: 67 per cent in Italy, 52 per cent in France, and 49 per cent in West Germany.[11] These are substantial differences.

It is true that the British economy is relatively 'open' to imports. But, to a surprising extent, imports to the UK are not a source of independent competition, but are controlled by the same multinational firms which also produce within the country.[12] The UK car market provides a vivid demonstration of the consequences of this. Despite being ostensibly involved in a free-trade pact as part of the EEC, British consumers pay significantly more for imported cars than do consumers in other European countries. The strategy appears to be to price imports high enough to allow the least-efficient local producer – British Leyland – to (just) remain in business.[13] The result, in 1981, was about 1 billion pounds in excess prices paid by British consumers to foreign-owned car firms.[14]

Thus, most markets in the UK are far from being fully contestable. What can be done? Not surprisingly, no single, simple policy will deal with the problem. The elasticity crisis is the result of deep-seated and complex forces operating over many decades; forces which were discernible in industrial economies in the time of Marx and Mill. But, contrary to the opinion of Marx, at least, I do not believe the erosion of elasticity – the drive to monopoly – to be irreversible. There are at least five useful policy actions that could be taken by a determined government.

First, *economic laws* have a role. While it may be unwise to attempt to proscribe ambiguous customs like 'predatory' pricing, there are plenty of anti-competitive practices blatant enough to be appropriate targets for legal action. Some of the existing apparatus of anti-monopoly legislation could possibly be prosecuted with more vigour. For example, in the case of the UK car market, recourse could be made to the competition policy legislation of the European Community.[15]

Radical action could be taken against mergers. Studies that have examined the consequences of the great 'merger boom' of the 1960s and 1970s find, almost without exception, that these have turned out to be disappointing, even to the firms concerned: the expected cost efficiencies just have not been realized.[16] Why not, then, simply ban all mergers involving any firm which has more than some set percentage – say 10 per cent – of its market? Certainly, some worthy mergers would thereby be blocked, but the results of the studies on this topic imply that, *on average*, market performance would be improved.

A particularly apt target for legal action is the practice of 'vertical integration' (mergers between buyer and seller) and the 'exclusive dealing' agreements that are a substitute for it. Why not outlaw this sort of thing? Who gains when breweries buy-out pubs, and/or strip them of 'free house' status? Why should petrol stations only be allowed to sell for one oil company?

All this may sound radical, but it is really quite conservative. What we should be doing is rebuilding the network of markets in the economy. Vertical integration and its like are simply devices for withdrawing goods from the market system as they pass through the various stages of production, and substituting internal operating procedures of bureaucratic firms. Every deal that we can force back onto the open market means more opportunities for other firms to get a piece of the action; more choice; more elasticity.

The second sort of pro-elasticity policy would make markets more contestable by increasing the threat to existing firms of entry by new (and therefore small) firms. Government may be able to help more with the fixed-cost expenses that bear relatively heavily on small firms. For example, it could ease the form-filling burden faced by small firms in their dealings with government departments. It could provide, for a fee, more marketing and counselling services aimed at smaller businesses. Governments can even do a good job of providing 'seed money' and venture capital, under certain conditions.

Of course, this involves bureaucrats making financial decisions, but bank managers are bureaucrats too. Publicly-funded development finance corporations have been successful before, at least when they stay clear of out-and-out handouts (grants), and work through properly commercial loans. Certainly, the British taxpayer has got a much better return, pound for pound, from the 'Council for Small Industries in Rural Areas' than from the National Enterprise Board's 'investments' in British Leyland.[17]

Thirdly, we should not neglect the consumer side of the market. Elasticity depends not just on what firms do, but also on how consumers react. We need expert consumers, looking for the best deal. A successful anti-inflation policy would be a big help, as it would allow consumers to focus on *relative* price changes, secure that their measuring rod of 'what a pound is worth' has not become obsolete since last they ventured onto the market.

But more could be done. Organisations such as the Consumer Institute do a good job of testing products and judging value for money (their success, incidently, is evidence in favour of price controllers being able to measure product characteristics objectively). They publish magazines which have a reasonably large following, but their findings might usefully be made more widely accessible. Why not set up an 'Anti-Bullshit Bureau', which would be empowered to add to any piece of media advertising, without warning and at the advertiser's expense, a counter-ad, including any relevant information, such as prices offered elsewhere, or results of expert tests, that the bureau considered likely to be of interest to the consumer. Such a scheme could at least provide employment for out-of-work satirists and comedians, and might well be very popular with the reading and viewing public. It would encourage informative marketing of superior products over the shoddy and the dross.

Fourth, while elasticity policies will assist the economy to achieve the adding-up goals of macroeconomic performance, the reverse is also true. In particular, full employment would remove much of the pain from the downward adjustments that are continually necessary in a flexible and efficient economy. In the era of low aggregate growth rates on which we seem now set (after the unusual boom decades of the 1950s and 1960s), expansion of one firm or sector will require contraction elsewhere.

Resistance to these downward adjustments is quite understandable in an economy of recession and unemployment. At present, the resources released by a declining industry are not, in general, directly re-employed in expanding firms — they become unemployed. With full employment this would not be so. Labour and capital made available by decline in some sectors would be eagerly absorbed in expanding firms and industries; and, in general, would end-up earning a better wage and profit, too. Thus, the elasticity-sapping resistance to downward flexibility would melt away. British Leyland could retreat to the product lines it is good at; British Steel could close its unprofitable plants. As taxpayers, consumers, and workers, we would all be better off.

Finally, government regulation — the pervasive system of rules and directives whereby the public sector intervenes directly in economic affairs — requires scrutiny. This topic is big enough for a chapter of its own.

20 Regulation

'No industry offered the opportunity to be regulated should decline it.'

OWEN & BRAEUTIGAM, *The Regulation Game*

Government's attempts to 'regulate' the private sector offer some vivid examples of the flaws of the managed economy. Recognition of these by perhaps a majority of economists, and by some politicians, has built up into something of a movement towards deregulation in last few years. This chapter attempts to sort out what the fuss is about, and to develop a governed economy approach to the problem.

Regulation, simply, is government telling business what it can and cannot do. Why does it bother? In our liberal capitalist economies most regulation is not intended to supplant market forces, as in centrally-planned economies. Rather, regulation is aimed at supplementing the market; at filling-in the gaps where markets cannot reach. There are thought to be two main types of these.

(1)   One gap is created by 'externalities': byproducts of the economic process that are not included in the prices paid for goods. Matters of health, safety and environmental impact are often involved here. For example, a firm may make use of a common-property resource such as a river to disperse effluent. If it does not pay for this use, it has no incentive to limit its effluent discharge, even though this may be increasing the costs (in water purification, say) of firms downstream. Another important example: the economic return perceived by firms from looking after the health and safety of their workers may not be sufficient to induce them to meet socially acceptable standards on these matters. Some intervention is therefore required.

(2)   The second sort of gap concerns economic performance. If markets are buffeted by big short-run swings in exogenous factors (weather, world prices) then firms may be pushed off the long-run growth path. To get efficient investment decisions, then, some intervention to smooth-out

169

the short-term fluctuations may be justified. The instability of 'free' markets is invoked to justify regulation of agricultural markets, as well as many transportation and service industries in which the source of instability is alleged to be excessive vulnerability to new firms entering. In terms of the concepts introduced in the last chapter, some regulation may be needed if markets are *too* contestable; too prone to disruptive swings in the number of firms involved.

Another economic market failure occurs when the technology of an industry makes it a 'natural monopoly' — an industry in which economies of scale are so marked that it is not efficient to have more than one firm supplying the market. To (hopefully) avoid exploitation of the market power accruing to a monopoly supplier, such industries are run either as government departments, or as heavily regulated private firms. For example, in Britain, telephone services are provided by the Post Office; in the US, by the Bell system.

This chapter focuses on economic regulation, which is of critical importance to the functioning of markets, and so for elasticity. Intervention to deal with externalities is treated in chapter 25.

Quite conservative estimates put the proportion of GNP subject to economic regulation at between 25 and 30 per cent.[1] About five percentage points, at most, of this is 'natural' monopoly; the rest comes from markets supposedly prone to destabilising forces in their natural state. Thus, government's influence on the economy through regulation may at least match in importance the economic impact of its above-the-line spending and taxing activities, This is certainly micro-meddling on a very large scale.

Does it work? A number of economists have asked this question over the last few years. With unusual near-unanimity, their answer has been 'No; not nearly as well as it should'. It is particularly interesting that economists on the 'liberal' side of the fence (notably Charles Schultze, Alfred Kahn, and Barry Bosworth) have been in the vanguard of a deregulatory movement in the United States. In their views on many social and economic matters, these economists are activist, Keynesian, natural inheritors of the tradition of Roosevelt's New Deal under which a good deal of the regulatory activity was initiated. It is not the principle of intervention in markets that upsets them, but, rather, the results in practice.

Five things seem to have gone wrong:

(1)　As noted, most economic regulation is intended to stabilise markets. It does this, in most cases, by licensing entry into the industry, and, often, by further limiting the segments of the market in which firms can operate.

Thus, there have been limits on the number of licences issued in most transportation industries, and restriction on market areas built-in to licences. Many service sector occupations have the number of practitioners, and the nature of the work they can do, set by licensing. The number and broadcast range of television stations is controlled.

That is, regulation has worked by limiting the competition faced by existing firms, either from outsiders, or from other firms in their industry. The point of this is to give firms security, so that they will be able to plan and invest successfully. The problem is that security leads to slack. Stability becomes rigidity. If firms are freed from competitive pressures they lose the incentive to keep prices and costs as low as possible, and to take the risks that are needed if new products and techniques are to be introduced.

There have been a number of case studies documenting the detrimental effects on efficiency of lack of competitive pressure.[2] Two examples: in an analysis of power generation in US cities, it was found that electricity costs in markets competed for by two or more power companies were about 11 per cent lower than in monopoly markets.[3] Rates for transporting poultry in the US dropped by 33 per cent after deregulation.[4]

(2) Entry and market-share regulation operate at the most micro level possible — on individual firms. Economic life at this level is extremely complex; too complex, in general, to be adequately encompassed in sets of rules and procedures laid down by an arm of high-level central government. The consequence is that regulation spawns all sorts of undesired and distortionary side-effects. Some of these were listed in chapter 10 (Canadian Dairy Policy) and chapter 15, which was concerned with the particular form of regulation known as incomes policy. Many other examples could be given. To note one: in Canada, the 'Crow Rate' (an anciently legislated and by now highly-subsidised freight rate for Prairie grain) which was designed to compensate the Prairie provinces for their distance from markets, may have encouraged grain production and export to the detriment of livestock and secondary grain processing, with a net effect of a *reduction* in the total value of Prairie agricultural production amounting to several hundred million dollars each year.[5]

Sometimes the unintended side-effects are beneficial. It has been reported that the catalytic converter that US car manufacturers are now required to fit to reduce carbon dioxide pollution actually led to an improvement in fuel economy. The reason is that, with the converter taking care of pollutants, engineers could tune engines for maximum fuel efficiency.[6] But it would seem unwise to rely on the good surprises outnumbering the bad ones.

(3)   Running the regulation business is costly. In 1979 there were 56 regulatory agencies in the US, with a total budget of $6 billion.[7] Adding a comparable amount for the private sector resources used in dealing with the regulators implies a very signficant sum diverted from productive use.

It is impossible to calculate with any accuracy the total value of the various costs directly and indirectly attributable to economic regulation. The estimate of one well-informed economist – Barry Bosworth, who directed President Carter's Council on Wage and Price Stability – is that regulation adds between three-quarters and one and one half per cent to the price level.[8]

(4)   Regulators are supposed to uphold the public interest rather than that of the firms of the regulated industry. But the 'public interest' is a woolly, diffuse concept, filtered through various politicians and consumer groups, who may not always agree. In contrast, the industry usually knows what it wants, and intensive, day-to-day contact with the regulators helps it to establish its point of view. The eventual outcome, as the Chicago economist George Stigler put it, is that the regulators get 'captured' by the regulatees.[9] Although it may begin with reforming zeal, the regulatory agency gets worn down into an accommodating pressure group representing the interests of 'its' industry in the governmental process. Thus, to take a notorious example, the US Federal Communications Commission was, until ordered to desist, acting as a vigorous defender of the monopoly position of the American Telephone and Telegraph Company.[10]

The capture phenomenon demonstrates the silliness of designing 'perfect' policies, which require perfect people to implement them. It is entirely understandable that the staff of an agency should come to identify their interests with those of the industry they are empowered to regulate. If the industry grows, so too will the agency, meaning promotions for its staff. A good working relationship between regulator and regulatee may lead to lucrative consultancy positions for agency officials after retirement. Even very honest officials find it difficult to maintain an aloof, arms-length relationship with people with whom they must do business every day. Empathy keeps breaking in.

(5)   Government's 'willing to do business with business' attitude, as demonstrated in micro-level regulation, gives an incentive for 'rent-seeking' behaviour (that is, the lobbying for goodies from the public purse). It seems that, just as individual officials are unable to maintain impartiality when implementing regulatory programs, politicians are not able to objectively sort out good from bad when legislating the programs into

existence. The pressures for log-rolling, pork-barrelling, trade-offs, and grand and petty larceny are irresistible.

The result in the United States, where the system of government is particularly prone to this sort of thing, is that official lobbying groups (called 'Political Action Committees', or PACs) have risen in number from about 600 in 1974 to more than 3000 in 1982.[11] This truly is a debilitating epidemic of single-issue politicking. The situation is not as bad in Britain, because party discipline in government is much stronger than in the US. The Prime Minister is not forced into endless compromising and concessions in order to govern. But the danger remains.

In summary: economic regulation is costly. When it involves, as most often it has, control over entry of new firms, and over the market shares of existing firms, it is likely to 'stabilise' industries into relatively inefficient and unadventurous units. Because the regulators come to identify their own interests with those of the industry, and because they have the power to act on these, it becomes difficult to get the necessary contraction in markets when changes in tastes and technologies demand a reallocation of resources.

All this reduces elasticity. Indeed, the reason that business interests, while ostensibly ideologically opposed to government intervention, in practice accept eagerly the regulatory embrace, is that this is an almost foolproof way of getting markets under control. It is true that most firms in regulated industries do not earn spectacularly high returns on their shareholders' funds. But there are rewards which, to the modern bureaucratic corporation, are more-than-compensatory. It is very difficult to go broke in a regulated industry. The profits earned will be steady, and adequate to attract funds needed to finance expansion. Freedom from competitive pressure can be enjoyed by managers in the form of a 'quiet life', and in the gentle padding of managerial salaries and perks.

Regulation – what could be called publicly-produced market power – has thus been entirely consistent with the trend towards privately generated market power documented in the previous chapter. What should be done about it?

The gist of the deregulation movement is quite simple – pull out; disband the agencies; let industries look after themselves; rely on market forces. The biggest and most celebrated act of deregulation so far attempted is that of the US airline industry. As chairman of the Civil Aeronautics Board, the economist Alfred E. Kahn presided over a drastic opening-up of routes and fares to new competition, and even managed to arrange for the eventual disbanding of the CAB itself.[12]

The final impact of airline deregulation is not yet known. So far, one major carrier (Braniff) has disappeared, which is consistent with there being some regulation-protected excess capacity. However, it is difficult, in 1983, to disentangle the effects of deregulation from those of the world recession, which has reduced profitability in even the best-run airlines. It is when the industry as a whole picks up that it will be easier to identify the consequences of greater competition.

Whatever the verdict on the airlines, the deregulation movement should be vigorously supported. Its thrust is towards opening-up markets (making them more contestable) and we must expect this to have a beneficial effect on elasticity and thus on economic performance.

Of course, there may be some industries which would be better regulated in the old way. But the problem with trying to do something about these is (to emphasise again one of the key points of this book) that government is inherently too distant from the market-place to be able to infallibly identify the worthy cases, and to successfully regulate them to the desired end. This means (1) that mistakes will be made, which are costly in themselves; and (2) that the fallibility of the policy-makers will attract the lobbyists and the rent-seekers, wasting a further slice of the GNP pie.

It is better to withdraw altogether from the micro-meddling game, in the expectation that the occasional opportunities for do-gooding thereby missed will be easily compensated for by the overall improvement in market efficiency. This is not a recipe for *laissez-faire*. Leave markets entirely alone, and they tend to coalesce into concentrated, low-elasticity units. But the policies suggested, in the previous chapter, to deal with privately-generated market power would rely on higher-level instruments – rules or laws which set general constraints on market behaviour, without depending on precise knowledge of how individual industries and firms operate. Most current economic regulation does depend on such detailed knowledge, and that is why it does not work very well.

Deregulation and competition policy are thus complementary. Competition policy tries to prevent the private sector from erecting barriers to new firms and to price competition; deregulation stops government from supporting these practices itself. The link is particularly close in those industries where professional or craft organisations are officially granted powers to set fees and control entry. Deregulation would remove the official sanction, and competition policy would discourage any less formal efforts to retain monopoly positions. Thus, for example, the public might see more competition on fees between lawyers, and more use of cheaper 'paralegals' on the less mysterious tasks, such as conveyancing and divorce settlements. (This is not to attack the useful job done by most professional associations in setting and enforcing quality standards. Such falls into the category of non-economic regulation, with which I am not here concerned.)

Finally, note that deregulation further illustrates the symbiotic link between successful micro and macroeconomic policy. Much, perhaps most, of the cyclical instability in individual markets that leads to cries for regulatory protection, is due to the swings in aggregate economic performance as the economy bobs up and down on the business cycle. Successful adding-up policies dealing with inflation and unemployment would damp down a large proportion of the aggregate cycle, and so would smooth-out conditions in individual markets.

In the other direction, successful deregulation would make markets more contestable, and increase elasticity in the system as a whole. This would result in an economy more responsive to monetary and fiscal policy, making easier the maintenance of non-inflationary full employment.

21 Labour, Work, and Women

'The invisible hand is all thumbs in the labour market.'

ARNOLD WEBER

One of the most distressing paradoxes of our lumpy economies is that, at a time when more than 10 per cent of the labour force does not have a job, a large proportion of the others are working more than they want. In total, there may even be too much work being done. The trouble is that the work is being done by too few members of the labour force, and often by the wrong people and for the wrong pay.

There may be no larger or more inert lump in the lumpy economy than the institution of the five-day, all-year-around work week. It has, of course, been whittled down over the years, from a norm of six days a week one hundred years ago, and from ten or even twelve hours a day to a little under eight, on average, now. But the assumption that everyone with a 'real' job would come to work every week-day, for all but two or three weeks each year, from youth to death or retirement, has remained virtually unchallenged until quite recently.

This is a silly and uncivilised way to run an economy. It is silly because it creates discontinuities which destroy elasticity. Employees must choose to do about 150 hours of work a month or no work at all. That makes it difficult to manage the adjustments required by changing economic and personal circumstances. And it is uncivilised because it treats work like a standardised commodity, over which the ostensible owner – the worker – has very little control.

It is true that a proportion of the work force does work part-time – that is, less than about 20 hours a week.[1] The availability of these jobs adds a useful dimension to choice in the labour market. But at present most of them are low-paid and unskilled (cleaning buildings and waiting on tables, for example) which are really only suitable for young people who do not need much money and have not yet permanently committed themselves to the labour force.

It is also true that an increasing though still small number of workers

176

have had access to 'flextime' (or 'flexitime') arrangements. These permit some choice in the starting and finishing times of a normal-length work-day.

But the target should be something much bigger than clocking-in and clocking-out times. People should be able to choose not just the timing of the working day, but also its total length; and the number of days, weeks, months, even years that they work. That is, people should enjoy, as a basic economic right, some sort of autonomy over their working lives consistent with the freedom that we take almost for granted in our personal and social existences. People should be free to work part-time at two very different jobs at once, to share child-rearing, to spend every Wednesday gardening or playing golf, to go hitch-hiking around Europe for three months every summer, to return to university for a year; all without any fuss from their employers.

Of course, employees should only be paid for the time they work, and in so far as promotion is based on actual experience rather than age, this must be calculated on the basis of hours on the payroll. Employees might still have to do as they are told when working – I am not here discussing 'industrial democracy', which is a different matter. But they would not have to accept being told which hours of their life they would be on the job.

The system in which employees choose how much work they will do, as well as when they will do it, has been given the name 'varitime': variable total working time.[2] There is certainly nothing new about the idea: millions of self-employed people practice varitime, and may even have become self-employed in order to do so. I, for example, have taken time from teaching and research in order to write this book, and took advantage of varitime to temporarily shift location by ten thousand miles: the first draft was typed in a house by the beach in New Zealand while the northern hemisphere was under snow.

What may seem radical is that *all* workers should have access to varitime. But such can be seen as just another step in the long struggle to free working people from the conditions of indentured servitude under which they were organised, to facilitate the rise of the factory system, in the last century. At each stage, progress has been resisted with squeals of anguish by employers, but once won, the improvements have been accommodated comfortably enough. No doubt epidemics of chimney fires were predicted when sweeps were forbidden to use little boys to do the dirty work. Certainly the periodic reductions in the length of the working day have aroused bitter opposition. In 1837 one of the leading economists of the time – Nassau Senior – set out to enquire into the consequences of reducing daily hours to ten. He argued, presumably sincerely but quite fallaciously, that such a reform would bankrupt industry, since this depended for its profit on the last – ie, the eleventh of twelfth – hour of work.

The legislation was finally passed in 1847, and catastrophe did not ensue. Such has been the pattern of most labour law reform – lengthy but unsuccessful resistance to the passing of the bill, followed by successful adjustment, and, eventually, almost total approval by employers and employees alike. Rare is the capitalist nowadays who would argue that the first Factory Act of 1802, which limited the hours of child apprentices in the mills to twelve a day, was too liberal.[3]

Such, I expect, would also be the consequence of legislation instituting varitime. There would be a big fuss at first, but soon we, and certainly our children, would wonder why we ever put up with anything less. The legislation would be complicated, and would need a lot of prior thinking-through and debate. Related issues such as the pro-rating of benefits, and the portability of pensions, would have to be dealt with.

But there does not seem to be a fundamental difficulty with varitime. Even assembly-lines, which are sometimes cited as being particularly un-suited to freer work arrangements, should not present an obstacle. On the contrary: because assembly-line work is so boring, it is particularly prone to that informal form of varitime called absenteeism. Something like 7.5 per cent of the workforce are absent for some reason each week, on average, with figures for routine factory jobs being even higher.[4]

This means that supervisors already manage to deal with a good deal of 'varitime', with this being awkwardly unpredictable, since, by the nature of absenteeism, the employer is not usually informed, if at all, until the last possible moment. Now, there is quite a lot of evidence that flexitime results in substantially lower absenteeism, and varitime would further help. Employees would have more opportunity to schedule non-work activities, and they apparently respond to greater freedom by showing more embarrassment about letting their employers down by failing to turn up when expected.[5]

Varitime would give a big boost to elasticity by widening the options available to both employer and employee. Instead of the 'all or nothing' choice between a full-time work-year and unemployment, both sides could choose from an expanded 'menu' of working arrangements. It would be easier, for example, for employers to reduce temporarily labour force levels when demand for their product drops.

Some adjustments would be needed. Because varitime gives more control to the individual worker, it takes power away from managers and trade unions, who have been used to settling between themselves the dimensions of everybody's working day. Managers, in particular, might have trouble learning to fully respect the new rights of employees. Some renegades would no doubt find ways of flouting the law, just as some now disobey minimum wage statutes and anti-discrimination laws. But once people get used to a law, so long as it is popular and perceived to be just, enforcement is not a big problem. The majority of employers would come to automatically respect their employees' right to operate on varitime, just as they now respect their unwillingness to work a twelve hour day.

What would be the overall impact of varitime? It is possible that voluntary reductions in hours worked by people already employed could exceed the increased working hours of the currently unemployed, so that total paid work done would decrease, and with it, measured GNP. But this would be no more than a by-product of people being better able to divide their time between paid and unpaid activites. Whatever the quantitative effect, people would be happier with varitime.

Breaking up rigidities in working time is one of two prongs of an elasticity-increasing labour market policy. The second concerns discrimination; in particular, discrimination against women.

Discrimination is defined as the situation of an individual's economic status being affected by some non-economically relevant attribute, such as their race, religion, class, or sex. I will here focus on sex discrimination, by which we mean, of course, men exploiting women. It is crucial to face up to the economic dimensions of sexual exploitation, because only then can we appreciate just how big an effort is needed to eliminate it. Women do about 60 per cent of the work and receive about 30 per cent of the pay. To put this another way, men get more than three times the money income for an hour's work than do women, on average.

I will explain how I arrived at these figures, because some of the assumptions used are debatable. Begin by noting that about 40 per cent of the 'official' (ie paid) work-force are women, whose pay averages 60 per cent of mens'.[6] This gives the figure of about 30 per cent for the proportion of pay received by women.[7]

Now, paid work is not the only useful work done in the economy. There is also volunteer work, which might be worth one or two per cent of measured GNP, but which we will not consider here.[8] And there is housework. A recent Canadian study put the value of housework, which is unpaid and not included in the GNP statistics, at between 35 and 40 per cent of measured gross national product. Nearly all housework is done by women. One American study found that women not in the labour force spent, on average, 55 hours a week on this activity (a figure which has not declined in fifty years), and working women 26 hours.[10] Another study, of men, discovered that, if there is a woman in their household, they do about four hours housework a week when employed, and about seven when unemployed.[11] Men do not do more housework if the woman is herself employed, and most of what they do is shopping.[12] For simplicity, then, we can ignore the male contribution to housework, and compensate by taking the lower bound of the Canadian estimate of the share of housework in GNP.

However, this number must itself be adjusted, since it is calculated valuing housework at what this would cost to have done professionally. Since nearly all professional household service providers are women, and thus relatively lowly-paid, the 35 per cent figure underestimates the actual amount of work done in the home as a proportion of the work that is included in GNP. Assuming that professional houseworkers receive the average female wage, and adjusting by the average male-plus-female wage, we get a figure of 50 per cent for the amount of housework as a proportion of measured gross national product.[13] That is, one third of the total work done in the economy, paid and unpaid, is housework. Then, adding this to women's 40 per cent contribution to the paid labour force, we get the figure of 60 per cent for the proportion of all work that is done by women.

These calculations involve several simplifications.[14] But it seems inescapable to conclude that women do more than half the work, whether or not the figure is 50 per cent more than men, as my 60:40 split implies. And it would be very, very difficult to crank-up the numbers enough to show that women's hourly remuneration equals that of men.

An extraordinary example of sex discrimination in action comes from the job experience of people who have had sex change operations. Martin Baily reports the findings of a study of 170 such people. All those changing from female to male earned more afterwards, whereas most of those going the other way ended up earning less.[15]

How is this exploitation managed? There seem to be three major control instruments:

(1)   The technological superiority of women over men in the bearing and nursing of babies is extrapolated into a presumed decisive superiority in all other domestic activities, such as cooking, cleaning, child-minding, and household management. (An exception may be fixing things that have broken, which is 'the man's job'.)

(2)   Out-and-out personal discrimination — paying men and women different amounts for doing the same job — remains, despite its illegality.

(3) More subtle, and legal, than personal discrimination, is what we could call occupational discrimination, the reserving of whole classes of jobs for one sex or the other, with subsequent adjustment of rates of pay.

Thus, women are bundled into the 'pink-collar ghettos' of the typing pools; into 'menial' service sector jobs, and into some factory industries, or to certain jobs within factories. Men get some manual labour jobs, most 'professional' and 'trade' positions, and nearly all of the management jobs in the hierarchies of government and business.

It does not really matter what the jobs are — that is, what is their intrinsic worth: so long as they are clearly divided by sex, exploitation can proceed. Thus, when, one hundred years ago the job of typist/secretary was done by men, its pay was well above the average pay of an industrial worker. Over the decades, the job has been infiltrated and finally taken over by women. What has happened to the pay? If I had had this book typed (rather than doing it myself on my wonderful word processor) the woman who would have done the job would probably have earned something like one half the rate of the male compositor who will set it up for printing.

There have been a number of attempts to explain male/female wage differentials by means of 'objective' personal productivity characteristics such as experience and education. None have been able to attribute more than half of the differential to these characteristics.[16] The rest is discrimination. Even the 'explained' portion should be queried. It is a fact that experience and education are closely related to pay. But why? Most economists have *assumed* that the relationship reflects differences in productivity, but this is very difficult to prove. Indeed, there is evidence that a major function of education and experience is as a 'screening device', to ration access to the limited supply of good, well-paid jobs.[17] Since women have difficulty getting access to higher education, and in building long spells of uninterrupted work, the screening works to preserve the majority of the good jobs for men.

Even accepting that some pay differences do reflect productivity differences — there are some highly-paid jobs (brain surgeon, airline pilot, orchestra conductor, for example) which almost everyone would agree are of above-average value — does not rationalise earnings differentials between men and women. We are left with the unanswered question: 'why, if not discrimination, do so few women get *access* to these productive well-paid jobs?' Neoclassical economists have trouble with this question. As one of them puts it

That employer discrimination could account for such a sizeable depression in female wage rates for such an extended period of time is
troublesome to anyone with even limited belief in the efficiency of the
price mechanism.[18]

So be it. But the usual reaction (as with another awkward fact — unemployment) is either to ignore the issue completely, or to try and explain it
away by some cunning theoretical sleight-of-hand. (The economist quoted
above goes on to develop an ingenious but question-begging rationalisation
in terms of the location decisions of couples.)

What can be done? The problem is certainly daunting in magnitude —
the amount of money involved in men's exploitation of women is far
greater than any conceivable exploitation of workers and consumers by
monopoly capitalists. Most men reading this will be systematic exploiters
of women, in either or both their business and personal lives. Many women
(those who fight their way onto the male earnings structure) exploit other
women. What else can they do? If you know any of the men who run
trade unions and left-wing political parties, you will know that many of
them are chauvinists. They follow a fine precedent set by Karl Marx, a
merciless exploiter of his wife and daughter.

Nothing short of a revolution in attitudes of men and of women will
breach the bastions of the sexist society. However, mundane economic
policy could be of assistance, in at least three ways:

(1)   Varitime, recommended above, would be a useful weapon for
women wishing to break-out from the housewife-plus-secondary income-
earner stereotype, since it would make it easy for a couple to share household responsibilities. Men would not necessarily be any keener to do their
part, but at least the usual excuse that paid work is a full time-or-nothing
affair would be removed.

(2)   Full employment would mean a tight labour market, which would
force employers to upgrade 'secondary' workers (women, blacks, youths)
to fill high-wage 'primary' jobs. On-the-job training and upgrading is a
major factor in increasing earnings, and past experience has shown that
recruitment of secondary workers to the primary labour force accelerates
in the upswings of business cycles.[19] Full employment also reduces the
resistance of unions to the opening up of good jobs to disadvantaged
groups, at least to the extent that such resistance stems from the union
members' fears for the security of their own employment.

(3) A vigorous anti-market power policy (chapter 19) would help, by cutting away some of the slack which is used to finance discrimination. This idea leads on to querying the fundamentals of firms, jobs, and the earnings structure, which will be the subject of the next two chapters.

Finally, we should consider the benefits of a non-discriminatory society. The morality of the matter is clear enough, and is quite sufficient to justify action. But this is a book about economics. Can we find economic re-inforcements for the ethical considerations?

As with so many issues, it boils down to elasticity. Like rigid working hours, discrimination amounts to a set of rules limiting the choices, and thus the efficiency and flexibility (the elasticity) of the economy. Reserving all of some jobs for women, and all of the others for men, amounts to a balkanisation of the market system. It is like drawing a line through the midlands of England, and forbidding any commerce to cross between north and south. It is inefficient because it means that about half the men and half the women are not able to do thé job they would be best at. It is sad to think of the brilliant female surgeons, pilots, and conductors that the world has missed out on: equally, it is sad to consider the talented house-husbands who have wasted their working lives in factories (or as incompetent surgeons, etc).

To conclude: I have pointed out in this chapter two big areas of the labour market where elasticity could, and should, be augmented by the breaking-down of artificial barriers that limit, in one case, the range of paid/unpaid, work/leisure choices, and in the other, the free access of different sexes to jobs. Now we move on to scrutinise the nature of the jobs themselves.

22 Hierarchy: How the Middle Class Does It

The focus thus far has been on how the pieces of the lumpy economy fit together. This chapter looks at the 'lumps' themselves – specifically, at what the people who work in firms and public sector organisations actually do, and how this is related to what they earn.

The most striking feature of the work-pay relationship is its formal hierarchical structure. Most jobs are neatly pigeon-holed into categories, which are then rather rigidly ordered on the income scale.

There are two types of ordering systems, or hierarchies. A majority of the work-force is employed in organisations in which there is an internal hierarchy of control relationships. Each employee has a place on an 'organisation chart' which generally looks like a pyramid. The workers at each level of the pyramid are responsible for workers at all lower levels. At the top is the chief executive, who is in charge of everyone. This type of hierarchy is called a 'bureaucracy'. Pay in bureaucracies is closely associated with one's level on the pyramid.

The second sort of hierarchy is the ranking of occupations. In most cases, it is possible to make a quite accurate guess about someone's income if their trade or profession is known. Doctors always earn more than nurses; carpenters more than labourers; cabinet ministers more than ordinary MPs.

These income hierarchies affect almost all of the labour force, including many people not employed in multi-level bureaucracies. Only a few loosely-structured occupations escape, such as artists, professional sportsmen, and criminals, whose incomes can vary from nothing at all to millions.

All this may be so well-known as to seem hardly worth writing about. Certainly, hierarchies are pervasive – they dominate both private and public sectors in our economies, and are common to both 'capitalist' and 'socialist' societies. But there is nothing trivial about their role. Hierarchies amount to a massive overriding of market forces: they supplant the actual productivity of a worker as a determinant of the worker's income, and they allocate resources within organisations by means of administrative controls, rather than through the price mechanism.

There are two sorts of reasons put forward to explain this interesting state of affairs. These can be called the 'economic' and the 'political' rationales for hierarchy.

From the economic perspective it is noted that the haggling and price-changing that goes on in markets is itself costly and time-consuming, so that it may be efficient to have some sequences of economic activities carried out in teams or organisations, within which market forces are suppressed in favour of routinisation and lines of authority.[1] This is obviously reasonable, and would be accepted as such by anyone bar an anarchist. But the economic argument does not necessarily justify *all* hierarchical structures, nor does it justify the income differentials associated with them. The process may have gone beyond economic sense. We will return to this below.

What about the 'political' function? Who gains from hierarchy? In his paper 'What do bosses do?', which generated a considerable controversy in radical circles a decade ago, Stephen Marglin argued that workers were bundled into factories, had their labour divided into simple repetitive tasks, and were ruled-over by a hierarchy of supervisors and their managers, all as part of the political process whereby capitalists gained control over the production and savings processes.[2]

Marglin's may be a valid analysis of the rise of hierarchy. But, by now, capital income is not a large fraction of the total (about 5 per cent in the US,[3] and is diffused largely among small investors and savings institutions, which play a small role in the actual running of businesses.[4] We should probably look beyond the owners of firms for the interests served by hierarchy, especially since it is pervasive in both public and private sectors of the economy.

Part of the answer can be found in the previous chapter: men exploit women, and do so by imposing hierarchies upon them. But this is not all of it. The income distribution is not a simple two-level construct, with nearly all the men on one level, and nearly all the women on the other. Rather, the aggregation of all the occupational hierarchies and bureaucratic pyramids is itself a pyramid, with relatively large numbers in lower income classes. Although some of the imbalance in this distribution is due to male/female inequality, there is still a lot of male/male inequality to be explained. For example, the 1978 Current Population Survey in the US revealed that about 20 per cent of full-time workers earned between $20 000 and $100 000, totalling nearly half of total earned income.[5] The great majority of this group, which I will call the economic middle class, were male,[6] but males were also a majority in the class earning less than $20 000.

It is the favoured position of this middle class that we should scrutinise. Why do doctors earn more than nurses, who in turn earn more than porters? One red-herring that must immediately be disposed of is the notion that pay differentials have to do with differences in the 'value' of the work. We could all agree that doctoring is in some sense more valuable than pushing stretcher beds along corridors, but still not be able to thereby justify the difference in salaries paid to doctor and porter. The price of something is determined not by demand (or value) alone, but by demand *and* supply together.

So, for example, a salt miner should not be paid differently to a gold miner, whatever the relative worth of gold and salt, so long as the two jobs are approximately interchangeable in skill and effort required. It is only when there are significant differences in what the miners supply — in the nature of the *work* — that we can expect the unimpeded interaction of supply and demand to throw-up differences in rates of pay.

Now, compared with a porter, the doctor's job is, on the plus side, more fun and carries higher status; and on the negative, more stressful and requires a longer training period. It may also be true that doctoring is intrinsically more 'difficult' than portering, in the sense of there being fewer babies born with the innate ability to be competent doctors than to be competent porters. In any case, it is conceivable that, in a system in which supply and demand set wages in competitive markets, the net effect of the pros and cons would be that doctors got paid more than porters. That is, there may be an economic justification for a differential. But can the size of the actual differential be so justified? The salary of a medical assistant, for example, is about five times that of a porter, in British hospitals.[7] Is this the outcome of free market forces?

It can be plausibly be argued that the inequalities of our income hier-, archies are far greater than those that can be defended on economic grounds. One well-known critic is Ivan Illich, who sees most forms of 'professional' activity as a conspiracy against lay people which is actually counter-productive in its effects on the quality of our health, housing, transportation and other services sold to us by the inhabitants of the upper levels of the occupational hierarchies.[8]

A more moderate view is offered by Randall Collins, in his book *The Credential Society*, who concludes that

The great majority of all jobs can be learned through practice by almost any literate person. The number of esoteric specialities 're-quiring' unusually extensive training or skill is rare.[9]

If correct, this implies that, in economic terms, the scarcity that generates the incomes of the higher-paid must be somehow contrived. There is, indeed, plenty of evidence of the middle class interfering on both sides of the market. On the demand side, the 'higher' professions lobby for monopoly positions (licensing requirements, for example) which prevent lower-level technicians from entering their market, and legitimise this with a mystifying fog of jargon and secrecy. Then, having gained some monopoly power, they protect it by controlling the supply side of their market, most often by imposing long formal training requirements

> It has been by the use of educational credentials that the lucrative professions have closed their ranks and upgraded their salaries; and it has been in imitation of their methods that other occupations have 'professionalised'.[10]

This works as a supply-limiting instrument because there is only a small subset of children (the sons, and to a lesser extent, the daughters, of the middle class) which has the appropriate cultural and financial background to successfully negotiate the long obstacle course of our education system. Certainly, a few of the more determined members of the lower class break through, and they are usually welcome enough (less so if black, Jewish, or female). But the substantial and persistent income differentials of our economy are witness to the success of the middle class in perpetuating their privileged position.

To summarise: it seems highly likely that the talents and efforts going into the occupations designated as high-paid are not sufficiently superior to those captured by other jobs to justify the substantial income differentials involved. Note that this is *not* to say that individuals are equal in their abilities (on which more below), but rather that the formalised criteria attached to each job are much more equal in their demands on ability than is implied by the hierarchy of differences in rewards.

So much for occupational hierarchy. What about the second great bastion of inequality – the bureaucracies in which most organised economic activity takes place?

The conventional argument proceeds in two steps. First, it is suggested that the logic of modern technology is such that only large-scale factories are efficient. Then, it is assumed that production workers in these big plants must be told what to do, and monitored to ensure that they do it. Such requires a higher level of supervisors, who must themselves be supervised, and so on, up the levels of the pyramid. There is some merit in this argument, but, as was the case with occupational hierarchies, it has almost certainly been taken too far. There is by now quite a lot of evidence against the acceptance of a 'technological imperative' ordaining large-scale production under bureaucratic control:

(1)   Studies attempting to explain differences in productivity across plants and across countries have found that what goes on inside the plant is much more important than simple plant size. In particular, what are called 'product-specific scale economies' – the degree to which a plant specialises in something that it does well – matter more than how big it is.[11] These sorts of efficiencies do not necessarily require large work-forces.

(2)   The 'logic' of technology may not be impartial. Scientists and technologists are problem-solvers, with limited time and resources at their disposal. Thus, they must *choose* which problems to focus on. It is likely that they have been induced to concentrate on the problems of large-scale production, rather than, say, work out how technology could be the servant of small organisations. That is, causation may run from the demand to have big firms to the supply of large-scale technology, rather than the other way around, as is conventionally assumed.

(3)   The division of labour into simple, repetitive tasks is unpleasant for the worker. This is a bad thing in itself, and it also leads to absenteeism, slackening, and industrial problems. In Britain, 1 per cent of plants with 25 to 100 employees had work stoppages in a typical year, whereas the equivalent figure for plants with 500 to 1000 employees was 16 per cent.[12]

(4)   It is not necessarily true that control must be exercised bureau-cratically. There is a lengthening list of examples of 'worker participa-tion' in management, from which it can be inferred that decisions can be made and implemented successfully, even in large organisations, in a quite democratic fashion.

(5)   The complexity of an organisation increases, perhaps exponentially, with its size. This means that the jobs at the top of the pyramid in a large bureaucracy may be very complicated indeed. There is alarming evidence that some of these jobs are just too difficult to be done successfully. Lord Stokes was an effective manager of Standard-Triumph, but neither he nor anyone else seems able to squeeze a genuine profit out of British Leyland.

In general, it seems that really big decisions, in either private or public sector, turn out to be mistakes more often than not.[13] So many things can go wrong, and so few can be predicted.

In summary, there is plenty of evidence that bureaucratically controlled large-scale production has been taken too far for efficiency.

Why? This leads on to the 'political' factors supporting hierarchical organisation. Bureaucracy tends to bloat because growth is in the interests of three powerful groups: owners, managers, and unions. Owners gain because increased size is one means of increasing power over markets, as discussed in chapter 19. Unions like market power, because they usually get a share of the profits that result, and also find it easier to organise and control workers in large plants. But the big gainers from size are managers – the people on the upper levels of the pyramid. Market power yields 'slack', which can be built-in to salaries and perks. And bigger organisations need bigger bureaucracies, which means more promotions, and higher-paid jobs at the top.

Indeed, quite simple rules of thumb appear to relate salary to 'responsibility' (the number of people directly or indirectly reporting to a manager) in bureaucracies. For example, in the large British chemical firm ICI, 'the number of executives on a particular salary level . . . is inversely proportional to the approximate fifth power of the salary at that level'.[14] What this means is that, if each manager has four direct subordinates, these will earn 75 per cent of the manager's salary.

Of course it is probably more difficult to manage 100 people than ten, and salaries reflect this. But this does not mean that hierarchy makes sense from a wider perspective. Difficulty need not equate with productivity, as the British Leyland example shows. Some very unproductive decisions are made by clever, industrious, highly-paid senior bureaucrats, in private and public sectors.

What I am suggesting is a reinforcement of the famous 'Peter Principle', whose discoverer suggested that people keep getting promoted in organisations until they reach their 'level of incompetence', where they stick around, doing a bad job.[15] My conjecture is that the likelihood of incompetence increases as we move up the hierarchy, because jobs get more difficult faster than ability and experience increase.

There is another irrationality. The essence of hierarchy is that pay is related to 'importance' – to position on the bureaucratic pecking order. This means that unusually successful production workers are rewarded by removing them from the jobs they are good at. The result, as noted by one chief executive, is

In nearly every major industry, the employee must become a manager to reach the top rewards. What this often does is turn good engineers or scientists into bad managers.[16]

There are occasional exceptions – people whose *mana* in the occupational hierarchy is big enough to override the usual bureaucratic rule. For example, in the National Health Service example used above, a 'Full-Time Consultant with A+ merit reward' earned slightly more than a 'Higher Directing Medical Officer – Civil Service', even though the latter, as a senior administrator, would presumably be above the consultant in the organisational pyramid. Some distinguished research scientists in the Canadian public service earn more than high-level administrators. Some professors earn more than their university president or vice-chancellor (though in many universities, this is not permitted).

But these are unusual exceptions to the general rule. Despite the evidence of their excesses, the structures of hierarchy maintain their dominance over the distribution of jobs and incomes. The next chapter examines what could be done about this.

23 Flattening the Hierarchies

What can be done about the excesses of hierarchy? This chapter offers some suggestions. First it is necessary to specify the alternative; to outline the characteristics of a more sensible and less inequitable organisation of work and production.

Note that the success (for the middle class) of the hierarchical income structure depends on the 'good jobs' being restricted to a minority of the work-force. What would happen, then, if the barriers to these jobs were broken down? This question was considered by Lane Tracy, in an enjoyable article published in the Harvard Business Review in 1972, not long after the publication of *The Peter Principle*.[1] If everyone in hierarchies rises to their level of incompetence, as claimed in that book, how then, Tracy asked, does any work get done at all? Peter's answer was that work was accomplished by employees not yet arrived at their incompetence level. But Tracy did not find this convincing:

> the accumulation of deadwood, particularly at the executive levels of our hierarchies, should be so great as to preclude any effective direction of the enterprise.[2]

'And so it does' might be one response, but Tracy had a more intriguing idea. He suggested the existence of a

> cadre of competent people to whom the Peter Principle does not apply. These people cannot be part of the organisational hierarchy, for there the Peter Principle operates at full force. And yet, to be in a position to carry out the necessary functions of planning, directing, and controlling the enterprise, such people must reside at all levels of the administrative hierarchy. What class of people fits this description? The obvious answer is *secretaries*.[3]

Secretaries are competent because of the barriers which keep them from promotion to their level of incompetence. That is, the whole grandiose edifice of bureaucracy is actually glued together by the under-paid efforts of a 'parahierarchy' of (women) secretaries, which Tracy calls a 'horizontal' hierarchy, because of the relatively small differences in salary and authority between secretaries throughout the bureaucracy.

Another major horizontal hierarchy is that of the production-level workers who actually turn out the goods and services. It looks very much as though the dominant economic class — white middle class males — lives largely off the efforts of the exploited members of parahierarchies.

The implication is that, if exploitation were eliminated, the present system would collapse. Tracy is quite cheerful about this since he believes, as I do, that the system is inefficient, and would be well gotten rid of. In its place would be a network of *horizontal hierarchies*. And what would this alternative look like? The essential feature of horizontal hierarchy is that

> differentials in pay and authority must be based on the skills of the person relative to his [sic] position, rather than on the position itself
> .... Such differentials would motivate a person to find the position in which he is most competent, rather than the 'highest' position.[4]

That is, there should be smaller differentials built in to the job, and more variation as the reward for doing it well. An excellent nurse could earn more than a mediocre doctor (though there would not be as many mediocre doctors as there are now, because people not suited to medicine would choose something else, rather than force themselves through medical school as a sure path to status and prosperity).

In principle, there is nothing revolutionary about horizontal hierarchies — they correspond to the way things operate now for that small minority of workers who work in the 'free' segment of the labour market — self-employed people, in particular. For example, there is no automatic schedule of incomes attached to the occupation of 'writer'. A book like this may bring in no money at all if it cannot find a publisher, or could make the author moderately rich, if it is a best-seller.

In practice, though, we are a very long way from an exploitation-free economy of horizontal hierarchies. What could be done about the situation? Certainly, government should not simply wade in and begin dismembering bureaucracies all over the economy. Such would be just the sort of 'micromeddling' consistently criticised as inappropriate throughout this book. The very problem of 'distance' from the action that dooms many top managers to incompetence would apply *a fortiori* to the intervention of government. We cannot expect the policy-maker to know how far flattening of the hierarchies should go, nor which ones should be dismembered, and which left alone.

Instead, we should apply a governed economy approach. That is, we should attempt to understand the economic factors that lead to dysfunctional behaviour, and do something about these. Then the system will itself choose which hierarchies should remain, and which are excessive. I have a few suggestions along these lines:

(1)   Note first that it cannot be simply a matter of 'equality of opportunity' – of ensuring that lower class children (and women, and minorities) get the same opportunities as the progeny of the middle class to qualify for the 'good jobs'. Given the arbitrariness of the occupational hierarchy, good jobs can only exist if supported by bad jobs. We probably already have too many doctors, lawyers, managers – certainly, everyone cannot fit in to the set of jobs presently pre-empted by the middle class. There should be equality of opportunity, of course, but it will have to be accompanied by a radical change in the job structure.

(2)   Certainly, 'equality of outcome' is not very interesting. People differ in the way they wish to divide their energies between paid work and other activities, and it is fair and efficient that the resulting differences in effort are reflected in differences in incomes. And it seems generally accepted that people fortunate enough to be born clever, or with some unusual talent, should benefit economically from this, just as people with good looks are expected to do well socially.

What should be aimed for is a job market in which people are able to choose the sort of employment that best fits their abilities and tastes, and be rewarded according to the productivity of their work. Productivity, note, is an economic, not a physical concept, which depends on both supply and demand – on both the effort and skill put into the job, and the economic value of the output resulting.

(3)   The pro-competition policies developed in chapters 19 and 20 would act against hierarchy. For example, a vigorous attack on the restrictive practices of professional associations would open up jobs presently reserved for the higher professions. The resulting direct competition and loss of *mana* for the professionals would erode their income advantages over others. Competition policy would also chip away at bureaucratic hierarchy. If big bureaucratic organisations are relatively inefficient, they must potentially be vulnerable to competition from other entrepreneurs employing more rational methods. Bureaucracy is sheltered by the monopoly slack in which large organisations are able to cocoon themselves: cut away the slack and they would have to 'shape up or ship out'.

(4)   Government should do what it can, using labour law and its own practices as a major employer, to 'decredentialise' the labour market, given that many of the educational qualifications demanded for middle class jobs are not much more than expensive and discriminatory rationing devices to restrict the flow of applicants. In most cases, the bulk of skills are acquired on-the-job, possibly augmented by attendance at courses and night classes while employed. In particular, it is not necessary to insist on a university degree before accepting someone for a managerial position. As late as 1970, more than half of the executives in the top income class in the US had no degree.[5]

Generalist arts and sciences degrees should be treated as consumer goods, not investment in human capital. If people wish to spend their time and money acquiring the gloss of a tertiary education, then fair enough; but such should not be taken by employers as evidence of having learnt anything specifically useful about working.

(5)   In all this, full employment would help a lot. By making labour scarcer it would force employers to make do with whatever workers were available, regardless of qualifications, and to scrutinise their internal bureaucratic procedures, with an eye to increasing productivity.

(6)   The progress of the feminist movement will be crucial. This is not just because women are at present the major exploited group, but also because certain principles which appear to be imbedded in feminist doctrine – 'co-operation rather than competition', and the querying of routinised authority relationships – are particularly appropriate to an economy of flattened hierarchies.

So how is feminism doing? Ground was gained during the 1970s, brightening that otherwise rather unproductive decade. But at its present stage, the women's movement may be responsible for an *increase* in economic exploitation. This is because it is still overwhelmingly a middle-class affair. Middle-class women have won better access to middle-class mens' jobs.

Thus the resentment of feminism of lower-class men and women is understandable, if short-sighted. More middle-class women in the scarce 'good jobs' means even less access to them for the lower class, and may therefore have *increased* inequality in the distribution of *family* incomes. Also, I have the impression, possibly mistaken, that a disproportionate number of feminist women are employed in the 'service' jobs – social work, the law, teaching – which exist largely as by-products of the male-dominated hierarchical economy. It will be when we see approximately

equal numbers of men and women as carpenters, rock musicians, economists and child-rearers, that we will have something big to cheer about.

(7)   A key achievement would be to break the rigid link between authority
and pay. It is this that forces the most able people to change from whatever they are good at to managing, in order to gain the rewards for their
ability. And it generates the incentive to create ever-taller hierarchies, since,
the longer the lines of authority, the more the manager gets paid. Management
should be treated as an occupation like any other, with good managers
paid more than bad ones, and no presumption that the manager of a group
of workers should automatically be the highest paid member of it. Government should at least experiment in its own departments with work-groups
run on these non-hierarchical lines.

(8)   It could be worthwhile to scrutinise the practice whereby managers
retain most of the profits of their firms for internal re-investment. Why not
require that *all* profits be remitted to their owners, the shareholders. The
dividend cheques might be accompanied by a letter from the management
asking for some of the money back, but at least re-investment would not
be automatic. The increased flow of funds would stir-up competition
in the capital markets, making it easier for new ventures to attract financing
– it would increase elasticity.

(9)   Elimination of exploitation would surely generate an irresistible
force to reform work. There simply would not be a labour force willing
to do all the boring and unpleasant jobs. This would be partly accommodated
by reorganising the work process – fewer and less important managers
with more worker participation; 'job-enrichment' to make work more
interesting and creative.

But there would remain an irreducible minimum of dull, dead-end jobs.
We could pay people more for doing this work – that is, pay more for bad
jobs than for more agreeable employment. When the bad jobs are physically
very demanding and/or dangerous – coal mining underground, for example
– this principle is already implemented to some extent. But most bad jobs
(for example, assembly line work, cleaning offices, waiting on tables) are
not very physically or mentally demanding, so that the people who would
choose to do them would be at the bottom of the ability distribution.

Thus, paying more for such work would amount to financially compensating people for their bad luck in being born dull. While I cannot see
any moral objection to this, it would be so far from the current practice
of any economy on earth that it cannot seriously be proposed as a feasible
policy.

The equitable solution, if no-one wants to take on something that must be done, is that *everyone* should do it – it should be shared. I am not thinking of the Chinese custom of sending the intellectuals off to the fields once a month, though this would probably do us no harm. Instead, why not have the children do the dirty work? Require every young person to spend a year or two immediately after leaving high school working full-time at one of the menial, dead-end, and low-paid jobs. Such could be in private or public sector, perhaps including service in the armed forces as one of the options from which a choice could be made.

As well as being eminently fair – after all, everyone who survives into adulthood must take a turn at youth – this scheme would have social and psychological advantages. Dead-end work is relatively easy to bear when it is known to be short-term. And middle-class children would benefit from some 'hands-on' exposure to how the rest of the world lives and works.

(10) Finally, something should be done to make our bureaucratic organisations more 'open'. For the people who work in them, big bureaucracies are like self-contained economies – job mobility is much easier within than between them. This is bad because it can trap people in job situations that do not suit them. And it encourages the growth-bias of bureaucrats – the ambitions of energetic personnel can only be satisfied within the organisation by having it grow, so that more layers of managers, and higher-paid top jobs, can be justified.

But we could get the benefits of size (security for some, opportunity for others) without the rigidities and biases, by amalgamating smaller production units into co-operatives. The co-operative would provide an umbrella organisation, guaranteeing the employment, pensions, and so on, of its members, but not restricting them to remain in a particular unit. Thus, an employee who tired of making widgets could apply for a transfer to the blobbles branch of the co-op. A particularly able person in one of the smaller production units could be promoted to a job in another, larger, unit, instead of being forced, as in a closed organisation, to promote its internal growth, whatever the economic rationale, as the only means of getting the rewards due to ability. Organisations within the co-operative would be *open* to each other.

This sounds something like the modern multi-divisional, or 'M-form' firm, which is a collection of semi-autonomous operating units reportable to a head office. The introduction of the M-form in General Motors by Alfred Sloan is credited as one of the great industrial innovations, rivalling in importance the assembly line as a means of building very large organisations without having them collapse under the inefficiencies of bureaucracy.[6] (Thus the M-form is a 'defensive' innovation — responding to the particular problem of loss of control due to extreme size. The motive for size itself remains of dubious economic merit.)

But co-operatives would differ from big firms in at least three respects:

(1)   There would not necessarily be any technical or marketing link between the operating units. Indeed, a large diversity of function is likely to be beneficial, because of the choice it gives members of the co-op, and for macroeconomic reasons, mentioned below.

(2)   Unlike nearly all large firms, the co-operative would be geographically concentrated. If people are to switch their economic function without mobility costs, they must be able to stay in their neighbour-hood. As a result, co-operatives would become political and social organisations in addition to their economic purpose.

(3)   As community-based organisations, we could expect co-operatives to be more democratic and less hierarchical than firms of similar size.

There are some approximate precedents for this model of co-operatives of open organisations. The Spanish Mondragon system is one that is quite well known,[7] and another is the communes of China.

Writing on the latter in one of his special reports for *The Economist*, Norman McCrae discerned a system of what he called 'village Keynesianism' — a policy of switching workers around the commune to keep all employed when demand fluctuates.[8] In the Chinese case, fluctuations appear to be of seasonal origin, resulting from the agricultural base of the communes' economies. In the off-season, workers are put onto manufacturing, or to building irrigation and other capital investment projects.

But co-ops could deal with the fluctuations of advanced capitalist economies, so long as they were sufficiently diversified. Microeconomic shifts in the demand for particular products could be accommodated by switching workers and capital from contracting to expanding activities. And macroeconomic swings in the total demand for goods and services could be fitted-in without unemployment by varying the number of people engaged on long-term investment projects, including work on the infrastructure — roads, utilities, recreational facilities — of the community in which the co-op was based.

If the co-operative system became widespread, it would greatly reduce the difficulty for central government of maintaining non-inflationary full employment. This is not just because each co-op would, in effect, be operating a do-it-yourself macroeconomic policy to deal with its own unemployment problems, but because, by taking quick and direct action at such a low level of the economy, the co-ops would nip in the bud the second-round 'multiplier' effects that cause a disturbance in one sector of the economy to have repercussions in others.

How could co-operatives of open organisations be fostered? They cannot be imposed from above, by government. They have to happen because individuals and communities *want* them to happen, and do something about it. All that writing about co-ops can accomplish is stimulate interest at this grass-roots level.

However, there may be some appropriate policies to facilitate formation of co-operatives. The legal system under which all economic activity takes place has been developed to serve conventional limited-liability, private ownership firms. This probably means that there are various impediments to alternative forms of microeconomic organisation which could be dismantled. The private sector capital market may not be very good at handling requests for funds from non-conventional business enterprises. Government may therefore be justified in using its existing development institutions as conduits for loan finance for co-operatives.

To conclude with a qualification: hierarchy is not entirely to be despised. There *are* goods best produced using large-scale techniques. And there is a role to be played by formal lines of authority and responsibility. Correspondingly, there are people who prefer doing relatively simple, repetitive tasks, and others who are gifted managers.

But the point I have stressed is that the supply of such jobs and people falls short of the demand placed on them in our bureaucratic economies. Thus, we should be aiming at a more sensible match between the difficulty distribution of jobs, and ability distribution of the workforce. This means, since ability is given, that the jobs must be adjusted to fit. At present there are too many jobs at the extremes of the distribution. There are not enough people with the leadership ability needed to competently take on the jobs at the peaks of the bureaucratic pyramids. And there are not enough workers whose talents or aspirations are limited to the repetitive banality of most present factory and office employment.

This chapter has suggested an alternative: a system of production units organised internally in 'flat' hierarchies, and open to each other within the network of co-operatives. I am not at all dogmatic about how this should be achieved, but it seems an attractive goal.

Part V
Policies: Special Cases

24 Productivity and Industrial Policy

'I am mystified. It appears that Okun's law has been repealed.'

ARTHUR OKUN

There is no more puzzling big number in economics than productivity – the per capita gross national product that determines a country's standard of living. Why are some mature industrial economies more productive than others? Why does productivity grow faster in some places than elsewhere? And, the biggest puzzle of all, what happened in 1974, when productivity growth virtually collapsed right across the world economy, never, it seems, to fully recover?

Interest in these matters runs particularly high in the English-speaking world. Of the 'big seven' OECD economies, Canada, the United Kingdom, and the United States had the fifth, sixth, and seventh highest growth rates of output per employee in the 1960–73 period.[1] After 1973, growth dropped in all seven economies, but Canada, the UK, and the US retained the bottom three positions.[2] Predictably, these figures have been greeted with cries of alarm and calls for action. This chapter will examine the seriousness of the productivity problem, and suggest what should, and should not be done about it, looking first at the cross-country differences, then at the general slowdown in growth.

It has always been difficult to explain why one economy has higher levels and/or growth rates of productivity than another. It is easy enough to devise a plausible set of factors to account for the workers in a particular industry or plant being more productive than workers in other plants. But when inter-country differences are examined, things are much less clear. Major factors that have been proposed include:

(1) *Differences in capital intensity.* The more equipment each employee has to work with, the higher should be their productivity. Surely this is reasonable, yet it has proved extraordinarily difficult to demonstrate.[3]

Labour productivity in Canadian manufacturing industries averages out at only 70 to 80 per cent of productivity in equivalent US industries, even though the capital/labour ratio (the amount of equipment and machinery per employee) is actually higher in Canada.[4] Growth rates of the capital stock in the post-war period up to 1960 were about the same in the UK and Japan, when productivity growth was much higher in the latter economy.[5]

(2) *Economies of scale* are sometimes suggested as sources of productivity differences. Yet the median plant size in the UK is twice or more the median size in France, Italy, Canada and Sweden – all countries with higher measured productivity than Britain's.[6] And analysis of plants in Canadian manufacturing industries has turned up very little evidence of bigger being systematically better than smaller.[7]

(3) *Technological progressiveness* is popularly believed to correlate with growth performance. It is hard to know how to measure this, but on one widely accepted indicator (expenditures on research and development as a proportion of GNP) the US did best, in 1971, and even the UK was higher on the list than Japan and Sweden.[8]

These are just three of the more important factors that economists have examined to explain international productivity differences; but everything considered, it seems fail to conclude that we have not succeeded. In what has been called 'the most systematic and imaginative effort' to explain the differences,[9] Edward Denison measured GNP per worker to be 41 per cent lower in Europe than in the United States in 1960. Less than a quarter of this difference was due to lower capital/labour ratios in Europe, and less than one eighth to economies of scale. Well over half of the productivity difference could not be explained, and was summarily attributed to the 'lag in the application of knowledge, general efficiency, and errors and omissions'.[10]

The unexplained, or 'residual', factor also dominated measured factors in accounting for growth rates within economies during the high-growth years of the 1950s and 1960s. In the neoclassical model that was believed to describe the growth process, the residual is interpreted as 'technical progress', an increase in the amount of output an economy can extract from its labour and capital stocks that is credited to the discovery and dissemination of improved techniques of production.

Given that the most casual observation of the real world reveals all sorts of improved processes and products in all sectors of the economy –

from supertankers to supermarkets — it seemed plausible enough that technical progress should play such a large role, if irksome to economists that something equivalent to a 'free lunch' should apparently be more important to growth than the intriguing trade-offs involved in allocating GNP between consumption and investment.

But neoclassical complacency has been shattered by the events of the last decade. Over the 1960—73 period, productivity growth in the seven largest OECD economies averaged 5.1 per cent annually. In the years from 1974 to 1980, the average was 2.1 per cent — a fall of 3 full percentage points.[11] Over the entire OECD group, only one country (Australia) did not have a slowdown in productivity growth after 1973.

As the bad news spread, there was a flurry of research interest, with disturbing results. The slowdown could not be blamed on a drop in one of the readily measurable economic inputs, such as capital formation or labour quality. Rather, it was the unexplained 'residual' factor that had collapsed. Denison, who was again at the forefront of the investigative effort, found that 2.1 percentage points of the 2.9 per cent drop in productivity growth in the United States came from the fall in his residual figure.[12]

The residual had turned on its inventor! For if a rationalisation in terms of technical progress was apparently reasonable during the fast-growth years, this was clearly not so of a sudden and universal collapse. How could the long, secular, wave of technological innovations dramatically dry up, in all places and all at once? There was a desperate search for alternative explanations. Many were offered — from ageing capital to lazy workers to over-investment in pollution-abatement. Denison gamely worked his way through seventeen of these. Some he rejected altogether; the others did not add-up to much. He was forced to conclude that what happened after 1973 is 'to be blunt, a mystery'.[13] That is, the residual is truly a 'measure of our ignorance'; or, more precisely, an indicator of the inadequacy of the neoclassical theoretical framework on which the growth accounting exercise had been built.

Thus, there are two problems: the real-world difficulty of productivity growth that lags in some economies, and has fallen everywhere, and the intellectual problem of not being able adequately to explain these events within the conventional paradigm.

The first of these problems generates a demand for policy action. But the second implies that it will be difficult to know what policies to implement. In particular, our ignorance about the underlying processes of productivity growth counsels extreme caution in getting mixed up in 'micro-meddling' activities that depend on precise knowledge about the workings of the system. Yet, alarmingly, the opposite has occurred. There has been a great surge of interest, particularly in North America, in something called 'industrial strategy', or 'industrial policy'. Details differ, but the proponents of industrial policy have in common a faith that government can increase productivity by intervening in the affairs of particular industries or even firms.

An ideologically mild form of industrial policy sometimes proposed by economists is the use of investment incentives applying not to particular firms but across sectors or over the economy at large. Such measures are usually justified with reference to one of the big 'macroeconometric' models in which modern economics' awkward synthesis of Keynesian and neoclassical doctrine is elaborated in hundreds of equations.

The fundamental neoclassical assumption of perfect competition implies that the rate of return to capital is forced to be approximately equal right across the economy. For some neoclassicists, the amount of investment generated by this competitive process will be optimal, and no policy intervention at all is desirable. Others, though, of more activist bent, perceive that the market-generated rate of investment may be too low, due to uncertainty about the future or to distortions elsewhere in the system such as too-high marginal income tax rates. Accordingly, they recommend general inducements to invest more; for example, a corporate tax cut.[14]

But evidence offered throughout this book, including the failure of the growth accounting studies noted in this chapter, strongly suggests that the economy is not neoclassical. In particular, there appears to be what was dubbed in chapter 9 a 'Band-X' of underutilised productive potential, which is generated, *inter alia*, by persistent differences in the efficiency of firms, including the efficiency with which they utilise capital equipment.

This means that, instead of stimulating investment and so productivity right across the economy, a tax break would probably *reduce* aggregate productivity, because it would only encourage investment by the less efficient firms who find themselves, quite properly, at the bottom of the queue when private sector investment funds are being doled out. In an imperfectly competitive economy, the more efficient (and thus more profitable) operators are constrained by sales, not shortages of funds, in their investment spending. Of course they would happily accept a tax cut, but as a windfall, not an inducement.[15]

There is another school of industrial policy proponents that contains few economists of any stripe. Indeed its members (often politicians egged on by interest groups) sometimes seem to deny the existence, in even imperfect form, of the market forces which are at the centre of the economist's world-view. Their idea is that government should descend to the micro-level of the economy and give money to particular industries or even firms. Policy-makers should pick 'winners' — the activities and organisations with potential for future growth — to 'get the economy moving again'.

Certainly, the potential winners are out there in the economy. But the key questions are: (1) whether government will do better than the private sector at identifying and encouraging them; and (2) whether they can intervene at all at this level without undesirable side-effects.

Past performance offers little comfort for this sort of industrial policy. When government steps where capitalists fear to tread, it usually puts its foot in it. Public sector bureaucrats do not make good venture capitalists. Ironically, to those who see a socialist tinge to this sort of public participation in business, the most spectacular failures have been with products aimed at the high-income end of the market — luxury sports cars and supersonic airliners in Britain; sports cars and executive jets in Canada.

But probably more disturbing than the success or failure of particular projects are the side-effects. The deep purse of government offers a security blanket to businesses which saps competitive vigour. And this same purse is an inducement to all entrepreneurs to divert energy from their proper function of producing goods and services towards qualifying for handouts. The worst example of these side-effects is undoubtedly the US armaments industry, which is effectively nationalised in every respect except for the profits.[16] One economist blames as a major cause of the decline in productivity growth in the United States the transformation of '20,000 prime contractors for the Department of Defense' from 'cost-minimising to cost-maximising' behaviour.[17]

The handout-seeking business was given the name 'paper entrepreneurialism' by Robert Reich, in his book 'The Next American Frontier'.[18] I have used this term, slightly shortened to 'paper entrepreneurship', as a synonym for what economists call 'rent-seeking behaviour'. Reich documents the enormous invasion of microeconomic affairs by government in supposedly free enterprise America, and the consequences of this for the perversion of the profit motive. Tax credits to industry were 1 per cent of GNP in 1950; 3 per cent by 1980. 40 per cent of the chief executive officers of the largest US firms now have a law or finance background; up from 13 per cent in 1950, when most executives were from marketing or engineering: that is, were trained in making and selling things rather than in trading paper assets. People with law degrees are *twenty five* times thicker on the ground in the United States than in Japan; surely this is close to an epidemic of litigiousness.

The enthusiasts of industrial policy would disburse vast sums of taxpayers' money on the basis of simple rules of thumb and dubious inferences of causality. Consider the relationship between size and economic success. It can be observed that the large firms in an industry tend to be relatively profitable. *Ergo*, cobble together a large firm and success will follow. This sort of reasoning led to British Leyland and British Steel, and the loss of billions of pounds of public money.

The fallacy is the assumption that success follows from size, rather than both being the consequence of a third factor. General Motors, Renault, Toyota became big *and* profitable because they were good at making automobiles. A thousand or so other manufacturers were not so competent, and went out of business. The problem with Britain's car industry before British Leyland was not that the firms were not big enough to be good, but rather that they were not good enough to be big. The hard fact is that European car assembly lines produce from 75 to 120 per cent more output than *similarly equipped* assembly lines in Britain.[19] Thus the formation of BL significantly reduced national productivity by artificially preserving some firms which should have been wound up, and probably also by impeding the progress of those manufacturers – Jaguar, Rover, perhaps MG – which are, or were, good performers in their niches of the industry.

The point applies to other attempts to find simplistic cures for lagging productivity. A favourite is research and development, or, more generally, any 'high-tech' activity. At least since Mr Harold Wilson and his 'white-hot heat of the technological revolution', there have been attempts to pick out and prod along firms and products at the 'leading edge' of technology.

But even granting a link between, say, research and development expenditures and productivity growth (and it was noted above that there really is not much empirical support for this) does not validate public policy intervention to increase research and development. Firms currently operating at the frontiers of knowledge may be more capable than average at increasing productivity. But if industrial policy is to deliberately increase high-tech activity in hope of thereby raising productivity, then firms must be induced to undertake reesearch that they would not otherwise have done. Since there are likely to be good reasons for the firms' reluctance to take on these activities on their own, it is foolish to expect the results to be as fruitful as the plum projects that they pick themselves.[20]

That the balloon of industrial policy has stayed aloft so long is probably to be blamed on a current of hot air emanating from Japan; or, to be precise, from westerners who claim some knowledge of the Japanese 'miracle'. The famous 'MITI' (Ministry of International Trade and Industry) is said to pick winners and losers, and divert resources towards one and away from the other. In fact this is not so. MITI has 'visions' of desirable future industrial structures. The current vision identifies a number of technological development tasks for the 1980s in such fields as energy, data processing, telecommunications, and genetics. It urges more R&D spending, public as well as private. And it sees a role for government in the development of high-cost, high-risk, long-lead-time technologies.

What the vision for the 1980s does not do is provide resources. It does not even propose budgetary priorities. At most, it presents a description of how some aspects of the Japanese economy and society might appear in the 1990s if MITI and its advisers are sufficently heeded by the budget makers and private investors — and if, in fact, the technologies listed in the vision prove to be feasible in commercial terms.[21]

That is, MITI engages in what the French call indicative-planning — sophisticated 'what if?' forecasting that can assist other peoples' decision-making. The key distinction between this and an activist industrial policy is that MITI does not have any money to spend. Therefore it is not required to be a better judge of investment opportunities than the private sector; nor does it generate the incentives for paper entrepreneurship.

All this may seem rather negative. I have argued that knowledge of the process of productivity growth is far too flimsy to support the super-structure of detailed micro-level policy intervention proposed by the advocates of industrial policy. What then should be done? To answer this, it is necessary to return to the distinction between inter-country differences in growth rates, and the slowdown that has afflicted all countries over the last ten years.

On the first issue, it will be argued that there really is not a problem at all. That is, policy-makers have no business worrying about the relatively low growth rate of the United States, or the relatively low level of per capita GNP achieved in Britain. Subject to one important qualification, which will be returned to below, the people in these countries are just about as productive as they want to be.

This assertion requires some substantiation. Consider the reasons that have been offered to explain productivity differences. It is not, as we have seen, a matter of inadequate investment in plant and equipment. Rather, differences are due to differences in the productivity extracted from a given plant. The 'Think Tank' that compared the British and European car industries found that slower-moving assembly lines, and more stoppages (due to poor stock control, labour disputes, and mechanical breakdowns) were responsible for the variance in output from similarly equipped plants.[22] Bacon and Eltis conclude:

If these faults apply to many British industries as they probably do —
it is unlikely that the car industry is unique — it will be evident that
much underproduction is due to failures by management and labour
on the shop floor. There is relatively little that governments can do to
put such matters right.[23]

But is there even anything *wrong* with low British productivity? The
British have a great deal of personal and social freedom. They have been
'unproductive' for a long time. It is plausible that they *choose* low productivity. Britain has a certain amount of wealth, in its energy reserves and
in the investment portfolios built up in its imperial era. It has a social and
environmental fabric pieced together over three centuries without revolution, civil war, or invasion. If the British had wished to alter their habits
and institutions to foster higher economic productivity, then surely they
would have done so by now. It is rather an insult to their spirit and intelli-
gence to imply otherwise, as do those local and foreign critics who lament
the 'British Disease'. Even in the midst of the Thatcher recession more
than 90 per cent of the British population consider themselves to be
happy with their lot — the highest in Europe after Holland. The disease
does not seem to be very uncomfortable.

The same point can be made about the United States, which, having
developed its own abundant natural riches to yield a material standard of
living unsurpassed for most of this century, seems now to be resting on its
laurels, so that, in so far as these things can be measured, a few European
economies are now ahead in the per capita GNP list. So what?

Contrast with the situation of the unfortunate Japanese — overcrowded,
resource-poor, caught on an economic treadmill of adding-value to other
peoples' resources and persuading them to buy back the final product, so
as to raise the money to pay for the next shipload of materials. The
Japanese growth rate is a product of desperation, not choice, and it
would be an unusual American or Britisher who would swap their relatively
relaxed and expansive lifestyle for the cramped regimentation of Japan.
What Western manager would put up with the routine at Japan's 'largest
outdoor management training school', where, along with martial arts
exercises at 5 am, and 25 mile forced marches in the dark, each manager
has to stand in front of the railway station and sing 'The Salesman's
Song' sufficiently loudly to satisfy an instructor standing 50 feet away?[24]

But there is one lesson that we can learn from the Japanese. Philip
Trezise gives the credit for 'a major role in the nation's economic achieve-
ments' to the 'monetary and fiscal policies that have underlain the relatively
steady course of the economy over 30 years'.[25] That is, government does

have a legitimate contribution to productivity – to maintain stable full employment at the macroeconomic level. Then business has the confidence to invest, and less reason to resist, along with unions, the reallocation of resources from declining to expanding industries.

The importance of macroeconomic conditions is vividly demonstrated by the second productivity puzzle – the great slowdown after 1973. The proximate cause of this is fairly obvious: the dramatic increase in oil prices initiated by OPEC at the end of that year. The direct consequences of higher oil prices were a transfer of wealth to the oil producers of about 2 per cent of OECD gross national product, and the instant obsolescence of a proportion of the energy-using business and private capital. No doubt the adjustments to this had some effect on productivity.

But the biggest factor was the recession induced across the OECD economies by governments trying (successfully) to neutralise the inflationary impact of higher oil prices. The eventual recession-induced loss of GNP was around three times larger than the original transfer of wealth to OPEC. It now seems clear that the decrease in capacity utilisation accompanying the recession was the culprit in the collapse of productivity growth.[26]

The real puzzle for economists is not explaining *what* caused the slowdown, but in explaining *why* it should have done so. In neoclassical theory, the combination of 'smooth' technologies and price-taking behaviour implies that the workers laid off in a recession will be of below-average productivity, so that the productivity of the unit should *rise* with declines in output. But in the lumpy, low-elasticity real world, firms are constrained by demand, not by price – they typically have excess capacity, meaning that they could expand output and reduce unit costs, if the extra demand were there. And conversely, a recession-induced fall in output increases costs per unit – productivity falls.

Thus, the great productivity slowdown, though unpleasant to live through, may at least help the case of those who would urge the feasibility and desirability of permanent full employment.

The long-run effects of full employment on productivity would also be beneficial. High and sustained levels of capacity utilisation give entrepreneurs confidence to invest in new plant and equipment. And a tight labour market reduces the resistance of firms and unions to the reallocation of resources from declining to expanding sectors, as noted above.

Along with the maintenance of full employment, there are other high-level 'framework' policies that would improve productivity. The elasticity-increasing measures suggested in previous chapters would improve the climate in which decisions are taken, without involving government in direct attempts to determine the precise course of events. It is the low-level, micro-meddling schemes proposed by the enthusiasts of 'industrial policy' that are fundamentally inappropriate to government, and would be of more harm than assistance to the goal of improving economic efficiency.

25 Being Sensible about Energy and the Environment

'Anyone who believes exponential growth can go on forever in a finite world is either a madman or an economist.'

KENNETH BOULDING

People are not the only resource of which the productivity must be monitored carefully. The high-growth years of the great post-war boom carried in them the seeds of a longer term dilemma: economic expansion chewed up increasing quantities of the basic primary inputs of which the supply was fixed or even decreasing.

The ensuing 'limits to growth' debate, which focused on environmental issues in the 1960s, and on depletion of energy in the 1970s, has often annoyed economists with its 'doomsday' scenarios of disappearing resources. Even on Spaceship Earth, the total potential availability of almost every resource, though ultimately finite, exceeds many decades or even centuries of depletion at current rates.[1] The real issue is *cost*. Up until about ten years ago, all the oil used cost less than $3 a barrel to produce. Now the known reserves of cheap oil are only a decade or so away from exhaustion. But the price is already much higher – around $30 a barrel – and at this price many other sources (the North Sea, for example) can be extracted profitably. At an even higher price – say $100 – tar sands, liquefication from coal, and other as yet unheard of reserves of oil will come on stream.

The point is that, with finite or depleting resources as with anything else, the price mechanism can do a job of balancing supply and demand. Naturally, we will be the poorer for using-up our low-cost resources (though not as poor as if we did not use them at all, of course), but market forces will handle the adjustment to high-cost supplies: there is no need for panic; nor for draconian acts by governments. The price mechanism certainly has a large and useful role to play, and policy-makers should be discouraged from getting in its way – for example by the ostrich-like

211

attempts of the government of Canada to set a 'made-in-Canada' price for domestic oil consumers.[2]

But there are two particular characteristics of resource markets that do justify some policy intervention.

First, there is the well-known problem of 'externalities'. In the classic example, an upstream plant uses a resource (a river) to dispose of its waste, but the effect of this waste on water quality is a cost imposed 'externally' to the plant, on downstream users of the river.

In principle, externalities can be dealt with by assigning property rights to the resource. When only a few people are involved (as in another classic, if esoteric, example, the case of one farmer's bees pollinating another farmer's orchard), these rights can be assigned to individuals (whether the perpetrator or the recipient of the externality gets the rights must be decided on equity grounds), and they can haggle-out an agreement between themselves. But, in many important cases, negative (bad) externalities affect whole populations — acid rain and foul air are examples — and then the property right can only be assigned to some political organisation representing the affected people. We are back in the world of public policy-making.

The second policy problem arises from the distributional implications of increasing resource scarcity. When oil is selling at the extraction cost of the marginal source (say North Sea Oil at $30 a barrel) there are still many 'infra-marginal' producers whose costs are $3 a barrel. The latter get very rich selling at ten times production costs. Now it can be argued that such wealth is a legitimate reward for the investors' good luck or good judgement in owning low-cost oil wells. But, even in 'free enterprise' societies, there are strong political pressures to get some of the money back. Thus the made-in-Canada pricing policy, wasteful though it may be, is politically justified as a means of redistributing wealth from the two million Albertans who own most of the oil and gas, to the twenty million plus citizens of the rest of Canada.

Dealing with both the externalities and the wealth-distribution consequences of resource use depends on the relationship between costs and depletion. Consider again the river example. Fish, it must be admitted, pollute rivers. But their excrement is quickly broken-up and recycled by the river's ecosystem. That is, the cost of the fishes' 'pollution' is zero, or even negative if it is a useful input somewhere else on the food chain. But on the other extreme, a large urban area discharging sewage into a river can literally kill it — destroy all life. That is, use of a resource (in this case the absorptive capacity of a waterway) is costless at low levels, but can be catastrophic above some threshold.

Against the costs must be set the benefits. Municipalities do not discharge raw sewage just to be mischievous; they do it to save the expense of a treatment plant.

The sensible goal of policy intervention is to ensure that, at the margin, the costs and benefits of using a resource balance each other. Three types of policy instruments have been used. Two of them are inappropriate; the third is a governed economy approach:

(1)   *Direct regulation is the traditional, and still the most common instrument used. Governments or their agencies instruct individual firms or regional authorities on permitted resource-use levels, and monitor them to ensure compliance.*

Like other attempts to secure satisfactory performance by issuing detailed orders to participants in the economy (see chapter 20), resource-use regulation makes heavy and unrealistic demands on the skill and probity of policy-makers. They must, in effect, have a detailed model of each user's impact on the resource, and be able to avoid the ever-present risk of being 'captured' by the regulatees.

There are many examples of regulation going wrong. Consider the story of standards for coal-fired utility boilers told by Robert Crandall to a United States Senate subcommittee.[3] Supported by environmentalists and midwestern coal miners, the Environmental Protection Agency (EPA) persuaded Congress to amend the Clean Air Act to require utilities to install best-available equipment to remove a proportion of the sulphur emitted when coal is burnt. This sounds harmless enough. But its effect, since all plants must have the equipment regardless of the sulphur content of the coal that they burn, is to encourage Midwest utilities to use the cheaper high-sulphur Midwest coal (hence the support of the miners), rather than the low-sulphur Western coal, even though the same total reduction in sulphur emissions could be obtained for about $1 billion less by burning low-sulphur coal and only partly treating the gases.

These are the classic consequences of micro-meddling — policy-makers, egged on by special interest groups, incurring unintended and costly side effects, and not necessarily even achieving the ostensible aim of their policy.

(2)   *A more 'economic' approach is to apply taxes or subsidies to resource-users. The tax or subsidy is set to match the value of the externality generated by the use of the resource.*

The advantage of this approach over direct administrative regulation is that people are encouraged to find the lowest-cost means of achieving the policy-maker's resource-use goal. In the coal-burning case, for example, the tax on sulphur dioxide emitted would equal the estimated environmental cost of the pollutant. Utilities would have an incentive to reduce emissions up to the point where the cost of abating another ton exceeded the tax per ton, and naturally would choose the least-cost combination of coal and emission equipment to achieve this.

The disadvantage is that a great deal of information is required; not only on abatement costs, but also on the market position of polluters. The response of two identical plants to a given tax will differ according to differences in their owners' ability to pass on cost increases (such as taxes) to customers instead of responding with the quantitative adjustments hoped for by the policy-makers.

Thus, although the tax/subsidy approach is generally preferable to direct regulation, it may still be too demanding in its informational requirements, given the 'distance' between policy-maker and the micro-level of the economy at which the resource-using decisions are made.

(3) *The governed economy approach to policy-making is to ensure that the goal is met, while giving micro-level agents maximum freedom to achieve adding-up in the most efficient way possible.* In the case of resources, the requirement is that use or depletion not exceed some set amount. The problem is similar to that of limiting total imports addressed in chapter 17, and the same policy instrument — marketable permits — can be proposed.

The idea is that government sell-off, to the highest bidders, 'licenses to pollute' (or to deplete, or whatever). The total number issued equals the policy goal, which therefore will be achieved, unless there is illegal activity (a problem for all policy). The policy-maker need not know in advance who will find it most costly not to pollute, nor the price at which the permits will trade — the market will sort this out, and yield an efficient pattern of pollution abatement in the process.

The EPA has already implemented a form of the permits system to control emissions of pollutants. Plants with a number of pollutant sources may be put under a 'bubble', which specifies the total emissions, while leaving the owner(s) of the plants to allocate these between the sources as they wish. Other arrangements being tried are 'offsets', which allow two firms to trade-off emissions between themselves, and 'banks', in which emission reductions can be deposited for later sale. These and other features and problems of marketable permits are discussed by Roger Noll.[4]

The big advantage of permits over taxes is that they ensure that the desired resource-use level will be met, whereas taxes require economists to *predict* how firms will respond. Since predictions are often wrong, the target will often not be met. Given the possible catastrophic consequences of over-use of resources, as when an entire ecosystem is irreversibly ruined, it seems essential that targets not be exceeded.

But the problems of working out desirable rates of pollution and so on should not be discounted. These are usually very microeconomic matters subject to considerable uncertainty. In many cases, the appropriate action for central government may be to ensure that property rights are assigned – that is, that someone owns the resource – and let owners and users sort out matters for themselves.

An important exception, which should be dealt with by national or even international authorities, is energy. Energy production and consumption are truly big numbers, of importance right up to the macroeconomic level, as the two OPEC price shocks, in 1973–4 and 1979, demonstrated.

The problem here is not depletion, despite the scares about running out of oil. The turmoil and supply disruptions that accompanied the big OPEC price increases raised concerns about the finiteness of fossil fuels, but the associated shortages were short-run. Low-cost fossil fuels will eventually run out, of course, but they will not do so overnight, and the time-path of prices will give plenty of warning. What does need to be dealt with are the disruptions from temporary shortfalls in supply, and the massive income transfers from consuming to producing economies.

Both problems would be manageable under a marketable permits system. Government would issue permits giving the right to purchase a given quantity of petrol. Once issued, these permits would be freely saleable at whatever price they could fetch in the market.[5] The number of permits issued could be reduced in times of temporary supply shortages. These cause problems, not because they imply that everyone has to make do with less petrol for a time (we can easily adjust our consumption habits to accommodate this) but because the fear of getting no petrol at all induces panics, queueing, and hoarding, which greatly magnify the disruption implied by the original shortfall.

The petroleum supply crisis in the United States, in the second quarter of 1979, had Americans committing every crime from auto theft to murder to fill their tanks. But the actual shortfall in supply was about 900 000 barrels a day – less than 5 per cent of demand (most of which was due not to cuts in imports from Iran, but to deliberate building-up of inventories by the refiners, encouraged by the Department of Energy).[6]

Much larger disruptions than this could easily be handled with the aid of a permits system. The price of permits would rise, of course, during the shortage; this would encourage people to find ways of economising on petroleum, and enable all users to be sure of easy access without queues or black markets.

How should petroleum permits be distributed by government? A good case, on equity grounds, can be made that access to a natural resource is a right to be shared evenly amongst the citizenry, and that this principle applies to energy as much as it does to, say, national parks. Then at least a portion of the available permits should be distributed equally between all adults. Those without automobiles or oil furnaces would be free to re-sell them for whatever value the market currently placed on them. It is utterly inequitable to have a rationing scheme that gives more to people with a car, and more still to people with two cars, as is sometimes suggested. It is, indeed, the relatively heavy energy users who are disproportionately responsible for shortages.

This applies to nations as well as individuals. The United States and Canada are extraordinarily profligate in their use of energy. The US, with 6 per cent of the world's population, consumes about 30 per cent of the energy used each year. The quantity of energy used per dollar of GNP in North America is nearly twice the amount in Japan and Western Europe.[7] A proportion of the difference is due to lower population densities in North America, but it seems clear that the biggest factor is differences in prices paid by energy users. For a long time, energy prices in Japan and Western Europe have been double or more North American prices,[8] and as a direct result the structure of both industrial and consumer use of energy has evolved differently.[9]

This difference in energy prices can be blamed for most of the bad things that have happened to our economies in the last decade. Suppose that the United States had always priced energy at around West European levels, and as a consequence now used about 40 per cent less crude oil, at current rates, around 5 million barrels a day, which is about equal to one third of OPEC's current production, and to current (late–1983) U.S. oil imports. It is unlikely that OPEC could have sustained either of its big price increases in the absence of US import demand for oil. For example, total Iranian oil production before the revolution that disrupted their exports and triggered the 1979 price shock was 5.8 million barrels a day.[10] Oil prices would probably still have increased, as the lowest-cost sources of supply were depleted, but would almost certainly not be at their present levels of around $30 a barrel.

The savings would be enormous. Even at OPEC's current low production rates of around 16 million barrels a day, a $10 a barrel difference in price is worth nearly $60 billion a year to the OECD and the developing economies. Even larger sums would have been saved by escaping the OPEC-induced worldwide recessions that followed the price shocks. The long-term trends towards declining economic performance that are the principal concern of this book would not be affected, but life in the short-term would have been much more pleasant.[11]

All this from price increases that would not cost anything, since they would be effected by taxes on gasoline use, as in Europe, which substitute for other taxes. Other indirect taxes could be lowered by the amount of oil-tax revenue so that the consumer price index would be, on balance, unaffected.

The failure of the Western oil consuming economies to counter OPEC with appropriate energy taxes must rank as the most costly mistake ever made in microeconomic policy. Pointing this out will not restore the millions of jobs and hundreds of billions of dollars lost over the last ten years, but it might help avoid perpetuating the error.

Finally, it is worthwhile noting, even though it does not seem to be very susceptible to policy action, that there is a factor of greater importance even than energy pricing (indeed, of unsurpassed importance) to the availability of natural resources. This factor is population. Resources show themselves to be limited when their price increases with higher utilisation rates (in contrast to manufactured goods, of which the price generally falls as volume increases). Furthermore, the price-utilisation relationship is usually non-linear — a doubling in output goes with more than a doubling of costs and price. Ecosystems, for example, are capable of absorbing a certain amount of pollution without damage: that is, up to a point, they are a 'free' resource. But thereafter costs may increase drastically, up to the critical level of catastrophe, when the ecosystem is destroyed by the pollution.

It seems clear that had the world's population stayed at its turn-of-the-century level (that is, at about half its present level) people alive today would be much better off. Reserves of $2 a barrel oil would last well into the twenty first century. There would be twice as many antiques, old houses, and desirable vacation-home locations available per person, and their prices would be a fraction of today's actual levels. The per capita costs of preventing pollution would be less. Cities would be smaller and less congested. Food would be a lot cheaper.

Against this, we might be less technologically 'advanced' in both civil and military activities. The space program would be way behind its present schedule, and so would nuclear technology (especially if less pressure on resources in the first decades of the century defused the tensions that allowed Hitler to come to power in Germany). Some economies of scale in manufacturing might not be as fully exploited as they are now, though a world market of even half the present size should still be large enough for an efficient international division of labour, so long as trade barriers were kept low.

On balance, it seems that we are faced with a distinct trade-off between the quantity and quality of life. It also seems likely that we have not, because of externalities, made the best choice from those permitted by this trade-off. It is a classic case of market failure: the costs in higher resource prices of another baby are spread across all humanity, whilst the benefits are largely concentrated on the parents who make the birth decision, and the baby's eventual family and friends. There is thus, in principle, a legitimate role for policy intervention to reduce the birthrate, though it is not clear just what action would be acceptable. At the very least, though, we should petition our governments to dismantle overtly pro-natalist programs such as child support payments, and to spend much more money on the dissemination of birth-control techniques.

I shall leave the last word on this undoubtedly controversial topic to the French mathematician and social philosopher Condorcet, who foresaw the 'limits to growth' nearly two hundred years ago, but was less prescient about humankind's ability to deal with it.

Men will know that the duties they may be under relative to propagation will consist not in the question of giving *existence* to a greater number of beings, but *happiness* . . . they will have for their object the general welfare of the human species, of the society in which they live, of the family to which they are attached, and not the puerile idea of encumbering the earth with useless and wretched mortals.[12]

26 Poverty: A Modest Proposal

'The issue of welfare is not what it costs those who provide it but what it costs those who receive it.'

DANIEL PATRICK MOYNIHAN

If government wants to reduce poverty, it should stop trying to eliminate it. Increasingly, government is relied on to weave a 'safety net' to support those at the lower end of the income distribution; a net paid for by taxes levied on the better-off. The trouble is, that though the taxes have been paid, the money has not always turned up at the other end – the net has holes in it.

This chapter will argue that the costly failure of governments' efforts to eradicate poverty is a natural consequence of the inappropriateness of the goal – of the distance between policy-makers and the poor. The appropriate thing for government to do is establish an economic environment in which the conditions that perpetrate poverty do not thrive. Rather than trying, with inevitably incomplete success, to take money from the rich and give it to the poor, government should be helping the poor get a decent chance to earn the money for themselves.

What are the dimensions of the problem? In a country with satisfactory average per capita income, poverty is by definition a 'micro' affair; an affliction of a minority of the population whose capacity to support themselves does not meet some social norm. But the minority is not insignificant. In Canada, for example, 614000 families and 851000 unattached individuals were, in 1978, below a poverty line officially defined as the need to spend more than 62 per cent of income on food, clothing, and shelter. These people were 10 per cent of all families, and 35 per cent of all unattached individuals.[1]

Although any poverty line is drawn arbitrarily, and a wealthy society's standard might seem luxurious in the Third World, it cannot be doubted that most of those counted as living in poverty, and many who are above the line, are leading thoroughly miserable lives.

The persistence of this large poverty-stricken minority, is, of course, direct evidence of the failure of anti-poverty policies. Indeed, it is even possible that the policies have made the problem worse. Until Lyndon Johnson declared his 'War on Poverty' in 1964, the official incidence of poverty in the United States had been falling – from 33 per cent in 1949 to 18 per cent in 1964. It continued to drop during the Johnson years, though by no more than before, then began to bottom-out. The lowest percentage achieved was 11.1, in 1973, and thereafter the figure has increased, reaching 13 per cent by 1980.[2] Yet the turn-around occurred during a decade in which government's transfer payments to the poor increased, in real terms, by more than two thirds. Indeed, by one calculation, just the increase in spending on social welfare programs between 1965 and 1975 would have been enough to give each of the 25 million people classed officially as poor in the US in 1975 $8000 a year, or $32000 for a family of four.[3] Clearly, the money is not getting through.

What has gone wrong? Examination of governments' anti-poverty programs shows that most of the money spent ends up benefiting people who are not poor, and good deal of the remainder is simply wasted.

There are two ways in which income can be redistributed: by giving people cash, or by giving them goods and services. The latter category includes free or subsidised health care, education, housing, and 'social' services. Each case raises issues of both efficiency and equity.

When the state produces things and gives them away, there is potential for inefficiency effects on both supply and demand sides of the 'market'. The costs of supplying services may differ between public and private enterprise. On the demand side, if something is given freely people may waste it – consume more than they would if they had to bear the costs of production. Even if access is limited by 'need', there are the administrative costs of establishing neediness, and the by now familiar incentive problem: it is worthwhile for people to go to some trouble (ie, incur some costs) just to qualify for the handout.

How do the various programs measure up to these efficiency criteria? Free hospital care is probably efficient on the consumption side – few people like being hospitalised, so there is unlikely to be much wasteful demand encouraged by a zero price. On the supply side, the US Medicaid and Medicare (for the poor and the aged, respectively) programs have shown alarming increases in costs.[4] But this is probably due to the power of the US medical interest groups, and their bias against low-cost preventional medicine, rather than to weaknesses in the concept of state-provided medical care. Most countries have not had such unpleasant experiences with inflation of health-care costs.

Services of general practitioners are rather different, since many people enjoy visiting their doctor, and so probably do so to excess in countries like Britain, where no fee is charged. It would be preferable to charge a user fee to cover at least a proportion of the costs — a fee which doctors could waive at their own discretion in the case of poor patients.

Education seems to be quite efficiently provided by the state. Up to the end of the secondary school level there is no problem with excess demand, because attendance is compulsory for all children. Thereafter, the situation is more flexible. I favour everyone getting vouchers entitling them to three years of post-secondary training or education (which could lead towards a university degree, or to a trade). Occupations with lengthier training requirements tend also to be the most lucrative, and are not obviously deserving of the taxpayers' subsidy. User fees for further tertiary education are therefore justifiable, with access assisted by readily available student loans and scholarships.

State-supplied housing is difficult to provide without waste. The difference between public and private sector rents locks people into housing situations which may not best suit their needs, and the lack of incentive for householders to maintain or upgrade properties means that administration and repair costs are probably higher than they should be. Other attempts to make housing cheaper, such as rent controls and subsidies, lead to distortions and unintended side-effects.[5]

Various social services provided by different levels of government (marriage counselling, family planning assistance, for example) are probably justifiable on the grounds of the beneficial 'externalities' they generate. We all benefit from living in an environment in which other peoples' personal and social problems receive some attention. And all would benefit, as pointed out in the previous chapter, from a lowering of the birth rate. This is not to admit any complacency about the supply side of social services — it was once reported that social workers in New York City spend three quarters of their time filling-in forms.[6] But all bureaucracies have administrative problems.

Overall, the efficiency aspects of publicly-provided goods and services do not seem worth a fuss, possibly excepting public housing. What, then, of the equity criterion?

An excellent argument can be made to the effect that a civilised and sensible society will provide free health care, education, and social services for all its citizens. But what cannot be argued is that this, the 'Welfare State', is run for the benefit of the poor; nor that it significantly improves their lot. True, Beveridge's original vision was of an attack on the 'giants' of 'Want, Disease, Ignorance, Squalor and Idleness',[7] and it was expected that the Welfare State would 'wither away' as the nation as a whole reached higher levels of prosperity.

But, far from withering away, the Welfare State has increased in importance. For example, in the ten years from 1961 to 1971 in Britain, the ratio of privately to publicly provided services dropped by one fifth in the school system and in the housing sector, and stayed about the same in hospitals.[8] Interestingly, part of the reason is economic growth itself, which has proceeded through productivity improvements in goods production. Education, health services, and perhaps housing, are not by nature susceptible to productivity increases, so that their price *relative* to the price of other goods and services has gone up, encouraging more people to avail themselves of the Welfare State, rather than pay for these services themselves.[9]

Thus, any initial redistributionary impact of the Welfare State (and note that it was actually intended to be a self-financing insurance scheme)[10] has been diluted as more and more of the middle class tax-payers have exercised their right to consume the services offered. As early as 1950 it was calculated that low income groups just about pay for the benefits they receive, through, among other things, the sales taxes levied on all consumers, rich or poor.[11]

Worse still, for the poor, is the fact that the middle classes tend to get more and better services out of the Welfare State. For example, the value of medical benefits obtained under the Ontario Health Insurance Plan was about 60 per cent greater for families earning more than $20000 annually than for families earning less than $4000, in 1974–75.[12] One American study found that between 30 and 90 per cent of those eligible were not using such programs, aimed at the poorest citizens, as Medicaid, Supplemental Security Income, food stamps and public housing.[13] It is well known that middle-class neighbourhoods have the best state schools, and it now seems that efforts to counter this with special efforts to 'upgrade' the educational levels of poor children do not do them much good anyway.[14]

It is a classic case of inappropriate policy-making in action. The Welfare State is not *designed* to discriminate against the poor — if anything, the opposite. But the architects of these schemes are too far from the implementation process to ensure things go as planned. In practice, in any social or economic transaction, the *consumer* or recipient has some input, and middle-class consumers are especially energetic and skillful at bending transactions to suit their interests. Naturally, it also helps to have middle-class folk like themselves on the other side of the deal — the administrators and professionals who deliver welfare services.

If the poor had the social skills and good connections of the middle classes, then they too could compete successfully for the attentions of the Welfare State. But with these capabilities, they probably would not be poor in the first place.

So much for payments in kind. What about the other allegedly re-distributionary policy instrument — cash transfers? Direct handouts to individuals absorbed about one quarter of the budgets of central and local governments in the United Kingdom in 1980. This is less than the more than 40 per cent that went on providing free or subsidised goods and services, but it is still a substantial sum — equal to 10 per cent of GNP.[15] The ostensible purpose of these transfers is to raise the incomes of needy people so that they can purchase a decent standard of living. There are various programs, falling into one of two categories, according to whether eligibility is statutory or determined by economic circumstances.

Statutory programs are sometimes called 'demogrants', because they depend on some demographic characteristic such as age (pensions), or family size (child allowances). The major payments set by economic cir-cumstances are unemployment benefits, and the various 'welfare' payments doled out to people who have exhausted their eligibility for unemployment insurance, or who are judged unable to work due to disability or family responsibilities.

There are major disadvantages to both types of transfers. Demogrants, of course, are costly — every payment to a needy old person or large family is matched by payments to all the other aged or fecund citizens who are well off. In fact, after allowing for the effects of the taxation system on the net amounts transfered, it turned out that, in Canada in 1975, the top 20 per cent of income recipients took home one third of family allowances, and above-average-income families received about one third of all transfer payments.[16] It takes a lot of demogrant dollars to get one dollar transferred to the poor.

Economic-eligibility programs are, by definition, targeted towards people in financial difficulties (though unemployment insurance increasingly benefits families which would not sink below the poverty line without it).[17] Such targeting is administratively expensive. The eligible poor must be identified and monitored, which involves humiliating 'means test', and unattractive discretionary behaviour on the part of officials.

And nearly all these income transfer programs have built-in inefficient behaviour incentives. I do not know if welfare and unemployment pay-ments foster 'welfare dependency' (erosion of individuals' capability to support themselves) but they surely do make *choosing* work less attrac-tive. This is because since benefits are cut-off or sharply reduced if the recipient earns anything from working, there is in effect a very high mar-ginal 'tax' rate on earned income.[18] One US study found that, after allowing as well for the costs of working (travel, clothes), and the loss of minor 'irregular' sources of income, it would actually end up *costing* a man on welfare $2.50 a week to have a job.[19] A marginal income tax effectively greater than 100 per cent is rather higher than the rates which get upper income groups complaining about 'loss of work incentive'. The problem is intrinsic to targeted transfers since by definition these must be eliminated as income from other sources increases.

Impatient with the costs, side-effects, and perverse incentives of our present systems of transfer payments, Milton Friedman suggested replacing them all with a 'negative income tax' (NIT).[20] The idea of a NIT is that every household gets an annual entitlement (a negative tax) of a certain sum, which is paid for by taxes levied on income earned.

In principle, a negative income tax can avoid the spillovers of demogrants, and the administrative and incentive costs of targeted transfers. But there is a problem. If the initial entitlement is to be adequate to keep a family with no other income above the poverty line, and if the marginal ('recovery') tax rate is not to be so high as to destroy incentives, then there would have to be a sizeable shifting of the tax burden to middle and upper income groups, to pay for the program. To take the case of Canada in 1980:

> If the support rate were designed to be barely adequate for a family of four, by present standards this would require a payment in the neighbourhood of $13000. If this amount were then combined with a recovery rate of 50 per cent, a break-even income level of $26000 would prevail — a level that would no doubt make even the most reform-minded finance minister blanch. Positive income tax rates above this level would have to be very high and rise very steeply in order to recoup lost revenue, a situation that might dampen work incentives at the middle and upper levels of the income spectrum.[21]

The middle and upper income groups have successfully resisted any major redistribution of income through the tax system,[22] and it is not likely that their resistance would suddenly evaporate at the sight of a NIT.

So something has to give. My suggestion is that the initial entitlement be lowered. If the $30 billion disbursed as transfer payments in Canada in 1980 were divided equally between the 15 million adult Canadians, each could get $2000 a year, with no change in the tax structure. The $2000 would be a 'social dividend' payable to all citizens surviving to adulthood. As a 'dividend' it could be supplemented by some of the income earned as 'rents' on natural resources, which, as argued in the last chapter, properly belong to everyone. And as a dividend it should be adjusted up or down as the country's gross national product rose or fell.

Such a scheme would naturally arouse protests from people concerned with the welfare of particular groups. Such concerns can, to an extent, be allayed:

(1) *The unemployed* would lose their benefits. But in a full employment economy, virtually all spells of involuntary unemployment would be short enough to be easily financed from personal savings and the NIT, which would also facilitate the high-elasticity 'varitime' labour market in which people would not always choose to work full-time work-years.

(2) *Single parents* would lose their welfare cheques. But a governed economy would deal with the environmental factors responsible for the plight of these households. Child care and family planning services should be available as part of the Welfare State. And Crown prosecutors should vigorously enforce child support.

(3) *The old* would lose their pensions. Perhaps the NIT should be increased after a certain age, paid for in part by a reduction in the size of the social dividend paid to young people, and in part by compulsory contributions from earned income, as at present. But the State need not assume all responsibility for the material comfort of old people. Publicly funded pensions may just reduce private savings for retirement by about the same amount.[23] What the State should do is use the legal system to strike-down compulsory retirement rules, and to facilitate the portability of private pension plans.

Still, some people would slide through into poverty, as they do now despite the present complicated and expensive array of income transfer programs. The problem is that high-level government simply cannot deliver a completely successful anti-poverty policy. If an individual feels strongly about the plight of the poor, more good could be accomplished by going out and finding a poor person and giving them some pounds or dollars (or, better, a good job), or, possibly, by giving the money to a local charity, than by handing it over to government with instructions to do something about poverty. Government will just lose the money, or spend it to some purpose that does not benefit the poor. In a stable and wealthy society with good state-provided education, health care and social services, poverty is essentially a micro-level problem, and can only be dealt with as such.

Nevertheless, there would be a lot less poverty in a successful governed economy. The key is sustained full employment. There are really two issues here – the *quality* and the *quantity* of work. On the first, it is alarming that, in Canada, for example, nearly half of the families living in poverty derive most of their income from wages; more than half of these from full-time, year-around work.[24] That is, many of the poor have regular jobs. The problem is that the jobs are no good – low-paid, obviously, and generally unpleasant in other ways as well.

Now, the important thing, for workers without marketable skills, is to get them out of the dead-end corner of the market, and onto the 'job ladder' leading to higher-paid, more attractive work. The impetus for this cannot come from the supply side of the labour market – we have noted the failure of education or training as a job-improving strategy. It must come from demand; from employers seeking-out potential workers, and giving them the chance to get experience and skills on-the-job.

Only a persistently tight employment market will induce employers to look further than their usual sources of upgradable labour to tap the resources of the working poor – the young; the old; the women; the ethnic minorities; the unschooled. Thus, it has been calculated that the economic position of blacks in the United States was significantly improved by the long expansion of the 1960s,[25] and that the slowdown of the 1970 impeded progress in reducing income inequalities by decreasing the number of workers getting on-the-job upgrading.[26] The process would be helped along from the supply side if an effort was made to share the bad jobs more equally, among young people, for example, as suggested in chapter 23. The goal must be to dry-up the pools of long-term low-wage jobs, and governed economy policies could go a long way towards achieving this.

Increasing the quantity of jobs would improve their quality at the low end of the market. As well, very low unemployment rates would reduce poverty directly. Recessions are not good times for the poor. One US study found that each percentage point increase in the unemployment rate reduces family incomes by 1 per cent for families at five times the poverty level, but by 3 to 4 per cent for families on the poverty line (and that only one third of the jobless heads of low-income families received unemployment benefits).[27] And no doubt these figures, which predate the Great Recession of the 1980s, underestimate the poverty now directly or indirectly attributable to unemployment, and thus underestimate the contribution to be made by a return to low-unemployment rates.

To summarise; the 'framework' policies of a governed economy would do better at reducing poverty than the present ragbag of direct, targeted programs that are designed to eradicate it. It is another example of the best being the enemy of the good; of the perfectionism of the managed economy getting mired in a morass of unpleasant surprises and unintended side-effects. It is foolish to expect ever to eliminate poverty. But much could be done to increase the economic competence of the poor, and to improve their chances of self-betterment. In place of a safety-net-with-holes, the governed economy would offer a springboard to economic success.

Part VI
Postscript

27 The Role of Economists

'Some of my best friends are neoclassical economists.'

T. HAZLEDINE

Economics has a long and dishonourable tradition of having, in Pigou's words, 'furnished for the ungodly blunt instruments with which to bludgeon at birth useful projects of social betterment'.[1] Although the last two centuries have witnessed slow but by now substantial improvement in the material well-being of the wage-earning majority, at almost every stage this progress was earnestly opposed by the economists of the day.

Thus Malthus persuaded Pitt to drop his plan for family allowances by arguing that giving to the poor actually made them eventually worse off (by inducing higher prices and a rise in population).[2] Nassau Senior's ridiculous argument that limiting teenagers' hours of work to ten a day would wipe-out all the profits of the textile mills helped delay the Ten Hour Bill for a decade.[3] The great social investigator Henry Mayhew (pioneer of the concept of the 'poverty line') had to deal with the entrenched orthodoxy of Victorian economists that poverty was due to the personal habits of the poor, and, in particular, could not be blamed on low wages.[4] When the anti-monopoly 'trust-busting' legislation was introduced in the United States at the end of the last century:

> About the only group in America other than big business outspokenly unconcerned about the trust problem were the professional economists. Many were captivated by Darwin's theory of biological selection . . . But in that unenlightened era, the views of economists concerning big business had little influence on public policy.[5]

Keynes' attempts to promote an activist concern with mass unemployment were directly opposed by the *laissez-faire* 'Treasury View',[6] and by the 'Unemployment? I see no unemployment' orthodoxy of most of his

231

colleagues, exemplified in the famously inapt timing of Lord Robbins' definition of economics as the study of the adaptation of 'scarce means to given ends'.[7] Robbins later advised the British government against commissioning William Beveridge to conduct an inquiry into full employment, 'on the ground that Beveridge was not a genuine expert on the unemployment question'.[8]

Beveridge went on to conduct a private inquiry, publishing his findings in the book *Full Employment in a Free Society*,[9] which had an influence second only to Keynes' *General Theory* in spurring the unprecedented commitment to full employment policies made in Britain, the United States and Canada at the end of the Second World War.

Nor are there signs that we have learnt from the errors of the past. The present appallingly high unemployment rates can be blamed in part on the doctrines of monetarist economics, with its fanatical focus on squeezing-out inflation, no matter the cost, and in part on the steady erosion of economic performance that has gone on since the 1950s, almost unnoticed by economists. This is a serious matter; worth some investigation. What is wrong with economists and/or with economics?

It should be noted at once that simple misanthropy is not to blame. Economists give nasty advice, but they are not personally nastier than the norm. His contemporary, Mrs Martineau, wrote that 'a more simple-minded, virtuous man, full of domestic affections, than Mr Malthus could not be found in all England'.[10] Lord Robbins, I believe, is a man of considerable decency, as well as distinction. And I can report from extensive experience of economists as colleagues that a kinder, more companionable bunch of people would be hard to assemble.

Indeed, a rigorous training in 'economic' modes of thought, whatever its drawbacks, does seem to inculcate a powerful distaste for non-economic traits such as prejudice or malevolence. This may be why a disproportionate number of academic economists end up being asked by their peers to run universities. Certainly, the chances of a black or female job applicant getting an absolutely fair hearing would be as high in that stronghold of the economic approach to everything — the Economics Department of the University of Chicago — as anywhere else in the labour market.

Nor is the problem that economists, while amiable enough, are dull. The average academic economist is a formidably well-trained creature, and economists feel, with some justification, a certain sense of superiority over other social scientists — smarter than sociologists, saner than political scientists. Thus economics differs from some of the other problem professions in that its failings cannot be blamed on the inadequacies of its practitioners.

In journalism and architecture, for example, the work of the best is undeniably successful; the trouble lies with the mediocrity of most of their colleagues. But in economics even the best foul up. The two giants of post-war economics — Milton Friedman and Paul Samuelson — are scientists of enormous ability, yet both, in different ways, are failures. Friedman's monetarism has failed to control inflation at an acceptable cost, and Samuelson failed to forestall monetarism by putting Keynesianism on a sound intellectual footing.[11]

So the problem must lie with economics itself; with what economists *do*. Now the question 'what is wrong with economics?' has been the main preoccupation of the previous 26 chapters of this book. It is not a simple matter. Yet the essence of the economists' error can be expressed very simply thus: in dealing with the model of perfect competition they illegitimately substitute an 'is' for an 'ought'.

It can be demonstrated theoretically that a world of perfectly competitive markets would have many attractive properties. At the microeconomic level, resources would be allocated efficiently. And the macroeconomic variables would be easily coped with — the system would tend to stay close to full employment, and any inflationary shocks could be easily countered by monetary policy at only a small and transitory cost in unemployment and reduced output. Thus the perfect competition paradigm has the property, always attractive, of bearing good news. The trains run on time in a perfectly competitive economy, and they are full of happy and productive workers and consumers.

Even better, for economists themselves, is the way in which the good news is borne. The tightness of the competitive world imposes constraints on economic agents which allow the theorist to construct satisfyingly sophisticated models of how markets function. No other social science has a body of real theorems to match those of neoclassical economics; none has models with the 'predictive power' of perfect competition. This must explain the economists' slip from normative to positive. The high-elasticity world of perfect competition has attractions as a *goal*. But economics has yielded to the temptation of assuming that something as good as this — for the world at large, and academic economists in particular — must be so *in fact*.

Thus a dangerous tension exists between the painful reality of deteriorating macroeconomic performance and the Panglossian picture painted by the neoclassicists. Much effort and ingenuity have been expended in devising schemes for disguising this tension. Unemployment is rationalised as 'natural', and cosmetic imperfections are slipped into the model to explain the temporary misperceptions that delay the effects of monetarist squeezes on the inflation rate.

It has become increasingly clear that these palliatives will not do. The tension between theory and fact will be relieved only after a major realignment of the two. Either the real world has to be changed to fit the model, or the model must be brought into line with reality.

I have argued that both strategies have a role. Much can be done to make markets conform more closely to the high-elasticity ideal of perfect competition, reinforcing a tradition of microeconomic policy activism that extends back at least as far as the United States' anti-trust legislation of the 1890s. But the theoretical framework must shift too. Imperfect competition with its accompanying low elasticities is an *intrinsic* characteristic of market life, and our theories and policy recommendations must accept this.

How radical a transformation is needed for a viable low-elasticity economics? Part of orthodox economists' resistance to even considering seriously a major paradigm shift seems to stem from a fear that their very way of life – the 'economic' approach to thinking – is at stake. We look at the existing alternatives: the obscurities of Marxism; the banalities of sociology; and shudder. There is a tendency to instinctively equate rejection of the neoclassical model with rejection of the basic building-block of economics – the notion of 'rational' behaviour by individuals mediated through the forces of supply and demand in markets.

I have tried to point out in this book that nothing so revolutionary is needed. On the contrary, the approach suggested here actually depends on taking the assumption of 'economic' behaviour a step further – from how the economic game is played to the rules of the game itself. Neoclassical economics assumes that agents maximise busily within the constraints of the 'price-taking' rule of perfect competition. But there is plenty of evidence that more money can often be made by working on the rule-book; by reducing elasticities in order to achieve a shift to price-making behaviour.

Thus we have an endless, and very 'economic' quest for control over markets by the participants in them. The consequence is loss of validity for the *laissez-faire* theorems. In technical terms, our present persistent mass unemployment is a sort of 'equilibrium', but it is not the best-of-all-possible-worlds equilibrium touted by neoclassical theorists. The low-elasticity economy has multiple equilibria – left to its own devices, it settles into stagflation, but there is no reason, in principle, why it should not operate at much more satisfactory levels of performance.

The governed economy approach to economic policy developed in this book is an attempt to set out a systematic approach to realising the potential for better performance. I have argued that policy should: (1) do what can be done to reverse the erosion of elasticity; and (2) counter, with 'adding-up' policies, the implications of low elasticities for macroeconomic performance. Some of the policies proposed (varitime; price controls, for example) may *look* radical. But, in fact, they are derived from a fundamentally conservative respect for the force of economic motives, and for the benefits of free markets. The only conceptual leap needed is to realize that truly free markets are not self-generating.

I am not alone in calling on my colleagues to make such a leap. But the critics within economics are still too small a minority. Economists are often accused of always disagreeing amongst themselves. My complaint, on the contrary, is that they agree too much. At the margin, on the technical details of policy advice, economists squabble, as do all professionals confronted with complicated problems. But they have largely agreed to leave undisturbed the foundations of the subject; the neoclassical assumptions that underly both Keynesian and monetarist theories.

Whatever the merit and fate of the various policy proposals offered in this book, it will have accomplished something of use if it opens a few cracks in the consensus that prevents economists from realising their potential as useful social scientists.

Notes and References

PART I   THE PROBLEM

2   CHARTING ECONOMIC DECLINE

1. The classic references are A. W. Phillips, 'The Relationship between Unemployment and the Rate of Change of Money Wage Rates in the United Kingdom, 1861–1957', *Economica*, vol. 25 (1958) pp. 283–99; and R. G. Lipsey, 'A Further Analysis', *Economica*, vol. 27 (1960) pp. 1–31. The Phillips paper is reprinted in J. R. Ball and Peter Doyle (eds) *Inflation* (Penguin, 1969).
2. Phillips actually plotted *wage* inflation, not price inflation, against unemployment.
3. Not quite equivalent, in fact, since the unemployment data differ. In the UK these are collected from figures on the number of people registered as unemployed. In the US and Canada, household surveys are used. The latter method tends to find a larger number of unemployed people.
4. See D. Grubb, R. Jackman and R. Layard, 'Causes of the Current Stagflation', *Review of Economic Studies*, Special Issue (1982), for an analysis of the relative importance for inflation of unemployment and import prices.
5. Sir Henry Phelps Brown, 'What is the British Predicament?', *The Three Banks Review* (December 1977). Phelps Brown has documented that there was no significant increase in the real income of English building-trade workers between 1215 and 1798 – a period of nearly six hundred years! In contrast, real earnings of manual workers have more than doubled since the Second World War.
6. A reasonable hypothesis may be that two World Wars and the intervening Depression left the world economy with a backlog of investment and trading opportunities which were exploited in the politically and economically stable post-war decades. As these 'easy' opportunities were used up, growth naturally slowed to rates which may be sustainable over the longer term. Note that this does not imply that our standard of living must *fall* from its 1960s level, just that it cannot be expected to increase so quickly as in those years. For a discussion from a historical perspective of the post-war boom, see W. Arthur Lewis, 'The Slowing Down of the Engine of Growth', *American Economic Review* (September 1980).

3   KEYNESIANISM: THE INCOMPLETE REVOLUTION

1. Edward F. Denison, *Accounting for Slower Economic Growth: The United States in the 1970s* (Brookings, 1979).
2. This quotation is from the Canadian White Paper, 'Employment and Income with Special Reference to the Initial Period of Reconstruction' (King's Printer, Ottawa, April 1945).
3. An entertaining account of the propagation of Keynesian ideas is given by one of those closely involved − John Kenneth Galbraith − in 'How Keynes came to America', *Economics Peace and Laughter* (Andre Deutsch, 1971).
4. Dornbusch and Fischer tell the story of this period in chapter 10 of the first edition of their *Macroeconomics* (McGraw-Hill, 1978).
5. W. W. Heller, *New Dimensions of Political Economy* (Norton, 1967); quoted by Dornbusch and Fischer, *Macroeconomics*, p. 297.
6. In chapter 19 of the *The General Theory*, in particular.
7. Galbraith, 'How Keynes came to America', p. 44.
8. Though the workers (a majority, in the example) who would keep their jobs without any cut in wages might well block it. Note too that in practice, most firms, especially in a recession, have some excess capacity, which means that unit costs fall when output is increased since various 'overhead' labour and capital costs can be spread over a larger volume of output. This means that a 25 per cent increase in output would require a small percentage increase in the work force.
9. For a technical exposition, see K. J. Arrow and F. H. Hahn, *General Competitive Analysis* (Oliver & Boyd, 1971).
10. R. W. Clower, *The Keynesian Counter-Revolution: A Theoretical Appraisal*, reprinted in Clower (ed.), *Monetary Theory* (Penguin, 1969). Axel Leijonhufvud, *On Keynesian Economics and the Economics of Keynes: A Study in Monetary Theory* (Oxford University Press, 1968). See also the article by Leijonhufvud in Clower's book.
11. Keynesians would not necessarily accept this interpretation of Keynes and *The General Theory*. One of the very best of them, James Tobin of Yale, has written: 'The predominant verdict of history is that, as a matter of pure theory, Keynes failed to prove his case' (that there could be a long-run equilibrium with unemployment). See 'Keynesian Models of Recession and Depression', *American Economic Review* (May 1975) p. 195. However, Tobin notes Keynes' arguments against the efficacy of falling wages as a demand-boosting instrument. This point is also recognised by Robert Eisner in the article preceding Tobin's in the same volume.
12. Arthur M. Okun, *Prices and Quantities* (Brookings, 1981).
13. For a technical survey, see Costas Azariadis, 'Implicit Contracts and Related Topics', in Zmira Hornstein *et al* (eds), *The Economics of the Labour Market* (HMSO, 1981). For a brief critical note, see pp. 175−6 of my paper in the same volume.

4   THE WACKY WORLD OF MARK II MONETARISM

1. For an interesting recent debate on the economics of Keynes, in which the wage stickiness issue is addressed, see the paper by Allan H. Meltzer, 'Keynes' *General Theory*: A Different Perspective', *Journal of Economic Literature* (March 1981), and the comments on it (with reply by Meltzer) in the same journal (March 1983).

2. Barro and Grossman wrote the classic paper, 'A General Disequilibrium Model of Income and Employment', *American Economic Review* (March 1971). For samples of their more recent views, see R. J. Barro, 'Second Thoughts on Keynesian Economics', and Herschel I. Grossman, 'Why Does Aggregate Employment Fluctuate?', both in *American Economic Review* (May 1979).

3. Milton Friedman, 'The Role of Monetary Policy', *American Economic Review* (March 1968); Edmund S. Phelps, 'Money-Wage Dynamics and Labor Market Equilibrium', *Journal of Political Economy* (July/August 1968). A good technical review of these developments is given by Robert J. Gordon, 'Output Fluctuations and Gradual Price Adjustment', *Journal of Economic Literature* (June 1981).

4. Thomas Sargent and Neil Wallace, 'Rational Expectations, the Optimal Monetary Instrument and Optimal Money Supply Rule', *Journal of Political Economy* (April 1975). See also Gordon, 'Output Fluctuations and Gradual Price Adjustment', pp. 504–12. For a non-technical critique, see Martin Neil Baily, 'Are the New Economic Models the Answer?', *The Brookings Review* (Fall 1982). An earlier version of Baily's paper appeared in *Science* (21 May 1982).

5. Robert E. Lucas, Jr, 'Tobin and Monetarism: A Review Article', *Journal of Economic Literature* (June 1981), p. 560.

6. E. S. Phelps *et al*, *Microeconomic Foundations of Employment and Inflation Theory* (Norton, 1970).

7. Ibid., p. 17.

8. James Tobin, 'Inflation and Unemployment', *American Economic Review* (March 1972).

9. Stephenson found that 90 per cent of US youths entering the labour market accepted the first job they were offered. See S. P. Stephenson, 'The Economics of Youth Job Search Behavior', *Review of Economics and Statistics* (February 1976).

10. R. J. Gordon, 'The Welfare Cost of Higher Unemployment', *Brookings Papers on Economic Activity* (1: 1973), reports studies finding the average search time of unemployed US workers to be 7.2 hours a week, of which 4.4 hours were 'newspaper and planning time'.

11. For the US see K. B. Clark and L. H. Summers, 'Labor Market Dynamics and Unemployment: a Reconsideration', *Brookings Papers* (1: 1979). For Canada, see A. Hasan and P. de Brouker, 'Duration and Concentration of Unemployment', *Canadian Journal of Economics* (November 1982)

12. J. P. Mattila, 'Job Quitting and Frictional Unemployment', *American Economic Review* (March 1974), found that workers who went directly from one job to another (that is, who searched on-the-job) showed a

median wage increase of more than 10 per cent, whereas those who changed jobs with an intervening spell of unemployment had a median wage change of about zero.

13. See James Tobin, 'Stabilization Policy Ten Years After', *Brookings Papers*, (1: 1980), pp. 58–61.

14. Tobin, 'Inflation and Unemployment', p. 7.

15. For a well-informed discussion on how well-informed are searching workers, see Okun, *Prices and Quantities*, pp. 37–43.

16. For a survey of this evidence, see my paper in Zmira Hornstein *et al* (eds), *The Economics of the Labour Market* (HMSO, 1981).

17. The ever-ingenious Robert Lucas has proposed another explanation of employment fluctuations, in terms of voluntary (of course) switching between work and leisure on the part of workers. This notion, too, seems to be empirically quite implausible. See Joseph G. Altonji, 'The Intertemporal Substitution Model of Labour Market Fluctuations: An Empirical Analysis', *Review of Economic Studies*, Special Issue (1982).

5 THE IMPORTANCE OF BEING ELASTIC

1. Robert E. Lucas, Jr, 'Tobin and Monetarism: a Review Article', *Journal of Economic Literature* (June 1981) p. 566.

2. For example, see Edwin Mansfield, *Microeconomics*, 3rd ed (Norton, 1979) p. 259. Mansfield admits that 'it is obvious that no industry is perfectly competitive . . . Nevertheless, this does not mean that the study of perfectly competitive markets is useless . . . a model may be quite useful even though some of its assumptions are unrealistic' (p. 250). My argument is that, in this case, the unrealism of the assumptions has been pernicious, not useful, since it has prevented macroeconomics from coming to terms with persistent unemployment.

3. For example, J. K. Galbraith, *Economics and the Public Purpose* (Andre Deutsch, 1974).

4. Oliver Hart, 'A Model of Imperfect Competition with Keynesian Features', *Quarterly Journal of Economics* (February 1982).

5. See the *Journal of Post Keynesian Economics*, published quarterly by M. E. Sharpe Inc., who also issue the admirable and less technical journal *Challenge*. Also recommended is the book of readings edited by Alfred S. Eichner, *A Guide to Post-Keynesian Economics* (Sharpe, 1979).

6. Keith Cowling, *Monopoly Capitalism* (Macmillan, 1982).

6 AN ELASTICITY CRISIS IN THE LUMPY ECONOMY

1. K. J. Arrow and F. H. Hahn, *General Competitive Analysis* (Oliver & Boyd, 1971), especially chapter 5.

2. R. H. Coase, 'The Nature of the Firm', reprinted in American Economic Association, *Readings in Price Theory* (London, 1953).

3. Sam Aaronovitch and Malcolm C. Sawyer, 'The Concentration of British Manufacturing', *Lloyds Bank Review* (October 1974).
4. See Tim Hazledine, 'Generalising from Case Studies: Sixty Reports of the UK Price Commission', Queen's University Discussion Paper 363 (October 1979). See also F. M. Scherer, *Industrial Market Structure and Economic Performance*, 2nd ed (Rand McNally, 1980) pp. 67–73; and Donald A. Hay and Derek J. Morris, *Industrial Economics: Theory and Evidence* (Oxford University Press, 1979) chapter 5.
5. For the UK, see Angus Deaton, *Models and Projections of Demand in Post-war Britain* (Chapman & Hall, 1975).
6. See Hay and Morris, *Industrial Economics: Theory and Evidence*, p. 529.
7. G. B. Richardson, 'The Organisation of Industry', *Economic Journal* (December 1972).
8. Okun, *Prices and Quantities* (Brookings, 1981).
9. J. S. Mill, *Principles of Political Economy*, Ashley edition, p. 242; quoted on p. 168 of *The Origin of Economic Ideas* (Macmillan, 1975), by Guy Routh, who points out that Mill himself went on to focus on 'competition' in his analysis.
10. Albert O. Hirschman, 'Rival Interpretations of Market Society: Civilising, Destructive, or Feeble?', *Journal of Economic Literature* (December 1982) p. 1473.
11. Andrew C. Sigler, 'Roundtable Reply', *New York Times*, 27 December 1981.
12. Paul W. MacAvoy, 'The Business Lobby's Wrong Business', *New York Times*, 20 December 1981.
13. Over the period 1960–70, the share of industrial jobs accounted for by firms with fewer than 500 employees declined from 56 to 51 per cent in the UK. See 'Small Business needs Beautifying', *The Economist*, February 25, 1978.
14. Aaronovitch and Sawyer, 'The Concentration of British Manufacturing', p. 15.
15. J. D. Gribbin, 'The Post-war Revival of Competition as Industrial Policy' (1977), Price Commission, mimeo.

PART II PRINCIPLES

7 THE POSSIBILITY OF FULL EMPLOYMENT

1. In their important study of labour market empirics in the US, Kim B. Clark and Lawrence H. Summers found the average duration of teenage jobs to be less than three months, compared to thirty months for 'prime-age males' (between 25 and 59). Women of this age group had jobs lasting 8.3 months on average. See 'Labor Dynamics and Unemployment: A Reconsideration', *Brookings Papers on Economic Activity* (1: 1979) table 10, p. 53.
2. Clark and Summers write, 'it appears that most unemployed accept

the first job offer they receive. According to the May 1976 survey, about 10 per cent reported that they had rejected a job offer', ibid., p. 55.
3. Dennis Maki, 'Unemployment: wrong ways to attack it', *Financial Post* (Toronto), 16 June, 1979.

8 INFLATION AND THE CURVE

1. G. C. Peden, 'Keynes, The Treasury, and Unemployment in the Later Nineteen Thirties', *Oxford Economic Papers* (March 1980).
2. R. G. Lipsey, 'The relationship between unemployment and the rate of change of money wage rates in the United Kingdom, 1861–1957: a further analysis', *Economica* (February 1960).
3. Barry Thomas and David Deaton, *Labour Shortage and Economic Analysis. A Study of Occupational Labour Markets* (Basil Blackwell, 1977).
4. Alan K. Severn, 'Upward Labor Mobility: Opportunity or Incentive?', *Quarterly Journal of Economics*, (February 1968).
5. Tim Hazledine, 'Distribution, Efficiency and Market Power: A Study of the UK Manufacturing sector', Ph.D thesis (University of Warwick, 1978).
6. For discussion of segmented labour markets, see the Symposium contributed to by Michael J. Piore, Dipak Mazumdar, and Bernard Elbaum, in the *American Economic Review* (May 1983), pp. 249–68.
7. Richard Kahn, *Journal of Economic Literature* (June 1970) gives an account of Keynes' and Beveridge's views on full-employment inflation. See also M. Kalecki, 'Political Aspects of Full Employment', *Political Quarterly* (1943), reprinted in Hunt and Schwartz (eds), *A Critique of Economic Theory* (Penguin, 1972).
8. 'The New Industrial State or Son of Affluence', *The Public Interest* (Fall 1967); reprinted in David Mermelstein (ed), *Economics: Mainstream Readings and Radical Critiques* (Random House, 1970) p. 498.
9. Robert J. Gordon, 'World Inflation and Monetary Accommodation in Eight Countries', *Brookings Papers on Economic Activity* (2:1977).
10. In Canada, for example, weekly earnings in manufacturing deflated by the Consumer Price Index were below their 1976 level in 1980. See Bank of Canada, *Review* (September 1981), p. S115.
11. See Rudiger Dornbusch and Stanley Fischer, *Macroeconomics*, 1st ed (McGraw-Hill, 1978), pp. 430–3; or 2nd ed (1980), pp. 460–3.
12. See may survey paper in Z. Hornstein *et al* (eds), *The Economics of the Labour Market* (HMSO, 1981), p. 176.
13. For example, see Robert J. Gordon, 'Output Fluctuations and Price Adjustment', *Journal of Economic Literature* (June 1981), and Louis J. Maccini, 'The Impact of Demand and Price Expectations on the Behaviour of Prices', *American Economic Review* (March, 1978).
14. Chapter 16 will explore the relationships between full employment, investment, and productivity.

9   IN SEARCH OF BAND-X

1. F. M. Scherer, *Industrial Market Structure and Economic Performance*, 2nd ed (Rand McNally, 1980) p. 469. For analysis of price umbrellas in Canadian industries, see Tim Hazledine, 'The Possibility of Price Umbrellas', *International Journal of Industrial Organisation*, 1984 (forthcoming).
2. Harvey Leibenstein, 'Allocative Efficiency vs. "X-Efficiency"', *American Economic Review* (June 1966). See also Scherer, *Industrial Market Structure . . .*, pp. 464–6, and Hay and Morris, *Industrial Economics: Theory and Evidence* (Oxford University Press, 1979), pp. 557–62.
3. Sir John Hicks once wrote that 'the best of all monopoly profits is a quiet life'. Quoted by Scherer, *Industrial Market Structure . . .*, p. 34.
4. S. Prais, cited by Hay and Morris, *Industrial Economics*, p. 245, who have a good discussion of this question.
5. See the references cited by Scherer, *Industrial Market Structure . . .*, n. 69, p. 37.
6. Keith Cowling. *Monopoly Capitalism* (Macmillan, 1982), p. 86–7. Cowling criticises several earlier studies which did not control statistically for monopoly power, since in highly competitive industries all firms must be of about equal profitability to survive. That is, only in industries with significant market power will there be the slack, the room to manoeuvre, that permits sizeable differences in reported profits to emerge.
7. Ibid., pp. 72–3.
8. G. D. Newbould, *Management and Merger Activity* (Guthstead, Liverpool, 1970); cited by Cowling, *Monopoly Capitalism*, p. 81.
9. Keith Cowling, *Monopoly Capitalism*, p. 82.
10. Of course, the tax system is set up so as to aid and abet these practices.
11. See Keith Cowling and Dennis Mueller, 'The Social Costs of Monopoly Power', *Economic Journal* (December 1978).
12. J. K. Galbraith, *Economics and the Public Purpose*, and *The Affluent Society* (1958, reprinted by Penguin Books).
13. See F. M. Scherer, *Industrial Market Structure . . .*, pp. 24–9.
14. The importance of discouraged workers was demonstrated in 1983's partial recovery from the recession. In Canada, for example, more than 80 per cent of the increase in jobs up to July 1983 went to people joining or rejoining the labour force, so that although employment increased by 3 per cent, unemployment hardly fell at all, dropping from 12.7 to 12.0 per cent. See 'Job Market Brightens', *Financial Post* (Toronto), 13 August 1983.
15. See chapter 20.
16. Tim Hazledine, *The Costs of Protecting Jobs in 100 Canadian Manufacturing Industries*, Labour Market Development Taskforce Technical Study No. 16 (Ottawa, 1981).
17. Walter J. Primeaux, 'An Assessment of X-Efficiency Gained Through Competition', *Review of Economics and Statistics* (February 1977).
18. P. Steer and J. Cable, 'Internal Organisation and Profit: An Empirical

Analysis of Large Firms', *Journal of Industrial Economics* (September 1978).

19. Hazledine, 'The Private and Public Costs of Monopoly Power'.
20. B. Klotz, R. Madoo, and R. Hansen studied the US firm-level data, and uncovered cost differentials similar in magnitude to those reported here for Canada. See 'A Study of High and Low Labor Productivity Establishments in US Manufacturing', in J. Kendrick and B. Vaccara (eds), *New Developments in Productivity Measurement and Analysis* (National Bureau for Economic Research, Studies in Income and Wealth, vol. 44, University of Chicago Press, 1980).

10 THE PRINCIPLES OF APPROPRIATE POLICY-MAKING

1. See chapter 20, where it is reported that the number of PACs in Washington grew from around 600 in 1974 to 2000 in 1980.
2. What follows draws on the analysis of Richard R. Barichello, *The Economics of Canadian Dairy Industry Regulation*, Technical Report E/I 2, Economic Council of Canada (Ottawa, 1981).
3. Ibid., table 10, p. 65.
4. Ibid.
5. E. Malinvaud, *Statistical Methods of Econometrics* (North-Holland, 1968), chapter 4.
6. For a balanced account of the US experience, see Dornbusch and Fischer, *Macroeconomics*, chapter 16.
7. For an absorbing non-technical account of how supply-side economics came to Washington, see John Brooks, 'Annals of Finance', *New Yorker*, 19 April, 1982.
8. An amusing and constructive analysis is E. E. Leamer's 'Let's Take the Con out of Econometrics', *American Economic Review* (March 1983).
9. Robert E. Lucas, Jr, 'Econometric Policy Evaluation: A Critique', in K. Brunner and A. H. Meltzer (eds), *The Phillips Curve and Labor Markets* (North-Holland, 1976).
10. G. Fromm *et al.*, 'Federally-Supported Mathematical Models: Survey and Analysis', Washington, DC, National Science Foundation RANN–C–804 (June 1974).
11. For an interesting account of these matters, see J. K. Galbraith, *The Age of Uncertainty* (BBC/Deutsch, 1977) chapter 7.
12. For an analysis of rent controls in Ontario, see Richard Arnott, with Nigel Johnston, *Rent Controls and Options for Decontrol in Ontario*, Ontario Economic Council, Policy Studies Series No. 2 (Toronto, 1981).

11 SPECIFYING POLICY INSTRUMENTS

1. For an account of US anti-trust policy, see Scherer, *Industrial Market Structure and Economic Performance*, pp. 491–6, and chapters 19 and 20.

2. Hay and Morris, *Industrial Economics: Theory and Evidence*, p. 614.
3. See Howard M. Wachtel and Peter D. Adelsheim, 'How Recession Feeds Inflation', *Challenge* (Sept/October 1977), who find that high-concentration industries tended to increase their price-cost margins in recessions, whereas low-concentration industries, at least until the 1960s, showed decreases.
4. For a survey of Canadian and US studies on minimum wages and their effects, see Edwin G. West and Michael McKee, *Minimum Wages: The New Issues in Theory, Evidence, Policy and Politics*, Economic Council of Canada and Institute for Research on Public Policy (Ottawa/Hull, 1980).

12 PROPOSAL FOR A GOVERNED ECONOMY

1. In the *New York Times*, 27 December 1981.
2. See the possibly devastating attack on Milton Friedman's doctrines by David Hendry and Neil Ericsson, 'Assertion without Empirical Basis . . .', Bank of England (1984).

PART III POLICIES: GETTING THE BIG NUMBERS TO ADD UP

13 PRICE CONTROLS AND INFLATION

1. James Tobin, 'Inflation and Unemployment', *American Economic Review* (March 1972), p. 15.
2. Recent papers by economists noting the costs in less efficient markets of inflation include David Laidler, 'Inflation and Unemployment in an Open Economy: A Monetarist View', *Canadian Public Policy*, Supplement (April 1981) p. 180; and H. S. Houthakker, 'Growth and Inflation: Analysis by Industry', *Brookings Papers on Economic Activity* (1: 1979).
3. Okun, *Prices and Quantities*.
4. Keith Cowling and John Cubbin, 'Hedonic Prices Indexes for United Kingdom Cars', *Economic Journal* (September 1972).
5. From unpublished calculations on Canadian price data, by Ida Albo and the author.
6. In my (1978) study of 51 UK manufacturing industries, I found no significant correlation between differences between the industries in productivity growth and differences in earnings per employee, over the 1958–73 period.
7. For discussion of the General Wage Order system in New Zealand, see John M. Howells, Noel S. Woods, and F. J. L. Young (eds), *Labour and Industrial Relations in New Zealand* (Pitman Books, 1974).
8. For references to other work, and some results for Canada, see my paper 'The Anatomy of Profitability in Canadian Manufacturing Industries', delivered to the Canadian Economics Association, Vancouver, June 1983.

14 ELEVEN FALLACIES ABOUT CONTROLS

1. Although these policies are not always successful in all respects (because they encourage rent-seeking by farmers), the stabilisation aspect seems to be useful.
2. Okun, *Prices and Quantities*.
3. For example, see *Road & Track*, October 1978, p. 33; and November 1978; p. 33, on Honda Accord prices.
4. E. L. Hargreaves and M. M. Gowing, *History of the Second World War: Civil Industry and Trade* (HMSO), 1952) p. 560.
5. Sir Arthur Cockfield, 'The Price Commission and the Price Control', *The Three Banks Review* (March 1978); and personal interview with Denys Gribbin, Price Commission, London, 18 May 1978.
6. D. Quinn Mills, 'Some lessons of price controls in 1971–1973', *The Bell Journal of Economics* (Spring 1975) pp. 26–7.
7. Hargreaves and Gowing, *History of the Second World War*, p. 648.
8. C. Jackson Grayson, Jr, 'Controls are not the Answer', *Challenge* (November/December, 1974).
9. W. H. Beveridge, *Full Employment in a Free Society* (George Allen & Unwin, 1944), p. 201.
10. For example, the *New York Times* reported (13 January 1980), that Americans would approve of 'wage/price controls' in the ratio 2:1, except for American economists, who were against them 1:3.
11. See A. J. Dawson, 'The Phillips Curve: an attempted identification', *Applied Economics* (March 1979). Dawson analysed wage increases in the UK and found expected price inflation to play a 'very significant' determining role, while the level of excess demand was not significant.

15 INCOMES POLICIES: HOW TO NOT CONTROL INFLATION AND GET EVERYONE MAD

1. See Peter Jay, Incomes Policy: Cycles of Failure', *The Times*, 27 June 1973 — a review article of a research report by Sir Richard Clarke.
2. Ibid.
3. Sidney Weintraub, quoted in 'The talk now is all about TIP', Canadian *Financial Post*, 16 May 1981.
4. For example, in a Symposium on inflation policy, George Freeman refers to some views that emphasise cost-push factors as 'seriously one-sided, if not highly eccentric' because of their neglect of market demand forces. See G. E. Freeman, 'A Central Banker Responds', *Canadian Public Policy* (Supplement, April 1981) p. 261.
5. 'Jenkin's 24 Hot Tips', *Observer*, 18 February, 1973.
6. Sir Alec Cairncross, 'Incomes Policy: Retrospect and Prospect', *The Three Banks Review* (December 1973) p. 18.
7. Gardner Ackley, 'Stagflation Swamp Revisited', *Across the Board* (The Conference Board, April 1978).
8. Ibid.

9. See Cockfield, 'The Price Commission and the Price Control', especially p. 22. Cockfield was the Chairman of the Price Commission from 1973 to 1977. For US experience, see D. Quinn Mills 'Some lessons of price controls in 1971–1973', especially p. 11.
10. J. R. Crossley, 'A Mixed Strategy for Labour Economists', *Scottish Journal of Political Economy* (November 1973) p. 215.
11. Mark A. Lutz, 'The Evolution of the Industrial Earnings Structure: the "Geological Theory"', *Canadian Journal of Economics* (August 1976).
12. H. C. Wallich and S. Weintraub, 'A Tax-Based Incomes Policy', *Journal of Economic Issues*, vol. 5 (1971).
13. Abba P. Lerner, 'Stagflation – Its Cause and Cure', *Challenge*, Sept/Oct 1977; Arthur M. Okun, 'The Great Stagflation Swamp', *The Brookings Bulletin*, No. 3 (1977).
14. Weintraub, 'The talk now is all about TIP'.
15. James A. Dalton and E. J. Ford Jr, 'Concentration and Labor Earnings in Manufacturing and Utilities', *Industrial and Labor Relations Review* (October 1977), found that highly concentrated industries tended to pay about $2500 more per year per worker than low concentration industries, and that unionisation had no significant additional effect. Studies that do find a statistical relationship between wages and unionisation probably do so because they omit concentration as an explanatory variable. Since degree of concentration and of unionisation tend to be correlated, omitting the former variable allows the latter to act as a statistical proxy for it.

16 ACHIEVING FULL EMPLOYMENT: THE CASE OF THE FAINT-HEARTED ENTREPRENEURS

1. Although much larger increases in spending were accommodated with relative ease during the Second World War.
2. For a recent analysis of the empirical evidence, see Peter K. Clark, 'Investment in the 1970s: Theory, Performance, and Prediction', *Brookings Papers on Economic Activity* (1:1979). Clark concludes that 'output is clearly the primary determinant of nonresidential fixed investment', and finds a capital price variable 'not very helpful' statistically (pp. 103, 104).
3. See the paper by Chang, Hilton and Yaseen in K. D. Patterson and Kerry Schott (eds), *The Measurement of Capital: Theory and Practice* (Macmillan, 1979).
4. See John B. Taylor, 'The Swedish Investment Funds System as a Stabilisation Rule', *Brookings Papers on Economic Activity*, (1:1982).
5. For a collection of papers evaluating various employment-creating programs, see Eli Ginzberg (ed), *Employing the Unemployed* (Basic Books, 1980).
6. For a survey, see John L. Palmer (ed), *Creating Jobs: Public Employment Programs and Wage Subsidies* (Brookings, 1978).

7. See the paper by Daniel Hamermesh in Palmer (ed), *Creating Jobs*.
8. Ibid., p. 110.
9. Alan S. Blinder, 'Inventories and the Structure of Macro Models', *American Economic Review* (May 1981), points out that, though inventory investment averages only about 1 per cent of GNP, it accounts for about 70 per cent of the peak-to-trough decline in real GNP during recessions.

17 TRADE AND EXCHANGE RATES

1. Quoted by William D. Nordhaus, in 'The Worldwide Wage Explosion', *Brookings Papers on Economic Activity* (2:1972).
2. M. Panic, 'Why the UK's Propensity to Import is High', *Lloyds Bank Review* (January 1975). Panic found the UK to have a higher propensity to import than West Germany or France, and that the share in imports of manufactured goods rose from 31 per cent in 1957 to 57 per cent in 1972.
3. Roger Opie, 'Towards a British Economic Miracle', *New Statesman*, 24 November, 1967.
4. For a technical account, see Ronald I. McKinnon, 'The Exchange Rate and Macroeconomic Policy: Changing Post-war Perceptions', *Journal of Economic Literature* (June 1981).
5. See Randall Hinshaw, 'Review', *Journal of Economic Literature* (June 1981) p. 603.
6. R. F. Harrod, *The Life of John Maynard Keynes* (Penguin, 1972), p. 354–6.
7. John F. Wilson and Wendy E. Takas, 'Differentiated Responses to Price and Exchange Rate Influences in the Foreign Trade of Selected Industrial Countries', *Review of Economics and Statistics* (May 1979), give estimates of responses to exchange rate changes in Canada, France, Germany, Japan, the UK and the US. They in fact find no evidence of a significant effect in the UK.
8. For a survey of pegged exchange rates, see John Williamson, 'A Survey of the Literature on the Optimal Peg', *Journal of Development Economics* (August 1982).
9. See various issues of the *Economic Policy Review* of the Cambridge Department of Applied Economics; for example, No. 3 (March 1977), article by Wynne Godley and Robert M. May, pp. 32–42.
10. See Nicholas Kaldor, 'The effects of devaluation on trade in manufactures', in *Collected Economic Essays*' vol. 6 (Duckworth, 1978), and Wynne Godley, 'Britain's Chronic Recession – Can Anything be Done?', in Wilfred Beckerman (ed), *Slow Growth in Britain* (Clarendon Press, 1979).

18 GOVERNMENT: THE DEFICIT AND WHAT TO DO ABOUT IT

1. See Sam Peltzman, 'The Growth of Government', *Journal of Law and Economics* (October 1980).

2. Calculated from the figures in the *Annual Abstract of Statistics* (Central Statistical Office, 1982). Allocations into categories made by the author.
3. Mervyn King, in the *Guardian*, 14 November 1973; cited by Stuart Holland, *The Socialist Challenge* (Quartet Books, 1975) p. 66.
4. In 1980, government expenditures on 'employment services' were 1.7 billion pounds, on 'other industry and trade' were 4.1 billion, and on agriculture were 1.6 billion; out of total expenditures of 90.7 billion pounds. See *Annual Abstract of Statistics* (Central Statistical Office, 1982).
5. A Brookings study found that 'the US tax system is essentially proportional for the vast majority of families and therefore has little effect on the overall distribution of income'. See Joseph A. Pechman and Benjamin A. Ockner, *Who Bears the Tax Burden?* (Brookings, 1974).
6. George Cooper, *A Voluntary Tax? New Perspectives on Sophisticated Tax Avoidance* (Brookings, 1979).
7. David Walker, review of J. A. Kay and M. A. King, *The British Tax System* (Oxford University Press, 1978), in *The Economic Journal* (March 1979) pp. 173–5. Kay and King also find that there is, in effect, no attempt to tax corporation profits in the UK now.
8. See 'Survey on Personal Finance', *The Economist*, 24 March 1979.
9. Carl P. Simon and Ann D. Witte, *Beating the System: The Underground Economy* (Auburn House, 1982), estimate the US underground economy at between 9 and 16 per cent of GNP in 1974. International estimates and comparisons are given in Vito Tanzi (ed), *The Underground Economy in the United States and Abroad* (Heath, Lexington, 1982).
10. For papers presenting arguments for and against the expenditure tax, see Joseph A. Pechman (ed), *What Should be Taxed: Income or Expenditure?* (Brookings, 1980). An analysis by economists involved in preparing the Meade Committee's report is the book by Kay and King, *The British Tax System*.
11. 44 per cent in the UK; 33 per cent in West Germany; 23 per cent in Switzerland, for example. See 'International Comparisons of Taxes and Social Security Contributions, 1970–79', *Economic Trends* (Central Statistical Office, December 1981).
12. See Tobin, 'Stabilisation Policy Ten Years After', n. 16, p. 40. A comprehensive empirical study of the economic effects of taxation is the volume *How Taxes Affect Economic Behavior*, Henry J. Aaron and Joseph A. Pechman (eds), (Brookings, 1981).
13. J. K. Galbraith, 'A Cure for the Economy', *New York Review of Books*, 2 June 1983, James Tobin, 'Reagan's Counterrevolution', ibid, 3 December 1981; Emma Rothschild, 'Reagan's Case Against the Economy', ibid, 25 April 1982.
14. The central governments of Canada, the US, Britain, France, West Germany, Italy, and Japan, have each been in deficit every year since 1974, according to OECD data (reported in the Toronto *Globe and Mail*, 23 April 1983).

15. William Nordhaus, 'The Imperfections of the Budget', *New York Times*, 22 March 1981.

PART IV POLICIES: INCREASING ELASTICITY

19 AGAINST MONOPOLY

1. 'People of the same trade seldom meet together, even for merriment and diversion, but the conversation ends in a conspiracy against the public, or in some contrivance to raise prices', quoted by Scherer, *Industrial Market Structure and Economic Performance*, 2nd ed, p. 167.
2. In a paper 'The Control of Monopoly', cited by J. D. Gribbin, 'The Post-war Revival of Competition as Industrial Policy' (Price Commission, mimeo, 1979) p. 9.
3. See Scherer, *Industrial Market Structure* . . . , chapter 9, for a survey.
4. See, for example, Harold Demsetz, 'The Crisis in Antitrust', in *Concentration, Oligopoly and Power* (The Conference Board information bulletin, June 1979).
5. Scherer, *Industrial Market Structure* . . . , pp. 509–13.
6. Tim Hazledine, 'Generalising from Case Studies: The Sixty Reports of the UK Price Commission', Queen's University Institute for Economic Research Discussion Paper No. 363 (October 1979) section III.
7. W. J. Baumol, 'Contestable Markets: An Uprising in the Theory of Industry Structure', *American Economic Review* (March 1982).
8. William G. Shepherd, 'Causes of Increased Competition in the US Economy, 1939–1980', *Review of Economics and Statistics* (November 1982).
9. Daniel J. Mitchell, 'Recent Union Contract Concessions', *Brookings Papers on Economic Activity* (1:1982) calculates that fewer than 2 million workers (out of a workforce of around 100 million) were directly affected by concessions, and points out that bouts of concessions have occurred before (after the Korean War; in the late 1950s; in the early 1960s) without having a lasting effect on bargaining behaviour.
10. Hay and Morris, *Industrial Economics: Theory and Evidence*, table 8.1, p. 240. The figures are for 1970.
11. 'Small Business Needs Beautifying', *The Economist*, 25 February 1978.
12. For an analysis of the role of international competition in UK markets, see Keith Cowling, *Monopoly Capitalism*, chapter 6.
13. See M. H. Ashworth, J. A. Kay, and T. A. E. Sharpe, 'Differentials between car prices in the United Kingdom and Belgium' (Institute for Fiscal Studies Report Series, No. 2, 1982) p. 38, who find that reduction of UK car prices to world levels would have been the 'probable result' of the liquidation of British Leyland, in the absence of an additional 300 million pounds annual subsidy.

14. Ibid., p. 36.
15. Ibid., chapter 6.
16. See Cowling, *Monopoly Capitalism*, pp. 82–3.
17. See Alan Butt Philip, *Creating New Jobs* (Policy Studies Institute, 1978); discussed in *The Economist*, 22 July 1978, p. 95.

20 REGULATION

1. See W. T. Stanbury and Fred Thompson, 'The Scope and Coverage of Regulation in Canada and the United States', in Stanbury (ed) *Government Regulation: Scope, Growth and Process* (Institute for Research on Public Policy, Montreal, 1980).
2. For a brief survey, see Scherer, *Industrial Market Structure and Economic Performance* pp. 466–8.
3. Walter J. Primeaux, 'An Assessment of X-Efficiency Gained Through Competition', *Review of Economics and Statistics* (February 1977).
4. 'Trucking Deregulation', *Consumer Reports* (June 1979) p. 360.
5. *Reforming Regulation*, Economic Council of Canada (Ottawa, 1981).
6. *Business Week*, 5 October 1974, p. 64.
7. 'Regulating the Regulators', *New York Times Magazine*, 10 June 1979, p. 104.
8. Ibid., p. 106.
9. George Stigler, 'The Theory of Economic Regulation', *Bell Journal of Economics and Management Science* (Spring 1971).
10. 'Regulating the Regulators', p. 108.
11. Barbara R. Bergmann, 'Lobbying: Shakedown on Capitol Hill', *New York Times*, 4 April 1982.
12. For his account of these and other events, see A. E. Kahn, 'Applications of Economics to an Imperfect World', *American Economic Review* (May 1979).

21 LABOUR, WORK, AND WOMEN

1. In Canada, for example, part-time workers were about 13 per cent of the labour force in 1980; up from 2.8 per cent in 1953. More than 70 per cent of part-time workers are women.
2. The idea often surfaces in newspaper and magazine articles. For a quite early reference, see 'It Started in Germany — And Keeps Growing', *Dun's Review* (March 1977) pp. 62–4.
3. These titbits of economic history are drawn from Guy Routh's *The Origin of Economic Ideas* (Macmillan 1975) pp. 148–60.
4. This figure is for Canada, and was reported by Wilfred List in the Toronto *Globe and Mail*, 24 September 1979. There is some confusion about whether Canadian absenteeism is higher or lower than absenteeism in other countries. List's figures put absenteeism higher in the US and France, for example, whereas Sidney Katz ('The Lost Weekday', *Financial Post Magazine*, 27 September 1980) claims that

these two countries, among others, have lower absenteeism rates than Canada. All sources agree, however, that absenteeism is a far more important source of lost workdays than strikes.

5. See 'Flexitime: A New Workstyle Catches On', *Dun's Review* (March 1977) p. 61.
6. These figures are based on Canadian data. See *Canadian Statistical Review* (March 1980) Section 4, Table 4; and David P. Ross, *The Working Poor* (Canadian Institute for Economic Policy, 1981), Table 2.2, p. 18.
7. Calculated as $(0.4 \times 0.6)/(0.4 \times 0.6 + 0.6 \times 1.0) = 0.29$.
8. An article in *Time* magazine, 7 August 1978, cited a 1974 study which found 1 in 4 adults in the US to be involved in volunteer work, with an annual value of around $50 billion.
9. 'What price housework? $80 billion', the Toronto *Globe and Mail*, 27 June 1978. Comparable US figures are reported by Reuben Gronau, 'Home Production: a Forgotten Industry', *Review of Economics and Statistics* (August 1980).
10. Joann Vanek, 'Time Spent in Housework', *Scientific American* (November 1974).
11. Reported by Gronau, 'Home Production', p. 410.
12. Vanek, 'Time Spent in Housework', p. 118.
13. $((0.4 \times 0.6 + 0.6 \times 1.0)/(0.6 \times 1.0)) \times 35 = 50$.
14. I have ignored the disposition of non-wage income, such as dividends and transfer payments, which probably are more evenly spread between men and women. I have also not allowed for the fact that most husbands do in fact 'pay' some of their income to their wives, in exchange for housework.
15. Martin Neil Baily, *Brookings Papers on Economic Activity* (2:1979) p. 434.
16. See the studies referenced by Robert H. Frank, 'Why Women Earn Less: The Theory and Estimation of Differential Overqualification', *American Economic Review* (June 1978).
17. Baily, *Brookings Papers* ... See also R. J. Flanagan, 'Segmented Market Theories', *Industrial Relations* (October 1973), who reports that 'recent evidence indicates that the link between schooling and income is far stronger than the link between achievement and income' (p. 260).
18. Frank, 'Why Women Earn Less', p. 360.
19. Wayne Vroman, 'Worker Upgrading and the Business Cycle', *Brookings Papers on Economic Activity* (1:1977).

22 HIERARCHY: HOW THE MIDDLE CLASS DOES IT

1. A. Alchian and H. Demsetz, 'Production, Information Costs and Economic Organisation', *American Economic Review* (December 1972).
2. Stephen A. Marglin, 'What do Bosses do? The Origins and Functions of Hierarchy in Capitalist Production', in Andre Girz (ed), *The Division of Labour* (Humanities Press, 1976).

3. Andrew Hacker, 'Creating American Inequality', *New York Review of Books*, 20 March 1980, p.21.
4. In 1977 72 per cent of US property income went to families with incomes less than $50 000. See Hacker, 'Creating American Inequality', p. 21.
5. Ibid.
6. Only 0.8 per cent of women had salaries of $25 000 or more in 1978. See ibid., p. 23.
7. Lord Taylor, 'How pay can be fairly controlled without a statutory policy', *The Times*, 14 April 1975.
8. Ivan Illich, 'The professions as a form of imperialism', *New Society*, 13 September 1973.
9. Randall Collins, *The Credential Society: An Historical Sociology of Education and Stratification* (Academic Press, 1979); quoted by Hacker, p. 25.
10. Ibid.; 'Creating American Inequality'.
11. For a survey of the evidence, see Scherer, *Industrial Market Structure and Economic Performance*, chapter 4. Scherer concludes that 'actual concentration in US manufacturing industry appears to be considerably higher than the imperatives of scale economies require' (p. 118). For a survey of the UK evidence, see Hay and Morris, *Industrial Economics: Theory and Evidence*, chapter 2.
12. The figures are for the years 1971–3, and are from the *Department of Employment Gazette*, November 1976; cited in D. T. Jones and S. J. Prais, 'Plant Size and Productivity in the Motor Industry: Some International Comparisons', *Oxford Bulletin of Economics and Statistics* (May 1978).
13. P. D. Henderson, 'Two British Errors: Their Probable Size and Some Possible Lessons', *Oxford Economic Papers* (July 1977).
14. A. F. and D. I. Trotman-Dickenson, 'The Distribution of Remuneration of Executives', *Economic Journal* (December 1979) pp. 919–20.
15. Laurence J. Peter, *The Peter Principle* (Pan Books, 1970).
16. Harold E. O'Kelley, 'How to Motivate and Manage Engineers', *New York Times*, 26 November, 1978.
17. Taylor, How pay can be fairly controlled . . . '.

23 FLATTENING THE HIERARCHIES

1. Lane Tracy, 'Postscript to the Peter Principle', *Harvard Business Review* (July/August 1972).
2. Ibid.
3. Ibid.
4. Ibid.
5. Hacker, 'Creating American Inequality', p. 22.
6. See Hay and Morris, *Industrial Economics: Theory and Evidence*, pp. 252–5, and Cowling, *Monopoly Capitalism*, pp. 83–94. For an analysis of the effects on profitability of the introduction of the M-form in Britain, see P. Steer and J. Cable, 'Internal Organization and Profit:

An Empirical Analysis of Large UK Companies', *Journal of Industrial Economics* (September 1978).

7. See Ana Gutierrez Johnson and William Foote Whyte, 'The Mondragon System of Worker Production Cooperatives', *Industrial and Labour Relations Review* (October 1977).

8. Norman McCrae, 'Agriculture goes right', in *The Economist*, Survey on China (31 December 1977) p. 15.

PART V POLICIES: SPECIAL CASES

24 PRODUCTIVITY AND INDUSTRIAL POLICY

1. The average annual growth rates were: Japan – 9.0 per cent; France and Italy – 5.7 per cent; West Germany – 4.7 per cent; Canada – 4.2 per cent; UK – 3.6 per cent; US – 2.8 per cent. *Source* OECD data, compiled by the Economic Council of Canada, in *The Bottom Line: Technology, Trade, and Income Growth* (Ottawa, 1983), Table 2–3, p. 9.

2. The figures for 1973–80 are: Japan – 4.7 per cent; France – 3.2 per cent, West Germany – 2.9 per cent; Italy – 2.1 per cent; UK – 1.7 per cent; US – 0.5 per cent; Canada – 0.2 per cent. *Source* ibid.

3. See M. N. Baily, 'Comment', *Brookings Papers on Economic Activity* (2:1979) p. 436.

4. See Michael Denny and Melvyn Fuss, *Productivity: A Selective Survey of Recent Developments and the Canadian Experience*, Ontario Economic Council Discussion Paper Series (Toronto, 1982) pp. 42–3.

5. Ibid., p. 38.

6. Joe S. Bain, *International Differences in Industrial Structure* (Yale University Press, 1968); summarized by F. M. Scherer, *Industrial Market Structure and Economic Performance*, 1st ed (Rand McNally, 1970), p. 94. Bain's data are for the 1950s.

7. See Tim Hazledine, 'The Anatomy of Market Power in Canadian Manufacturing Industry', paper presented to the Canadian Economics Association Meetings (June 1983).

8. Economic Council of Canada, *The Bottom Line*, Table 4–1, p. 37.

9. I. B. Kravis, 'A Survey of International Comparisons of Productivity', *Economic Journal* (March 1976) p. 25.

10. E. F. Denison, assisted by J. P. Poullier, *Why Growth Rates Differ* (Brookings, 1967) p. 332. Quoted by Kravis, 'A Survey . . . '.

11. Calculated from Economic Council of Canada, *The Bottom Line*, table 2–3, p. 9.

12. Edward F. Denison, *Accounting for Slower Economic Growth: The United States in the 1970s* (Brookings, 1979). Summarised in *The Brookings Bulletin*, vol. 16, No. 2.

13. Ibid., quoted in *The Brookings Bulletin*, p. 8.

14. As a quite typical example, see the Economic Council of Canada's *Eighteenth Annual Review: Room to Manoeuvre* (Ottawa, 1981)

p. 84. One Council member, R. B. Bryce, who is probably the most distinguished practitioner of macroeconomic policy that Canada has had, noted his reservations about the neoclassical econometric model underlying the Council's recommendations, and about the policy conclusions drawn from the model (ibid., pp. 95–8).

15. Another experienced member of the Economic Council, Kalmen Kaplansky, entered a Dissent to this effect (ibid., p. 98).

16. For a horrifying exposé of this industry, see James Fallows, *National Defense* (Random House, 1981).

17. Seymour Melman, 'Decision Making and Productivity as Economic Variables: The Recent Depression as a Failure of Productivity', *Journal of Economic Issues* (June 1976).

18. Robert B. Reich, *The Next American Frontier* (Times Books, 1983). See too Reich's articles in *Atlantic Monthly* (March and April issues, 1983).

19. Robert Bacon and Walter Eltis, *Britain's Economic Problem: Too Few Producers* (Macmillan, 1976), p. 112.

20. The debate on industrial policy is particularly vigorous in Canada, when constant comparisons with the great southern neighbour can induce feelings (mistaken, in my view) of inadequacy in size and performance, and consequent calls for remedies. The pro-high tech etc. view has been most vigorously espoused by the Science Council of Canada, eg John Britton, James Gilmour, and Mark G. Murphy, *The Weakest Link – A Technological Perspective on Canadian Industrial Underdevelopment* (Science Council of Canada, Ottawa, 1978). Notable attacks on the doctrine by economists are Donald Daly, 'Canada's Comparative Advantage', Economic Council of Canada Discussion Paper (Ottawa, 1979), and R. J. Wonnacott, 'Industrial Strategy: A Canadian Substitute for Trade Liberalization', *Canadian Journal of Economics* (November 1975).

21. Philip H. Trezise, 'Industrial Policy is not the Major Reason for Japan's Success', *The Brookings Review* (Spring 1983) p. 15. This article is excerpted from Trezise's book, *Industry Vitalization: Toward a National Industrial Policy* (Pergamon Press, 1982).

22. Bacon and Eltis, *Britain's Economic Problem*.

23. Ibid.

24. Reported by Peter McGill of the *Observer* (London); reprinted in the Toronto *Globe and Mail*, 4 July 1983.

25. P. H. Trezise, 'Industrial Policy', p. 18.

26. See J. W. Kendrick, 'International Comparisons of Recent Productivity Trends', in W. Fellner (ed), *Essays in Contemporary Economic Problems: Demand, Productivity, and Population* (American Enterprise Institute, Washington 1981), and Organisation for Economic Co-operation and Development, *Productivity Trends in the OECD Area*, Working Party No. 2 of the Economic Policy Committee, Note by Secretariat (October 1979). For a survey, see Andrew Sharpe, 'A Review of the Productivity Slowdown Literature' (Long Range and Structural Analysis Division, Department of Finance, Ottawa, October 1982) (draft).

25 BEING SENSIBLE ABOUT ENERGY AND THE ENVIRONMENT

1. For a sanguine analysis of resource availability, see Julian L. Simon, *The Ultimate Resource* (Princeton University Press, 1981).
2. For an analysis of Canadian energy policy and alternatives, see Tim Hazledine, Steve Guiton, and Lorraine Froehlich, 'OPEC and the Value of Canada's Energy Resources; A Long-Run Simulation Model', Economic Council of Canada Discussion Paper (Ottawa, 1984).
3. See Robert W. Crandall, 'Curbing the Costs of Social Regulation', *The Brookings Bulletin* (Winter 1979).
4. Roger G. Noll, 'Implementing Marketable Emissions Permits', *American Economic Review* (May 1982).
5. Marketable permits for petrol have been suggested, by, among others, C. Henderson, in *The Inevitability of Petroleum Rationing in the United States* (Princeton Center for Alternative Futures, 1978).
6. Philip K. Verleger, Jr, 'The US Petroleum Crisis of 1979', *Brookings Papers on Economic Activity* (2:1979).
7. Sachs gives ratios (primary energy in oil-equivalent per unit of Gross Domestic Product) of 1.14 (Canada); 1.05 (US); 0.85 (UK); 0.60 (Japan); 0.58 (W. Germany); 0.50 (France). See Jeffrey D. Sachs, 'Comment on paper by William D. Nordhaus', *Brookings Papers on Economic Activity* (2:1980) p. 395.
8. See Joel Darmstadter, Joy Dunkerley and Jack Alterman, *How Industrial Societies Use Energy* (Johns Hopkins University Press, 1977) Table F−2, p. 264.
9. See, for example, ibid., figure 4−2, p. 59, for a graphing of household consumption against energy prices.
10. Verlegar, 'The US Petroleum Crisis', p. 463.
11. William Nordhaus has constructed a model of the world oil market, and used this to analyse the effects of oil taxes. In his scenarios, the benefits range from $400 billion to $1400 billion, and he suggests that the optimal tax lies between $25 and $50 a barrel above current OECD taxes. There is some hypocrisy in Nordhaus and other American economists recommending higher oil taxes without pointing out that other OECD economies have had relatively high taxes in place for decades; it is the US (and Canada) whose cheap-oil policies have given OPEC its power. See William D. Nordhaus, 'Oil and Economic Performance in Industrial Countries', *Brookings Papers on Economic Activity* (2:1980).
12. From Condorcet's *Esquisse*, written in 1793. Quoted by Mogens Boserup, 'Fear of Doomsday: Past and Present', *Population and Development Review* (March 1978) p. 135.

26 POVERTY: A MODEST PROPOSAL

1. David P. Ross, *The Working Poor: Wage Earners and the Failure of Income Security Policies* (Canadian Institute For Economic Policy/ James Lorimer & Company, 1981) pp. 5−6.

2. These and following figures are from Charles A. Murray, 'The two wars against poverty: economic growth and the Great Society', *The Public Interest* (Fall 1982).
3. William E. Simon, 'US welfare subsidizing the middle class', the Toronto *Globe and Mail*, 31 July, 1978; excerpted from Simon's *A Time for Truth* (McGraw-Hill, 1978).
4. See Karen Davis and Cathy Schoen, *Health and the War on Poverty: A Ten-Year Appraisal* (Brookings, 1978).
5. See Peter D. Salins, *The Ecology of Housing Destruction: Economic Effects of Public Intervention in the Housing Market* (New York University Press, 1980); reviewed by Walter Goodman in the *New York Times Book Review*, 10 August, 1980.
6. James Reston in *New York Times*, 23 November 1966; cited by Peter F. Drucker, *The Age of Discontinuity* (Heinemann, 1969) p. 204.
7. William Beveridge, *Social Insurance and Allied Services* (HMSO, 1942).
8. See Tim Hazledine, 'Unbalanced Growth in the Welfare State', *Scottish Journal of Political Economy* (November 1976) Table 1, p. 227.
9. See ibid. for a formal model of this process of 'unbalanced growth'.
10. Beveridge, *Social Insurance and Allied Services*, p. 2.
11. See Findlay Weaver, 'Taxation and Redistribution in the United Kingdom', *The Review of Economics and Statistics* (1950) pp. 201–13. Weaver's findings are discussed by Alan T. Peacock and P. R. Browning, 'The Social Services in Great Britain and the Redistribution of Income', in Peacock (ed), *Income Redistribution and Social Policy* (Cape, 1954).
12. Reported by Stan Oziewicz in the Toronto *Globe and Mail*, 22 June 1978; from a study carried out by Pranlal Manga for the Ontario Economic Council.
13. Alvin L. Schorr, 'Loose Welds in the Social Compact', *New York Times*, 23 July 1979.
14. Lester C. Thurow, 'The Failure of Education as an Economic Strategy', *American Economic Review* (May 1982).
15. Figures calculated from the Central Statistical Office's *Annual Abstract of Statistics*, 1982.
16. Ross, *The Working Poor*, pp. 83–4.
17. See Economic Council of Canada, *Annual Review* (Ottawa, 1978) chapter 6.
18. Ross, *The Working Poor*, pp. 84–5.
19. Study cited by Daniel Patrick Moynihan, in the *New Yorker*, 13 January 1973.
20. Milton Friedman, *Capitalism and Freedom* (University of Chicago Press, 1962) chapter XII. See Ross, *The Working Poor*, pp. 64–70.
21. Ross, *The Working Poor*, p. 66.
22. Lester Thurow reports the finding of Joseph A. Pechman and Benjamin A. Okner (*Who Bears the Tax Burden?* (Brookings, 1974)) that the variance of tax rates 'within each income class is much larger than the variance across income classes. The tax system is both progressive

and regressive'. See L. C. Thurow, 'The Economics of Public Finance', *National Tax Journal* (June 1975) p. 191. Cited by David G. Davies, 'Measurement of Tax Progressivity: Comment', *American Economic Review* (March 1980).

23. See E. Philip Howrey and Saul H. Hymans, 'The Measurement and Determination of Loanable-Funds Saving', *Brookings Papers on Economic Activity* (3:1978) p. 679.
24. Ross, *The Working Poor*, p. xiii.
25. Richard B. Freeman, 'Changes in the Labor Market for Black Americans, 1948–72', *Brookings Papers on Economic Activity* (1:1973).
26. Thurow, 'The Failure of Education as an Economic Strategy'.
27. E. Gramlich, 'The Distributional Effects of Higher Employment', *Brookings Papers on Economic Activity*' (2:1974).

PART VI POSTSCRIPT

27 THE ROLE OF ECONOMISTS

1. A. C. Pigou, *Wage Statistics and Wage Policy*, Stamp Memorial Lecture, 1949 (Athlone Press, 1951). Quoted by Guy Routh, *The Origin of Economic Ideas* (Macmillan, 1975) p. 105.
2. See Routh, *The Origin of Economic Ideas*, pp. 111–14.
3. Ibid, pp. 159–60.
4. See Eileen Yeo, 'Mayhew as a Social Investigator', in *The Unknown Mayhew*, ed E. P. Thompson and Eileen Yeo (Penguin, 1973).
5. Scherer, *Industrial Market Structure and Economic Performance*, p. 493.
6. For an interesting re-interpretation of the attitude of the British Treasury to Keynes, see G. C. Peden, 'Keynes, The Treasury, and Unemployment in the Nineteen Thirties', *Oxford Economic Papers* (March 1980).
7. Lionel Robbins, *An Essay on the Nature and Significance of Economic Science* (Macmillan, 1935).
8. Jose Harris, *William Beveridge: A Biography* (Oxford University Press, 1977) p. 434. Reviewed by Warren J. Samuels in the *Southern Economic Journal* (July 1978).
9. George Allen & Unwin, 1944.
10. Quoted by Keynes in his essay on Malthus in *Essays in Biography* (Macmillan, 1933) p. 132.
11. A most interesting assessment of Samuelson's contribution is made by his brilliant protegé, J. E. Stiglitz, in the latter's 'Review' of George R. Feiwel (ed) *Samuelson and Neoclassical Economics* (Kluwer-Nijhoff, 1982), in the *Journal of Economic Literature* (September 1983).

Index